A History of Leisure

Related books from Palgrave Macmillan

Jeffrey Hill, *Sport, Leisure and Culture in Twentieth-Century Britain* (2002)

Hayden Ramsay, *Reclaiming Leisure: Art, Sport and Philosophy* (2005)

Ken Roberts, *The Leisure Industries* (2004)

Chris Rojek, *Leisure and Culture* (1999)

A History of Leisure

The British Experience since 1500

Peter Borsay

palgrave
macmillan

First published in 2006 by
PALGRAVE MACMILLAN
Houndmills, Basingstoke, Hampshire RG21 6XS and
175 Fifth Avenue, New York, N.Y. 10010
Companies and representatives throughout the world.

PALGRAVE MACMILLAN is the global academic imprint of the Palgrave Macmillan division of St. Martin's Press, LLC and of Palgrave Macmillan Ltd. Macmillan® is a registered trademark in the United States, United Kingdom and other countries. Palgrave is a registered trademark in the European Union and other countries.

ISBN 13: 978–0–333–93081–6 hardback
ISBN 10: 0–333–93081–9   hardback
ISBN 13: 978–0–333–93082–3 paperback
ISBN 10: 0–333–93082–7   paperback

This book is printed on paper suitable for recycling and made from fully managed and sustained forest sources.

A catalogue record for this book is available from the British Library.

A catalog record for this book is available from the Library of Congress.

10 9 8 7 6 5 4 3 2 1
15 14 13 12 11 10 09 08 07 06

Printed in China

To Clare and Sarah

CONTENTS

LIST OF TABLES

PREFACE

A GLORIOUS IRRELEVANCE?

When, on Tuesday, 11 September 2001, the twin towers of the World Trade Center in New York were demolished by two hi-jacked Boeing planes, it was obvious that it was one of those defining moments in history. The conjunction of a phenomenon that both was happening and had happened – of history being made – added hugely to the significance of the spectacle. That it was revealing itself on the television screen, and was accompanied by an inescapable frisson of excitement, made it difficult to avoid the comparison, however distasteful, with a media sporting occasion. The unpredictability of the drama in the USA, and in particular the regular deployment of flashbacks and expert analysis to construct and reconstruct the history of the event, were uncannily familiar to a habitué of live TV sport. Interminable replays and pundits' assessments had ensured that Michael Owen's wonder goal and David Beckham's infamous ankle flick in the 1998 World Cup match in France between England and Argentina were already part of the sport's and the nation's history even before the match was completed.

Yet, of course, there is a difference between what transpired in New York in 2001 and France in 1998: one was political, the other simply a piece of leisure; one deadly serious, the other just a game.

This was brought home in the response of the sports world and the media to the events unfolding in New York, when they agonized over whether it was appropriate for essentially frivolous activities to continue in the aftermath of the awesome occurrences in the USA. On the following Saturday David Davies in the *Guardian*, under a headline 'Ryder Cup stares into the abyss', reminded readers, 'as the US and the rest of the world wrestle with the morality of continuing with a triviality such as sport in the face of the monstrous wrongs that took place in New York and Washington, there are doubts as to whether the event can take place'. By Monday the decision had been taken to postpone the tournament for a year. That weekend's English Premiership fixtures went ahead, but with a respectful pre-match minute's silence. However, this only prompted Will Buckley in the *Observer* on Sunday to thunder, 'How can a minute's silence preceding an hour-and-a-half's screaming of abuse at irrelevant footballers contesting a trivial game constitute "the paying of respects"?' On Monday Martin Kelner in the *Guardian* defended the continuation of the weekend's football, but only on the grounds of exposing its insignificance: 'What convinced me even more, though, of the wisdom of resuming football on Saturday was the spat between Alan Shearer and Roy Keane, and that between Robbie Fowler and most of the Derby team. These conflicts, which belonged in the column marked "handbags", would on normal weekends have taken up far more newsprint than they deserved, but for once everyone seemed to recognise their glorious irrelevance.'[1]

Here, in the tragedy of the twin towers, was an opportunity to place pleasure in perspective, to put the rampant hedonism of a consumer-oriented culture in its place, by drawing the line between real life and leisure. Yet the golf was only postponed (and this was probably due more to the players' anxiety about their personal security than to any sentiment of propriety), the Premiership matches did take place, and Roy Keane, seemingly unrestrained by the events across the Atlantic, did 'handbag' Alan Shearer. No doubt the crowd also roared as these two protagonists played their gladiatorial parts. Was this serious or was it not? Was it reality or play? This is the question which troubles any historian of sport, or more broadly leisure. It is not one which, on the face of it, agitates historians of wars, politics, government, religion and such like. They deal in matters which appear self-evidently real and serious. By comparison, is not leisure so much cultural froth on the hard realities of history, a mere – and the word seems to encapsulate the marginality of the whole subject – pastime? The answer is No, *and* Yes. No, not only because sporting events continued, largely unhindered by the tragedy of 11 September; not only because outside the USA, sportsmen and women, musicians, actors, crowds, and audiences, after a brief payment of respects, continued to behave in much the same manner as if the event had not occurred; not even because in the United States itself it soon became a matter of democratic and patriotic duty for Americans to continue their recreational pursuits as a sign of defiance, in stadiums that became focal points of national identity in a way which no formally sacred structure was able to compete with. But primarily because for the vast majority of those living in at least the western world, something which approximates to leisure consumes a large (some might say increasing) portion of our incomes, time, and physical and psychic energies.

And yet, yes. We do conceive leisure as superfluous and frivolous. This is not to deny that there are 'serious' pastimes that are widely practised and considered to be improving. None the less, even they have to be fitted into 'unobligated' time, and in establishing priorities they must always play second fiddle to career, work, and family. Moreover, as the response to 11 September accurately gauged, we feel morally obliged to acknowledge that, when brought face to face with the realities of life, leisure is 'trivial' and 'irrelevant'. All this could be attributed to a deeply inbred Protestant anxiety about pleasure. But there are also strategic reasons of personal and social psychology why leisure should adopt a mask of triviality and unreality. By conceiving leisure as non-essential, by treating it as a mimetic and symbolic experience,[2] powerful energies can be generated and manipulated, without destabilizing the operation of the 'normal' world. People are able to behave in ways which under normal circumstances would appear threatening and dangerous, but which become acceptable under the implicit understanding that an invisible but impermeable barrier separates the recreational sphere from that of everyday existence. At the same time the notion of separate spheres opens up the possibility that areas of experience can be entered that would be impossible to access in real life; that leisure reaches parts of the human psyche other modes of activity can not. Thus leisure is *both* real and unreal, trivial and serious, and we continue to believe that it is irrelevant at the same time as behaving in a manner which suggests the opposite. As Mike Marqusee has argued, 'the beauty of football, like other games, lies in its sublime pointlessness. . . . The paradox is that precisely because it is utterly trivial, sport becomes saturated with meanings.'[3] It is this ambivalence which makes leisure such a powerful, irreplaceable, and unique aspect of the human makeup.

PURPOSE, SCOPE, AND STRUCTURE

In one sense my intention in writing this book is simply to establish the importance of leisure to the study of British history. Such a mission – which made sense 50, even 25 years ago – might seem unnecessary today. Leisure has been part of the wave of writing on British social and cultural history which originated in the late 1950s and early 1960s, and in which Richard Hoggart, Raymond Williams and Edward Thompson were such a powerful influence.[4] There is now a wealth of highly researched literature on what may be broadly called 'recreational subjects'. Yet there is still a need to assert the significance of the subject. This reflects the continuing legacy of traditional approaches to history in which it was simply impossible to conceive of alehouses and race horses on a par with the machinations of church and state, or even to imagine that they might be in some way interconnected. But just as much a threat as past attitudes regarding what is legitimate are those of the present and future. Increasingly the tendency among those operating at what is conceived as the cutting edge of academe has been to collapse leisure into the broader categories of cultural and theoretical studies. On the one hand, this is an admirable trend. It raises the level of analysis above the obsessive and hagiographic cataloguing of detail associated, for example, with the older forms of sporting or theatre history; it introduces powerful conceptual tools developed in the social sciences; and, above all, it encourages a holistic approach to the subject. On the other hand, there is the danger that everything becomes reduced simply to culture and theory. This runs the risk of distancing the observer from the nitty-gritty of recreational experience, undermining the significance of structural economic and social inputs, and losing all sense of the categories – however imprecisely and artificially constructed – in and through which we live our lives. Work, religion, education, leisure and such like, despite the loose boundaries separating them, constitute for the modern Briton distinctive territories.

One of the aims of this book, therefore, will be to advocate the case for leisure, both contemporarily and historically. This approach involves walking an intellectual tight-rope. If culture is too amorphous a category, could not the same be argued for leisure? Surely it would make more sense to study, as most have done, the separate areas that constitute recreation. But this poses a problem, where to stop? Having embarked on the process of categorization, at what point should one stop? What constitutes a meaningful destination? If sport, why not soccer, bowls, curling, angling, or horse racing; and if racing, why not national hunt, flat, or point to point? All these forms of leisure possess their own separate organizations, rules, and rituals. However, these categories can easily become prisons, narrowing the vision to the point at which study becomes a closed system in which the chronicling of arcane conventions, extraordinary events, superstars (animal and human), and glorious performances are justified in their own terms. If meaningful analysis is to take place, a line has to be drawn between categorization and generalization. The argument of this book is that leisure constitutes a valuable boundary, high enough up the specificity–universality spectrum to obtain the broader vision, yet low enough to make sense of what is being observed. So, for example, it is hoped that historians of sport can learn something that they might otherwise have missed, by placing the subject in the broader context of leisure. The best historians of sport have always instinctively done this, but the aim here is to make the process more explicit. As Pierre Bourdieu has argued, the 'space of sports is not a universe closed in on itself. . . . We are altogether justified in treating sporting practices as a relatively autonomous space, but you shouldn't forget that this space is the locus of forces which do not apply only to it. I merely mean that you can't study the "consumption" of sport . . . independently of the . . . consumption of leisure in general.'[5] To facilitate this approach, a thematic agenda has been adopted. Individual recreations will not be studied in their own right, but as phenomena which contribute to a range of wider social forms and processes. The thematic approach is further emphasized by eschewing a straightforward narrative and chronological framework. If historians of different types of recreations and eras can see a commonality of analysis, and questions are raised about the conventional history of leisure that have remained largely concealed, this book will have served its purpose.

The years 1500–2000 are chosen, as will become clear, to take the long-term perspective, and above all cross the 'great divide' that the Industrial Revolution is often taken to constitute in the history of leisure. However, this is not a comprehensive study of leisure in Britain during the last half-millennium. It is unlikely, given the present state of knowledge, that such a study could be written. The gaps will be clear enough. The years before 1700 are treated less intensively than those after that date, while I have only scratched the surface of the mass of work in sociology, geography, anthropology, media studies, cultural studies, and tourism which explores contemporary society. Some areas of leisure have been treated in greater depth than others. This reflects in part the secondary literature, in part my own interests. Though the geographical boundaries of this study are formally those of the British Isles, England receives the lion's share of the attention and Ireland is treated only cursorily. None the less, it was felt to be important that an attempt was made to obtain a British perspective, because the fates of each of the four nations, in leisure as much as in politics, have been so closely bound to each other, and because the contrasts between the areas provide a valuable comparative framework. Though the themes explored in each of the chapters are large and important, I am conscious that other authors would have cut the cake in different ways. They might have examined some subjects in far greater detail than I have. Professionalization, cultural transmission, religion, and the civilizing process are, for example, all topics which would justify special treatment. The structure adopted therefore reflects my own particular, but it is hoped coherent, vision of the subject.

In the broadest terms the book moves from exploring the structural to the cultural dimensions of leisure. The Introduction tackles the key issues of definition and chronology. What is leisure; is the concept valid throughout the period 1500–2000; and is it possible to detect phases of change in the history of leisure? Chapters 2 to 4 explore the interaction between leisure and economic, political, and social structures. They do so by focusing on three issues that have been central to historians' treatment of these subjects: commercialization, the state, and class. The last of these, while constituting a way of perceiving the structure of society, is also one of the poles around which people build a sense of who they are. In Chapter 5 a range of identities is explored; self, gender, ethnicity, age, family, community, and club. Identity is often closely linked to place (the subject of Chapter 6), which examines locality, region, and nation. Place is also part of the larger space–time continuum investigated in the final part of the book. Chapter 7 addresses space through the themes of tourism and the town–country dialectic, while Chapter 8 assesses the relationship between time, work, and leisure, before exploring typologies of time and memory and the recreative past. The book concludes by re-visiting, in the light of the themes examined in the main body of the text, the core problems raised in the Introduction, of chronology and definition.

P.B.

ACKNOWLEDGEMENTS

Such is the nature of the professional practice of history that to succeed one has to specialize. One of the pleasures in writing this book has been the opportunity to read a variety of exciting books and articles, from several disciplines, that focusing exclusively on my own period and specialism would not have justified. My debt to these authors will be clear from the notes and bibliography. This book could not have been written without the work that they have undertaken. Nor could it have been compiled without the support of the staff of several libraries, in particular the National Library of Wales and the University of Wales, Lampeter. I am grateful to the latter institution for allowing me periods of study leave in which to research and write this book, and for my colleagues in the history department for their ongoing support. I also owe a debt to the anonymous readers who commented on the original proposal, and the two readers who made detailed and helpful reports on the finished manuscript. I am grateful to Jeremy Black, who set the ball rolling; Terka Acton and Sonya Barker at Palgrave Macmillan for their sympathetic guidance and assistance; and my copy-editors Jocelyn Stockley and Valery Rose for preparing the manuscript for the press. Over the years I have picked the brains – and benefited from the feedback of conference and seminar papers – of many fellow historians on the subject of leisure, but for specific kindnesses I would like to thank Gary Cross for responding with such alacrity and supplying a copy of his study of Anglo-American leisure; Alastair Durie, Christiane Eisenberg, Michael Schaich, Keith Robbins and Jon Stobart for sending me offprints; my postgraduates Laura Williams, David Lloyd, Anne Phillips and Mike Benbough-Jackson from whom I have learnt so much; Neil Evans for providing offprints and attempting to set me straight on Wales (only the text will tell if he has succeeded); and John Jenkins, whose encyclopaedic bibliographic skills and knowledge of sport I have drawn heavily on. My Welsh friends will never forgive me for preferring football to rugby, and my children have sat through tedious hours of sports and opera broadcasts in the car, and suffered the torment of château and country-house visiting. This book is dedicated to Clare and Sarah as recompense. The influence of Anne is present throughout this study. She will recognize the books of hers that I have stolen and the ideas that I have borrowed.

1

INTRODUCTION

DEFINITION

Most histories of leisure wisely eschew any concerted attempt to define the subject, depending instead upon a common-sense meaning shared between writer and reader. There is much to be said for this approach. Detailed definitions can tie a noose around a subject which later restricts the scope of investigation. Moreover, in the case of leisure, the subject's very imprecision – its capacity to flow into other areas – is fundamental to its functional effectiveness. None the less, in a work where the case is being made for the study of leisure, some attempt at definition is unavoidable. Two basic approaches can be adopted; the negative, which emphasizes what leisure is not (its 'extrinsic contextual elements'), and the positive, which focuses on what it is (its 'intrinsic qualities').[1] The first of these methods, though it avoids having to tackle the beast directly, requires all the other animals in the jungle to be identified; that is, it necessitates some description of the various categories of experience, other than leisure, through which we live our lives. Very roughly these may be delineated as work, education, religion, civil life (which includes politics and voluntary work), and ordinary life (a big bag that encompasses 'necessary' activities like sleeping, resting, eating, and sex). Leisure can thus be defined as what is left once these categories have been removed. Since the areas outlined above can be conceived, in one form or another, as 'obligations', then leisure is often defined in terms of what transpires in 'discretionary or unobligated time'.[2] This is encapsulated in the *Concise Oxford Dictionary*'s definition of leisure as 'free time, time at one's own disposal'.

The most important single category against which leisure is commonly defined is 'work'. *The International Encyclopedia of the Social Sciences* declares that 'leisure . . . consists first and foremost in freedom from gainful employment in a place of business', and the Routledge *Social Science Encyclopedia*, which brackets leisure under the alphabetical entry for 'work', defines it, among other things, as 'time free from work and other necessary activities'.[3] That the meaning of leisure is closely tied to the nature of work is undeniable. But giving work such a dominant role in characterizing leisure raises several problems. First, for the historian of the *longue durée* it smacks of a time-tied definition, forged in the satanic mills of Industrial Revolution Britain. Has work always been so important that it determined all other areas of people's lives? Secondly, what is meant by work? A notion tied too tightly to activities for which there is an overt material or economic return would exclude tasks such as unpaid caring, child-rearing, and domestic duties. None the less, such activities exert as much influence as paid work on the lives of those involved, imposing constraints upon them and limiting their unobligated time. Moreover, because these tasks have traditionally been undertaken predominantly by women, defining work in crude economic terms will skew the notion of leisure in a masculine direction. Thirdly, what of people who do not work; the part-employed, the underemployed, the unemployed, and those, by choice or otherwise, outside the labour market – the retired elderly, young children, the disabled, the sick, the country gentleman, and the playboy? At any one time they might constitute a sizeable element, perhaps a majority, of the population. Are they all, by virtue of not working, in a permanent state of leisure? If such a position is not tenable, then how much leisure do they experience, and what exactly, if it is not work, determines the nature of this experience?

Fourthly, the notion of work defining leisure rests on the assumption that it is possible to distinguish clearly between the two activities. This is far from obvious. Music, for example, has accompanied many work situations, and was particularly common among miners, textile workers, and sailors. The so-called 'waulking' songs of the Hebridean weavers were sung while hand-shrinking the cloth, so as to ease the effort involved and organize the production schedule, while shanties were deployed by sailors to develop co-ordination and team work to facilitate the completion of strenuous tasks like hauling the sails or lifting the anchor.[4] Singing and modulated sound also played its part in agricultural work.[5] Even in non-manual jobs, music, through electronic mediums such as the radio and CD player, is today frequently employed, 'to reproduce an aesthetic environment of "working" and to circumscribe within that environment "Where the mind can go" '.[6] Some places of entertainment have also serviced the world of work, notably the alehouse and pub, which from at least the sixteenth century until the twentieth century acted effectively as an employment exchange, and until the truck legislation of the 1870s, as a wage office.[7] Conversely, some sites of work have become places of pleasure. Redundant mines, mills, and docks have been turned into 'working' museums, and active plant, like the Bulmers cider brewery in Hereford and the Sellafield nuclear reprocessing plant, have become the object of 'factory tourism'.[8] Perhaps the most serious problem in trying to distinguish between work and leisure, and therefore defining leisure in terms of non-work, is the fact that a significant and growing proportion of the population are employed in the leisure 'industry'. For a professional footballer or pop star the experience of a match or gig is not the same as that of their audience. However, performers of this type rarely see their 'work' in the same light as would a miner, farm labourer, or accountant. Something of the task and occasion rubs off, so that they operate in a marginal world between work and leisure.

The difficulties in defining leisure negatively are compounded when investigating areas outside work. Education for the conventional pupil and student might seem a clearly defined category of experience, equivalent to work, against which leisure can be defined. But for those attending night classes in painting or car maintenance, and retired people taking a university degree, education will often be primarily a form of recreation. And what should we make of the seventeenth- and eighteenth-century tour? It might be read as a form of holiday. However, the Grand Tour often contained some formal element of training in dancing, fencing, languages, and other social graces. Celia Fiennes, the intrepid tourist of Augustan England, was clear about the didactic function of travelling:

> if all persons, both Ladies, much more Gentlemen, would spend some of their tyme in Journeys to visit their native Land, and be curious to inform themselves and make observations . . . the Ladies might have matter not unworthy their observation . . . and thence studdy how to be serviceable to their neighbours especially the poor among whome they dwell. . . . But much more requisite is it for Gentlemen in general service of their country . . . especially those that serve in parliament.[9]

Charitable duties, alluded to by Fiennes, were not for eighteenth-century polite society simply a branch of civil life. Inputs of leisure would also be involved, through, for example, the arrangement of charity balls, concerts, and festivals.[10]

The boundary between religion and recreation is also blurred. In pre-modern Britain leisure occasions were closely tied to the festivals of the Christian calendar. Douglas Reid has claimed of nineteenth-century Britain that 'much church-going could be defined from a utilitarian point of view as having the essential social qualities of other leisure-time pursuits, namely their voluntary, non-remunerative, pleasure-seeking nature', and Richard Holt argued that 'the blanket labelling of sport as a "religion" is too vague to be meaningful but when applied to specific national forms, to rugby in Wales or football in Scotland . . . seems sufficiently powerful to qualify as "an elementary form of religious life" '.[11] The fusion of the sacred and the profane emerges most strikingly in the custom of the wake, especially but not exclusively associated with Ireland, where the sombre proceedings of commemorating the dead could descend into a scene of bacchanalian revelry, much to the horror of the church.[12]

Defining leisure negatively is, therefore, problematic. In particular it runs the risk of undervaluing what it describes. Leisure becomes what is left when all the more important and serious areas of life have been accounted for. Most strikingly this is seen in definitions which revolve around work, in which an often very narrow, highly masculine notion of labour is prioritized, and taken to be the engine which propels the entire social machine. However, it is equally tenable to place leisure in the driving seat, and to argue that people do not recreate themselves to relieve the toil of work, but labour in order to provide the resources with which to recreate themselves. The so-called 'leisure preference' is one several historians have recognized and governments have feared.[13] Theories of leisure based on non-obligated time, though they may drop any formal reference to work, suffer from the same disadvantage. There is always the idea that there are 'obligations' that are more important than pleasure, the pursuit of which cannot be conceived of as an end in its own right. What is needed, therefore, is a positive definition of leisure which isolates its intrinsic qualities.

This is easier said than done, because of the problem of not only determining what these characteristics might be, but, having identified them, demonstrating that they are in some way specific to leisure. Joffre Dumazedier argues that

the positive functions of leisure can be summed up as follows. (1) . . . a chance to shake off the fatigue of work . . . (2) . . . escape from the daily boredom of performing a set of limited and routine tasks. (3) . . . leisure makes it possible for the individual to . . . enter into a realm of self-transcendance where his creative powers are set free to oppose or reinforce the dominant values of his civilization.[14]

Though acknowledging the distinction between negative and positive traits, we find even the positive ones outlined have a strong sense of the negative, and this applies to most definitions which accommodate a notion of 'freedom'.[15] What is often meant is 'freedom from' rather than 'freedom to', and even in the latter case it is often unclear what sort of experience is being envisaged; freedom to do what? The pursuit of pleasure might be the answer.[16] However, quite apart from the problem of accommodating recreations which embrace elements of pain and punishment, and there are surprisingly many of these, the notion remains too intangible to be satisfying. In the interests of specificity, therefore, I would suggest the following three 'intrinsic' characteristics: symbol, play, and the 'other'. By *symbol* is meant a notion of representation; a surrogate, image, or metaphor for some other phenomenon. So, for example, the birds in a cockfight or mounts in a horse race could be said to represent their owners and those who bet on them, and a piece of landscape to represent a nation. By *play* is meant something synthetic, unreal, and experimental; a self-contained activity without obvious consequence or significance, a mere game. Hence, especially in the wake of 11 September, sport can be portrayed as 'trivial' and 'irrelevant'. There is a fundamental social convention that leisure, however our experience might suggest otherwise, is not to be taken seriously; that as the spectator exits the cockpit, the theatre, the sports' stadium, the club and pub, he or she leaves the fantasy for the real world. The notion of a fantasy world is also implied in the idea of the 'other'. This need not be confined to a specific location, though in the case of tourism and the holiday, place is of vital significance, but can embrace any experience which is 'other' than that conceived of as normal.

A number of points need to be made about this 'definition'. It is not free from the criticism of definition by negation, especially in the context of the 'other'. This recognizes the fact that intrinsic to the concept of leisure is the existence of other categories of experience without which it could not exist; and, indeed, that these categories constitute a mutually supportive and inter-dependent package, in which none could operate without the presence of the others. The three characteristics outlined are not exclusive to leisure, but are present in some degree in all human activities. The argument here is that leisure is particularly saturated with these traits, and that they are present in this specific combination. Perhaps the closest alternative fit to leisure on this definition is religion, with its high levels of symbolic behaviour and the presence of the 'other'. But, much as a sacred ritual might resemble theatre to the agnostic, there can be no denying the ultimate reality and seriousness of religious worship to believers, for whom God and the afterlife are no fiction and game. If religion lacks the element of play, the same might also be argued of a range of activities – reading, gardening, craft hobbies, and such like – that could be described as 'serious' leisure. Such pastimes often 'mimic' work or education. This has the advantage of legitimizing leisure in a society in which work and learning are dominant ethics. The promotion of 'rational recreations' during the Victorian era can be read in this light. However, gardening is not the same as agricultural labouring, pleasure reading as structured learning. In both cases, embedded in and defining the recreational forms are elements of play.

Such a line of argument does not exclude the possibility that a particular activity – though we might define it in terms of its predominant characteristic – can embody a mixture of two or more categories of experience. An evening class might be *both* educational and recreational, charitable work *both* a branch of civil life and a pastime. Equally, the *same* activity might occupy different categories, depending upon its intrinsic qualities. Take the example of a meal. Everyday eating – breakfast, the lunchtime snack, and the run-of-the-mill dinner – would be part of ordinary life. Symbolic behaviour and play would be present, but they would be operating at a non-intensive subconscious level. The central aim would be to feed. The 'other' would be almost wholly absent. Compare this with a funeral wake, a Shrovetide Feast, a harvest festival dinner, the office Christmas party, or a romantic restaurant meal, where the participants would be well aware that these are out-of-the-ordinary occasions. Special food and drink, some with mood-changing qualities, would be consumed, and in volumes which would normally be considered excessive. Some of the food might be 'exotic', drawn from foreign areas of the world; much would be steeped in tradition – the Christmas turkey and pudding in England, Shrovetide Fastyn Cock (roasted oatmeal dumplings) and Sauty Bannock (cakes of egg, salt, and meal) in northern Scotland[17] – invested with special meaning. There would be a common awareness that the feasting is there to facilitate a wider purpose, such as the encouragement of a personal relationship, the marking of the year, and the celebration of the family or community. In other words, the event would be freighted with symbolic meaning, a piece of leisure rather than simply a part of ordinary life.

HISTORY AND LEISURE

A central problem in characterizing leisure is whether the concept has a historically stable meaning. Hugh Cunningham, refusing to come to any simple exposition of the category, has argued that 'For a historian . . . it [leisure] cannot be pinned down to a neat one-sentence definition, for it is precisely the change in its use that is significant.'[18] Many commentators have taken this argument one step further, suggesting, directly or by inference, that leisure is a product of the Industrial Revolution, and that before the late eighteenth century it scarcely existed. Dumazedier contends that

> for leisure to become possible in the life of the great majority of workers, two preconditions must exist in society at large. First,

society ceases to govern its activities by means of common ritual obligations. . . . Second, the work by which a man earns his living is set apart from his other activities. . . . These two necessary conditions exist only in the social life of industrial and postindustrial civilizations; their absence from archaic and traditional agrarian civilizations means the absence of leisure.[19]

John Clarke and Chas Critcher take the view not so much that leisure was absent before the nineteenth century, but that it could not be separated from work, and was therefore effectively indistinguishable as a category of experience; 'looking overall at the trends evident by the 1840s, the clearest impression is of the wholesale changes in the rhythms and sites of work and leisure enforced by the industrial revolution. It was during this period that what we have come to see as a discrete area of human activity called "leisure" became recognisable.'[20] Many commentators would share the perspective that industrialization generated separate spheres of work and leisure.[21] Given the view that recent trends in post-industrial and post-modern society have tended to merge the spheres together again,[22] it might be contended that it was only for two centuries that a distinct phenomenon of leisure existed.

This is not the argument adopted here. One of the central purposes of this book is to argue the case that leisure can and should be explored across a long time span, and that the failure to do so distorts our understanding of it. Though transformations of a radical nature in the form and character of leisure have occurred, there are also underlying continuities, based on the defining qualities outlined above, which make it permissible to examine the same category of experience in 2000 as in 1500. The door to such an approach was opened by Peter Burke in 1995. He noted that 'Implicitly or explicitly, most recent work [on leisure] has been based on one central hypothesis, that of a fundamental discontinuity or great divide between pre-industrial and industrial society. According to this view, in medieval and early modern Europe, as in other pre-industrial societies, the modern idea of leisure was lacking.' Questioning the viability of the 'discontinuity thesis', he identified a series of 'discourses' (educational, legal and political, theological–moral, and medical) and sources and pieces of evidence (courtesy guides, recreational treatises, paintings, villa vacations, academies, the use of time, and rational recreations) which pointed to the 'invention of leisure in early modern Europe'.[23] In fact since the early 1970s, and J. H. Plumb's argument for the 'commercialization of leisure in eighteenth-century England', 'the great divide' had been slipping backwards in time to a point well before the classic era of the Industrial Revolution. Moreover, as early as 1980 Hugh Cunningham, in a strikingly innovative study of *Leisure in the Industrial Revolution*, expressed grave doubts about 'the implicit assumption that society before the Industrial Revolution may be satisfactorily described in such terms as "traditional", "pre-industrial" or "the old society" ', and proclaimed 'continuities . . . as much the theme of this book as changes'.[24]

As it turned out, the principal challenge to Burke's view has come not from a historian of industrial Britain, seeking to defend the 'great divide', but from a historian of Europe, Joan-Luis Marfany, aiming to dismantle divides *per se* (though not notions of change). Marfany considered leisure, and a consciousness (especially among the lower orders) of the difference between recreation and work, to be a feature of medieval society; and argued that the early modern 'invention' of leisure was a specifically elite response to a growing separation of duties and pastimes, and a feeling that the former were becoming increasingly burdensome.[25] How far it is appropriate to go along the road of demolishing *all* divides is a matter for debate. Burke finds 'neither the continuity thesis espoused by Marfany nor the opposite thesis of sharp discontinuity are completely satisfactory', and warns of the dangers of 'anachronism'.[26] There is clearly a risk of imposing modern conceptual categories on pre-modern society. Focusing on symbol, play, and otherness is an attempt to use elements which could be applied equally to modern and pre-modern patterns of behaviour. Sometimes the distinction between pre-modern and modern pastimes is taken to be that the former is predominantly ritualistic and embedded in a festive culture, while the latter is rationalistic (an abstract measure of skill) and autonomous. This is not entirely convincing. For all the efforts of commentators to clothe modern sport in a scientific discourse, the behaviour of the fans and performers is intensely ritualistic; and though we do not share many of the festivals of our ancestors, modern society has shown a remarkable capacity to 'invent' new types of festive culture and 'reinvent' traditional festivals.

These issues will be elaborated upon later. An important question is: To what extent were pre-industrial people conscious of a phenomenon called 'leisure', as opposed to individual pastimes? Amongst the elite there appears, in particular from written evidence, to be, as Burke has argued, an awareness of a generic notion of pleasure. However, at the level of popular culture, where little evidence of conscious categorization as such survives, the position is far from clear. Would those attending an alehouse or a bull fight have seen the common characteristics of these activities? The same question could be asked of parallel pastimes today, and the answer may not be as clear cut as some might imagine. I would guess that in pre-industrial society there would be some awareness that the mixture of symbol, play, and otherness did produce a particular type of experience, but that it is unlikely that for most people a single concept like 'leisure' would have been used, or available, to describe this.

Though the linguistic point is an important one, the unavailability of labels does not of itself preclude the existence of common experiences. Historians of pre-industrial politics and religion will readily examine the past in terms of these categories without agonizing as to whether their subjects conceived of their worlds in these terms. Persisting with the idea that, to put it crudely, we have leisure whereas our pre-modern ancestors did not simply prevents the exploration of an important phenomenon across the *longue durée*. To argue in this manner does not exclude the possibility, indeed the likelihood, of radical change – it simply allows the character of this change to be plotted, and the elements of continuity to be identified; or, in the words of the sports historian Richard Holt, it permits 'the tension between timeless impulses and historical time' to be properly explored.[27]

CHRONOLOGY

It will be clear from the above discussion that I do not see the chronological point of departure for this book, 1500, as a 'great divide'. Given the apparently limited nature of research on recreations and pastimes in medieval Britain it would be difficult to make any firm pronouncements on the period, other than that people engaged in a wide variety of pastimes and recreations, some of which bear more than a passing resemblance to those followed today. The year 1500 is chosen partly for pragmatic reasons: that from this date there is a relevant secondary literature available on which (tentative) judgements can be based, that the early modern period is one with which I have some research familiarity, and that to attempt coverage of more than five centuries would be too tall an order. In part the choice of date also reflects a view that the Reformation is important in understanding leisure. Caution should be exercised in making too much of this; above all one should be aware of the risk of succumbing to the myth of the kill-joy puritans. However, the Reformation was a sea-change event in the cultural life of Britain and Europe, and, as Peter Burke makes clear, the theological–moral discourse was one area where new notions of leisure were being forged. The finishing point of *c*. 2000 was the product of a variety of decisions. First and foremost was the need to cross the threshold of the Industrial Revolution. When it became clear that many historians of leisure see the late nineteenth century as even more important than the late eighteenth century, it was felt necessary to carry the story further. Stopping at the Second World War would have made sense. The sheer volume of secondary material that could be said to be relevant after this date is overwhelming. None the less, even a passing acquaintance – no pretence is made that the post-war literature is being surveyed in any other than a fragmentary fashion – with this output suggests that it is here that the notion of radical change is most prevalent and consequently most in need of a little historical perspective.

It is no part of this book's agenda to argue for a leisure stasis. That said, a thematic as opposed to a chronological approach has been adopted. This may lead to a lack of clarity as to the processes of change under way, and give a misleading impression as to the strength of continuity. It may be helpful at this stage, therefore, to outline some of the broad phases of change suggested by historians. Though the 'great divide' has overshadowed much work on the subject, in practice a range of more flexible time boundaries have emerged as historians tackling different aspects of leisure, and operating from different perspectives, have established their own chronologies. One factor which complicates the issue is the manner in which change is mediated through a range of variables, such as town and country, region, social class, gender, and individual pastimes. So a particular recreation, or form of a recreation, may experience its own internal life-cycle – such as the 1960s dance craze for the twist – the rise and fall of which does not, of itself, reflect the fortunes of leisure as a whole. Similarly, there are differing regional experiences; the seaside holiday and the modern game of cricket made much faster initial progress during the eighteenth century in the south than in the north of England, and the Depression of the 1930s – and its consequent impact on recreational life – was much more keenly felt in some areas of Britain (such as South Wales and the north-east of England) than others.

Whilst acknowledging the importance of such variables, six main phases of change have been postulated for the period 1500–2000. First, Ronald Hutton finds strong 'evidence for the accumulation of communal customs and for the elaboration of the ritual year in England between about 1350 and 1520'; in other words, for a late medieval making of 'merry England'.[28] Such an enrichment of the nation's recreational culture made the second phase, that instigated by the Reformation of the 1530s, all the more distinctive. Though any crude notion of a sudden Protestant crackdown on pleasure is difficult to sustain, there appears a long-term but uneven and highly contested process of attrition by which England was deprived of some of its traditional merry-making, such as mumming, maypoles, church-ales, and summer games.[29] In Scotland the process bit deeper with the onset of a more rigorous Calvinist reformation.[30] Underpinning change was a re-evaluation of the categories through which people lived their lives. Keith Thomas has argued that 'only in the sixteenth century does the fundamental economic importance of labour as a factor of production seem to have been explicitly recognized. . . . It is in the religious teaching of the post-Reformation period . . . that the positive merit of hard work is most clearly asserted.'[31] Such a valorization of work did not necessarily imply a wholesale abandonment of leisure. However, it did require a reassessment of how work, leisure and religion – and, indeed, education, civil life, and ordinary life – interacted. A third phase was entered in the years after the Restoration of Charles II in 1660. The 'attack on secular merry-making [was] called off for half a century', and more positively, Britain witnessed the Enlightenment and what has been called 'the commercialization of leisure', a process involving the placing of high-status pastimes into the market place, and their expansion and reformulation along more urban and polite lines.[32] Some of these changes had been anticipated in the late Tudor and early Stuart period, with the rise of the spa town and horse racing, and the flowering of the Elizabethan and Jacobean commercial theatre in London.

Though traditionally the late eighteenth century has been demarcated as the point of 'take-off' for the fourth phase, the Industrial Revolution, there is plenty in the economic development of Britain since the late seventeenth century to indicate a marked quickening in industrial growth before the 1780s. Indeed, it could be argued that the commercialization of leisure was part and parcel of the same economic process as industrialization. Moreover, one of the features most associated with the Industrial Revolution, the attack on popular recreations and customs, was anticipated during the Reformation phase. The tendency among historians now is to stress not the narrowing of the recreational world of the common people, the so-called 'leisure vacuum', but the 'efflorescence of popular leisure in the later eighteenth and early nineteenth centuries'.[33] Yet the notion of the 'great divide' remains difficult to shift and it may be unwise to push too hard. The short-term impact of industrialization on certain regions and social groups was considerable, and the long-term consequences of it, and the attendant urbanization, were to be huge for the entirety of Britain. This prompts the question: At what point did industrialization and urbanization bite so deeply that they stimulated a quantitative and qualitative change in leisure *en masse*, penetrating most regions and social classes? Many commentators would point to this fifth phase originating at some point between the mid-nineteenth century and the First World War. Peter Bailey, in a review of the recent literature on the history of leisure, sees 'a general confirmation of the middle years of the nineteenth century as marking the emergence of a recognizably modern leisure', adding that 'the most crucial stage in this general transformation comes in the last quarter of the century'.[34] Hugh Cunningham finds 'widespread agreement that a new phase in the history of leisure opens up in the mid-nineteenth century'.[35] Historians of sport are especially keen to see the origins of modern games in the mid- to later Victorian years, Neil Tranter concluding that 'there is no doubt that the period between the mid-nineteenth century and the outbreak of the First World War was characterised by a notable transformation in the scale and nature of Britain's sporting culture'.[36] Key factors in this transformation are the continuing impact of industrialization and urbanization – in the latter case so that more people were living not just in towns but in very large cities and conurbations – a rise in the real incomes of a large sector of the working class, and the rapid development of the communications (especially rail) network, integrating the supply and demand for leisure.

Where the next divide comes is more difficult to say. Bailey argues that after the First World War 'leisure continued to expand, mostly in reinforcement and extension of pre-war patterns'.[37] Individual forms of entertainment, such as the music hall and cinema, declined and rose in a compensatory swing; other pastimes like the seaside holiday consolidated their hold on the broad mass of the population; and the Depression of the 1930s exacerbated regional differences. But there seems no compelling case to argue that leisure entered upon a new phase. The same could be argued for the years immediately after the Second World War. The nearer one gets to the present, the greater the difficulty given the reduction in long-term perspective, in establishing significant trends, and the greater the risk of dramatizing the level of change recently or currently under way. However, Arthur Marwick's proposition 'that there was a self-contained period . . . commonly known as the "sixties", of outstanding historical significance in that what happened during this period transformed social and cultural developments for the rest of the century', and Jonathon Green's view that the sixties constituted the 'pivotal decade' of the twentieth century, are plausible.[38] Marwick's 'cultural revolution' was not an exclusively British phenomenon, and it may be that what most characterizes this sixth phase is not so much a distinctive set of values, as the internationalization and globalization of leisure through developments in the media, communications, and transport. To what extent the sixties represented the high-point or the dissolution of modernity; how far they were separate from or anticipated postmodernism; and to what extent postmodernity and post-Fordism constitute a new phase in the history of leisure or simply a late modernist version of modernity is unclear. In the confused situation of the contemporary scene it may be best not to pronounce on the existence or otherwise of a further phase in the history of leisure.

2

ECONOMY

The economic history of leisure has not, with some notable exceptions, received a great deal of attention.[1] Seaside holidays, May Day frolics, and street gambling have found it hard to compete with heavy-weight subjects like crop yields, railway construction, banking, and textile manufacture. Underpinning such differential treatment may be an anxiety as to whether there is such a thing as a leisure economy. Even if the answer is 'Yes', there may be a feeling that the 'leisure economy' is simply a by-product of a 'real' economy of manufacture and commerce, parasitic on and potentially threatening to its success.

The position adopted in this book is that leisure is as fundamental a part of the economy as any other sector, that this goes not simply for the contemporary scene but also historically, and that the notion of parasitical and productive sectors is untenable, reflecting a moral rather than an economic standpoint. This does not, however, address the question: How far does leisure constitute a *distinctive* sector within the wider economy? It is this question which underpins the discussion in the following chapter. The first part will explore the arguments which seek to 'normalize' the leisure economy by demonstrating how it related to an influential model of economic change, commercialization; and by examining the forces of demand and supply. The second part will investigate those characteristics of leisure which may be argued to make it 'abnormal' or peculiar.

Discussion is hampered by three major problems, one practical and the other two theoretical. First, if the economic history of leisure is generally under-researched, then that of the years before the eighteenth century constitutes a virtual wasteland. Secondly, in examining what is distinctive about the leisure economy problems of definition become acute. Were harvest dinners a form of celebration or a payment in kind? Is the construction of a cinema a facet of the building or the entertainment industries? Thirdly, built into our understanding of economics and economic history are notions of normality. By and large the norm for the early modern and modern periods is taken to be a capitalist, profit-orientated economy, operating on a principle of 'rationality', occupied by a male workforce, and comprising agricultural, commercial, and industrial sectors. To conform, leisure must approximate to this norm. But why should leisure itself not set the norm? The point is particularly apposite since some of the characteristics often attributed to the leisure economy, such as utility-maximization and high risk taking, can often be seen in the so-called normal economy. The rash of investment in high-technology shares in the late 1990s must challenge notions that the financial markets and big industry automatically operate to an abstract model of 'rational' economic behaviour.

COMMERCIALIZATION

Historians of leisure have generally worked hard to incorporate the development of leisure into the capitalist narrative of economic development. In this way leisure takes a place alongside that of the other sectors contributing to the story of British economic progress. Within the grand economic narrative there are a number of sub-narratives. For historians of leisure, by far the most important of these is commercialization. The centrality of the idea to the development of leisure is suggested by the fact that it, unlike industrialization, earns a separate entry in the ABC-Clio *Encyclopedia of World Sport*, where it is defined as 'that aspect of the sports enterprise that involves the sale, display, or use of sport or some other aspect of sport so as to produce income'. The entry goes on to warn that 'the commercialisation of sport is not a cultural universal, but a product of unique technical, social, and economic circumstances'.[2] Much of leisure historians' time has been dedicated to exploring how these unique circumstances came together to transform traditional forms of pleasure into new forms of income-generating products. Thus discussion of the economic history of leisure is invariably framed in terms of factors like markets, wealth, income, prices, consumers, commodities, products, capital, investment, and technologies.

Three broad schools of commercialization have emerged, focused on the eighteenth, nineteenth, and twentieth centuries, though within these, important sub-phases have been identified. Inspired by J. H. Plumb and his thesis, first fully articulated in 1972, of 'the commercialisation of leisure in eighteenth-century England', the century or so after the Glorious Revolution of 1688 has been portrayed as the crucible of a new leisure economy.[3] This involved the placing of high-status pastimes and products into the public market place. John Brewer argues that in the early eighteenth century, church and state reduced their role as patrons of the arts, creating a 'cultural vacuum' into which poured the providers of commercial leisure.[4] Music, theatre, and painting became highly marketable products,[5] Peter Clark and Rab Houston maintaining that in the art world 'a dense network of informal clubs gathered together artists and patrons on a more equal footing, de-emphasising old-style, seigneurial patronage relationships in favour of more commercial arrangements'.[6] A crucial development was the widespread adoption of the subscription system by which recreations and luxury products – such as horse-racing prizes, musical concerts, and books – were funded on a collective basis, providing a halfway house between the patron and the anonymous market place.[7] Quite at what point during the long eighteenth century commercialization began to make a really telling impact is a moot point. David Solkin sees the 'advent of the exhibitions' from the 1760s dramatically altering the visual arts as 'The market . . . began to intrude upon the consciousness of the public sphere . . . prompting a recognition that the self-determining laws of commodity production had come to play an increasingly predominant role in determining the directions that culture was to take.'[8] Simon McVeigh's study of concert life in London also emphasizes the latter part of the century as a turning point, while it is clear that many of the entertainments that contributed to the upsurge in popular leisure detected by Hugh Cunningham and Adrian Harvey in the late eighteenth and early nineteenth century 'were frankly commercial in nature'.[9]

Locating the commercialization of leisure in the long eighteenth century has the effect of de-prioritizing the significance of the Industrial Revolution. Mike Huggins has argued that horse racing was already a commercialized recreation in the early nineteenth century, and that the sport was 'transformed to only a minor extent by the processes of capitalism, urbanization and industrialization'.[10] However, for most who occupy the nineteenth-century school these three factors would be of decisive significance, and the crucial watershed would be the latter part of the century as industrialization created the context in which the production of leisure became, as never before, a business- and consumer-orientated enterprise. Pamela Horn contends that 'it was the commercialisation of leisure which was to be the most striking feature of the final years of the [nineteenth] century', and James Walvin proposes that 'the central feature of the transformation of English recreations in the last quarter of the [nineteenth] century is that the new forms depended essentially on forms of consumer goods and services which . . . were functions of an expanding economy'.[11] Music hall[12] and popular publishing[13] have both been identified as part of this process, but sport is often taken to be the area of leisure most affected. Wray Vamplew argues that 'commercialised spectator sport for the mass market became one of the economic success stories of late Victorian Britain', and Neil Tranter that 'we must not lose sight of the fact that, in essence, the sporting culture of late nineteenth- and early twentieth-century Britain was quite unlike anything that preceded it. Sport, in its modern, organised, commercialised and extensive form was truly an "invention" of the Victorian and Edwardian age.'[14]

For historians of the twentieth century the transforming influence of commercialization did not stop at 1914. Stephen Jones contends that 'the process of commercialisation was unfinished in the 1890s' and it was only during the inter-war period that 'entertainment and leisure became big business'.[15] Joseph McAleer similarly accepts the Victorian contribution, but argues that 1914–50 'represents the first time the mass reading public was commercially managed and exploited in a recognizably modern way'.[16] What McAleer calls the 'mass commercialization of popular publishing'[17] is something which Richart Hoggart associates far more with the years after the Second World War,[18] while developments in the media and sport, and crucially the interaction between the two in the later twentieth century, have led many commentators to see this as the period in which leisure was finally exposed to the full force of the market place, leading Richard Holt and Tony Mason to adopt the concept of 'hyper-commercialization' to describe the economics of sport in this period.[19]

That so many historians, dealing with very different eras, have resorted to the same economic concept to describe and account for the changing character of leisure is potentially problematic. Just as the middle class are always said to be rising, as we shall see, so leisure is always said to be commercializing. Is it plausible that the same engine is driving the machine at all times, or are we seeing here the unwitting expression of a common ideology among historians? It could be argued that there is a degree of specificity to the chronology, in that those pressing for evidence of an early impact of the market place on leisure have generally not pushed the boundaries back before the late seventeenth century. However, to what extent is such an analysis simply the product of a lack of research? Medievalists now readily see commercialization as a powerful force in transforming the general economy and society of England since at least 1000, if not before.[20] With an increasingly monetarized, exchange-based, and market-driven economy, and more and more people living in towns, was it possible that leisure remained aloof from this process? One commentator has referred to the 'commercialization of the tournament' in the twelfth and thirteenth centuries,[21] and work on topics as varied as popular publishing, the theatre, and alehouses before 1660 suggests a recreational culture in which at least sectors were already well attuned to providing for the market.[22] It is hard to conceive that it could have been otherwise, with 200,000 people occupying London by 1600, and perhaps double that number by the middle of the seventeenth century.[23]

If commercialization is omnipresent in the worlds of both early modern and modern recreations, how great is its value as a model in accounting for the changing economic history of leisure? One approach is to treat commercialization as a long-term process, already well advanced by the early modern period, in which a growing proportion of output and GNP is transacted through the market, involving exchanges in kind or money. Following this model, leisure would be drawn continuously and increasingly, though perhaps at a rate slower than other sectors, into the commercial economy. The commercialization of leisure could thus be portrayed as an ongoing process in which the market grabs an ever-increasing share of output. In such a scenario the arguments for an eighteenth-, nineteenth-, and twentieth-century commercialization of leisure are not contradictory, but represent higher and higher levels of market penetration. This is plausible, but it does raise a number of problems. First, there is an assumption of a progressive process of commercialization. Is this tenable? Periods of stagnation and even retreat might be expected, even though little attempt has been made to identify these. Secondly, is there an end game, a point at which leisure will become entirely commercialized?

If so, what economic model will then come into play? Thirdly, can the argument for higher and higher levels of commercialization be demonstrated convincingly? Is contemporary leisure as commercialized as the model of progressive market penetration would suggest? There are many recreations today, often delivered through the voluntary sector – such as visiting, walking, reading, amateur dramatics and sports, and community social events – which involve comparatively low levels of monetary exchange but deliver a high degree of output in terms of time consumed and pleasure derived. How commercialized are these activities, and, more to the point, how much more commercialized is leisure in 2000 than in 1900, 1700, and even 1500?

Given the present state of knowledge many of the questions raised above cannot be answered. They may be unanswerable. This should not necessarily prompt an agnostic response. Common sense suggests that in absolute terms there is a good deal more commercialized leisure produced and consumed than ever before. The long-term growth in the population, personal wealth (one index of real incomes suggests a growth from 100 in 1801, to 113 in 1851, 240 in 1901, 363 in 1951, and 702 in 1981),[24] and GNP would make such an outcome virtually inevitable. Moreover, leisure would be a major beneficiary from the tendency for a growing proportion of any extra income earned, as personal wealth expands, to be spent on non-essentials. So though we may remain open-minded about whether leisure as experienced by consumers is more commercialized than at some particular point in the past, it is perfectly reasonable to argue for a great increase in the volume and scope of leisure products available in the market place. However, in turning to commercialization to explain the development of leisure, what is needed is not a universal model of change that can (and has tended to) be applied to all periods, but one that recognizes the manner in which the model has changed over time. Critical to such an approach is a focus on the factors of demand and supply, and how, historically, variations in these have influenced the commercialization of leisure.[25]

DEMAND

Commercialization is premised upon there being a demand, or more precisely a potential demand, for a product. A crucial determinant of demand is the volume and distribution of wealth. Concern with this underpins the work of many historians of leisure, and can be used to argue for the commercialization of leisure being a phased process. Four broad stages have been detected. First, there is the pre-commercialization phase, embracing the years before 1660. The vast majority of the population are considered too poor to possess the resources to spend on non-essentials like leisure. The few in society who do enjoy substantial personal wealth, the crown, aristocracy, and gentry, are too small in numbers to constitute a genuine market, and their demand can be satisfied by the mechanism of the patron–client relationship. The second phase, originating in the late seventeenth century, witnesses the rapid expansion in the numbers and wealth of the middling orders (manufacturers, wealthy tradesmen, and especially the professions), under the influence of a commercial and 'industrious' revolution. This not only generated new demand for status-accruing cultural products, but pressurized the traditional rural elite to expend a greater proportion of their wealth on conspicuous consumption, and for the first time created a genuine public market in leisure. The Industrial Revolution, in its early manifestations, accelerated this process, expanding further the middling orders, increasingly releasing their women from the burden of work, and adding a number of skilled workers to those with 'surplus' wealth. However, it was only from the later nineteenth century, the beginning of the third phase, that the real income of the working class as a whole began to rise – as a consequence of growing money wages and falling food prices – to a level where its huge potential as a consumer of leisure was first properly released. The 'substantial increase in working-class spending power' has been seen as the 'foremost' economic variable behind the late Victorian commercial revolution in sport.[26] Quite how much of this working-class potential was released and when is unclear. Andrew Davies has argued that what determined the lifestyle and recreational habits of early twentieth-century Salford's working class, and this could include the families of skilled workers, was poverty not wealth.[27] Thus the absorption of the working class into the leisure market place was a patchy and protracted phenomenon, heavily influenced by variables of region, occupation, and gender. None the less, most would argue that the third phase was the point at which a genuinely mass market emerged in leisure. Davies himself acknowledges that there was a rise of around 30 per cent in the standard of living of British working-class families between 1899 and 1936.[28] What characterized the post-1945 fourth phase was not so much the introduction of new social classes into the leisure market, as the overall escalation of the volume of personal wealth, fuelled by expanding credit arrangements such as hire purchase agreements; the introduction of social groups – particularly the young, women, and the aged – whose limited access to wealth had traditionally restricted their role as consumers of leisure;[29] and the internationalization of demand.

In the model outlined above, the commercialization of leisure is a function of expanding wealth, percolating through society, from the top downwards, in a series of chronological phases, each characterized by the absorption of a class or social group/s into the market place for leisure, until the whole of society is encompassed. One example to illustrate this process would be the holiday resort. Spas emerge, under a mixture of royal, aristocratic, and gentry patronage, as places of fashionable health cure in the later sixteenth and early seventeenth century. However, it is only after 1660 that they proliferate and become, in Daniel Defoe's words when describing Bath, 'the resort of the sound, rather than the sick'.[30] Upper middle-class demand plays its part in this, but the impact of the middling orders as a whole becomes crucial in the growth of the seaside resort (which emerges first in about the 1730s), and the third wave of spa development from the later eighteenth century.

London artisans influenced resort development in Kent from the early nineteenth century, but working-class demand only kicked in on a major scale in the late nineteenth century. Even then it was focused most strongly in the north-west of England and its resorts, and it was probably only after the First World War that the working-class seaside holiday became a universal phenomenon. In the later twentieth century, rising affluence throughout society encouraged holidays overseas, diverting demand from domestic into foreign resorts, but not destroying the former, as the market for holiday-making became a more complex and pluralistic phenomenon.[31]

The appeal of a this model of change is that it treats the commercialization of leisure as a phased process, and provides a coherent account, located within an evolving social structure, of why these phases should appear when they do. Its schematic elegance, however, hides a messier reality. It is unlikely that the landed elite were the only market for leisure before 1660, or that the lower orders only made a significant presence after 1870. Moreover, it would be quite wrong, in recognizing the role of the working class in the late nineteenth and twentieth centuries, to ignore that of the middle class.[32] The model also has little to say about other factors which structured the nature of demand, such as urbanization. It is clear that London was a critical influence in the location of the early spas and seaside resorts, as later Edinburgh and Glasgow were to be for the Scottish resorts, and the textile towns of Lancashire for the resorts of the north-west of England.

Towns, as the economy's shop window, also played a vital part in the long-term trend towards 'consumerization', a subject for which the historical discourse parallels closely that of the commercialization of leisure. Phases of intensified consumption have been detected in the late seventeenth and eighteenth centuries (Neil McKendrick refers to a 'consumer revolution'),[33] the later nineteenth century (which Hamish Fraser characterizes as 'the coming of the mass market' and Thomas Richards as a period when 'the commodity became and remained the one subject of mass culture'),[34] the inter-war years and 'the new consumerism',[35] the years after 1950,[36] and the later twentieth-century world of 'post-Fordist consumption' (with, in John Urry's words, 'consumption rather than production dominant', and 'almost all aspects of social life . . . commodified').[37] Some historians of consumption are well aware of the problems of chronology posed by finding consumer revolutions at multiple points in the past, and have called for a more guarded and nuanced approach.[38] The point here is not to develop a critique of the concept – it would no doubt follow closely that articulated earlier in relation to commercialization – but to explore its relationship to the structuring of demand for leisure. The links lie not only in the obvious fact that leisure is a consumer product, but also in that the very act of consumption, particularly in the form of shopping, is a recreation.[39] As early as the 1720s Daniel Defoe could claim 'to have heard, that some ladies . . . have taken their coaches, and spent a whole afternoon in Ludgate-street, or Covent-Garden, only to divert themselves in going from one mercer's shop to another . . . having not so much as the least occasion, much less intention, to buy anything'.[40]

SUPPLY

By and large a demand-led view of economic change has held sway among historians of leisure. But supply also has an important role to play. Five factors have been highlighted: technology, capital, entrepreneurship, cartelization, and professionalization. There is a risk in assuming that technologies compel people to behave in a certain way, and in attributing economic growth simply to new innovations. Tia DeNora labels this 'technologism', and argues instead for 'the social–technical *mélange* through which forms of agency and social order(s) are produced'.[41] Bearing this caveat in mind, the impact of technology can be seen as twofold. First, there are direct innovations in the equipment designed to deliver leisure. So, for example, the introduction of the piston valve system into brass instruments in the early nineteenth century made it possible to keep them in tune across the entire range of notes, which made learning and playing the instruments easier, and facilitated their mass production at a cheap price. In golf, the replacement of the feather-packed ball by gutta-percha balls, and later machine-made rubber-strip 'Haskell' balls, extended the hitting range and length of courses. Of 'major significance' in enhancing the appeal of grouse shooting was the introduction of breech-loading in the 1860s and the use of smokeless cartridges in the 1870s, which made it possible to shoot faster. It is said that the arrival of the drop-frame, chain-driven, safety cycle with pneumatic tyres did more than anything else to open up cycling to the whole new market that women constituted.[42] Examples of this type could be replicated endlessly. It remains the case, however, that many pastimes – such as running, football, rugby, and cricket – are basically simple in character, and offer little potential for technological innovation. One answer has been to create 'pseudo-technologies'. Sports clothing is one example, where those who purchase accoutrements, such as running shoes, are encouraged to believe that their performance will be markedly enhanced, though the improvement at best could only be marginal. More to the point, many who buy the items of leisure wear concerned never engage in competition.

In low-tech sports, of greater importance has been the indirect impact of technology, where innovation has played a critical part in the process of commercialization. Transport is one key area. In the eighteenth century the introduction of turnpike roads eased the movement of race horses around the country and made possible a national network of meetings, while in the following century the rise of the railways 'revolutionized sport by widening the catchment area for spectators and enabling participants to compete nationally', having a dramatic impact on sports like horse racing, fox hunting, and cricket.[43] The expanding suburban and national rail network sustained the London theatre and touring companies against the loss of the working-class audience to the music hall, drawing in clientele and providing access to provincial and indeed imperial markets.[44] The nationwide, working-class based, competitive brass band and choral movements of the nineteenth century would probably have been impossible without the railways. As Gareth Williams argues, it was the 1,500 miles of track laid in Wales between 1840 and 1870 'that enabled the South Wales Choral Union to steam into history'.[45] Improvements in road, river, and sea transport, and the rise of coach (seventeenth century), steam boat and railway (nineteenth century), and motor vehicle and air travel (twentieth century) have been central to the growth of the tourist and holiday industry. This has been so not only in widening the range of locations to be visited, and the geographical and social markets to be exploited, but also because travel itself became part of the tourist experience.[46] Paradoxically, the railway and motor car, though reducing journey times, enhanced the potential for extended personalized touring,[47] and in the case of the cruise liner the mode of transport became the holiday experience itself.

Transport technologies have a magnetic appeal to academic and popular historians alike that can lead to their significance in the commercialization of leisure being overrated. The British network of spas and seaside resorts, and the traditions of domestic and foreign tourism, were, for example, established well before the arrival of the railways, 'which did not, in themselves, cause' the 'large-scale expansion of the seaside holiday market'.[48] The same tendency towards exaggeration also affects treatment of the media. None the less, it is hard not to acknowledge the importance of the arrival of printing (in Europe *c.*1440, and in Britain in 1476). A major market in popular and not just elite literature emerged from the sixteenth century,[49] and from the end of the seventeenth century newspapers and journals widened the opportunities for recreational reading, as well as being used to advertise fashionable goods and leisure events.[50] It is difficult to distinguish, as in the case of transport, between the media's roles as a delivery mechanism and as a source of leisure in its own right. Sport, gambling, and the media have been inextricably intertwined from the origins of the newspaper press. For the large numbers who never attended horse races or football matches, but who by the late nineteenth century regularly bet on their outcomes, sport was something refracted largely through the media. The rise of electronic means of communication has accentuated this process even further – the dramatic growth of internet betting is a case in point – and blurred even more the distinction between means of delivery and modes of pleasure. Film, radio, television, walkmans, compact discs, MP3/WMA players, and the internet are not simply platforms for performances created elsewhere, but are integral to the entertainment product itself. After the Second World War the arrival of terrestrial television, and later of cable, satellite and digital forms of delivery, transformed the economics and form of professional sport, and the music industry has become geared increasingly towards distance and, generally, non-live delivery of its products.[51]

So-called media moguls, such as Kerry Packer and Rupert Murdoch, played an important part in the above processes. An important variable in the supply of commercial leisure has always been entrepreneurialism. In the 'captains of industry' tradition of British economic history the tendency has been to highlight the influence of certain heroic innovators and businessmen: James Burbage as a theatre entrepreneur in Elizabethan London, Ralph Allen as the business genius behind the Georgian spa of Bath,[52] Thomas Cook of Leicester as the pioneer of the Victorian tourist industry,[53] and in the modern era the football chairman–tycoon, such as Jack Walker at Blackburn and Roman Abramovich at Chelsea. Historically, however, far more important in promoting the commercialization of leisure have been the mass of small-scale entrepreneurs, such as the peripatetic actor–managers of eighteenth-century England, who despite operating businesses on a shoestring managed collectively to establish a national network of commercial theatres; or the myriad of petty bookmakers, frequently operating on or beyond the edge of legitimacy, who nurtured what may have been the most common pastime in late Victorian and Edwardian Britain.[54] Among leisure entrepreneurs one of the most important groups was the drinks trade. For the vast majority of our period the alehouse or pub, for the common people, and inn and tavern, for the better off, was the most important single commercial social institution for the majority of the adult male population. Numbers on the ground were impressive. Between the 1570s and the 1630s the number of alehouses in England doubled from around 25,000 to 50,000 (though growth levelled off during the later seventeenth century), reaching a ratio of one (licensed and unlicensed) establishment for around every 100 people. By the late nineteenth century there were around 100,000 on-licensed premises. However, the growth in the population meant that the ratio of hostelries to persons in 1900 was around 1:300 (though pubs were larger by this stage), and as rival outlets for drink (such as clubs, bars, restaurants, and off-licences) and rival recreational attractions proliferated in the twentieth century the ratio had risen to over 1:600 by the 1960s.[55] It was through the offices of the alehouse keeper, publican, and innkeeper that commercialized leisure was developed in its early stages, and, as the vital public interface with the mass of the population, was diffused through society as a whole. It is they who provided the venues for a multiplicity of indoor recreations – such as theatre, assemblies, concerts, games, and club and society meetings – as well as sponsoring and servicing outdoor sports and events, from cricket and curling, to pigeon-fancying, fishing, and football.[56]

Sponsorship was a key aspect of the drink trade's interest in leisure. Prizes would be offered and rooms provided in anticipation of the business that this would attract. Civic authorities in England and Scotland since at least the seventeenth century were investing significant sums in racing prizes and up-market leisure facilities, such as formal walks and gardens, in order to attract the gentry and their families to town.[57] Local government in spas and seaside towns had a special interest in promoting leisure, but these locations also attracted investment in resort facilities from private interests like the railway companies.[58] The growth in private sponsorship has proved an important factor in fuelling the expansion of commercialized leisure. In the later twentieth century the arts and sport were particular beneficiaries. The latter

proved a highly effective platform from which to access mass consumer markets, particularly once the visual media started to beam
the names and products of sponsors to huge national and global
audiences. The drink and tobacco trades have been especially
prominent (in 1988, sports sponsorship and associated activities
accounted for more than a quarter of the drink industry's total
advertising budget of £158 million),[59] reflecting a long-standing
association between leisure and recreational drugs. Though in
recent decades sports equipment and clothing firms have also
been heavily involved in promoting leisure, a great variety of
businesses, from insurance to mobile phones, have realized the
benefits of sponsorship. This proved a lifeline for many professional
sports suffering from declining spectator numbers after the 1950s,
and has strengthened the commercial basis on which the physical
recreation industry is run.[60]

Some sponsors now commit substantial sums of money to sport,
such as the £300 million deal the sportswear multinational Nike
negotiated with Manchester United.[61] This reflects the fact that as
commercialization intensified it both contributed to and was itself
enhanced by a change in the scale of entrepreneurial operations.
The influence of the petty bourgeois business person, such as the
myriad of holiday landladies and fish-and-chip fryers celebrated by
John Walton, should not be underestimated.[62] However, the
long-term trend was towards an increased scale of operations. New
pastimes would burst on the scene with a proliferation of small
entrepreneurs attempting to cash in on the craze. Over-supply and
competition would drive many of these businesses to the wall, leav-
ing those that survived to grab a larger share of the market. Many
of the small spas which sprang up in the late seventeenth century
enjoyed only a transitory existence, unable to compete with the
larger, better-equipped centres like Bath and Tunbridge Wells. Race
meetings underwent two major phases of rationalization – after
earlier phases of proliferation – in the mid-eighteenth and late
nineteenth centuries.[63] The smaller music halls in London, whose
numbers had mushroomed from their introduction in about 1850,

were already by the 1860s being displaced by the bigger establishments, and syndicalization, first introduced in the cities of the north of England and central Scotland, spread across the nation in the 1890s.[64] Similarly, the initial undergrowth of tiny cinemas, prompted by the introduction of film after 1900, was by the 1920s being pruned back by the appearance of larger auditoriums and cinema chains such as Odeon Theatres, Gaumont British, and Associated British Cinemas.[65] Even the bookmakers, perhaps the most prolific of the petty leisure entrepreneurs, were to find that legalization in 1960 was to prove not their salvation but their death knell, as the mass of betting shops originally opened were cut back (from a peak of 15,782 in 1968 to 9,400 by 1992), and the industry became concentrated in fewer and fewer hands. By the late 1980s three leisure conglomerates, Hill/Mecca, Coral, and Ladbrokes, controlled over 40 per cent of the betting shops.[66] The expansion of the package holiday has had a similar effect upon the tourist industry.[67]

Though new types of leisure always allowed scope for the small-scale entrepreneur to make an impact, the broad thrust towards integration and cartelization is clear enough. Some would argue that it is reflected in the trend in British and European football, both round and oval ball, towards super-leagues and within these to the hegemony of a handful of super-clubs. The 1960s and 1990s were especially important as 'transitional decades' in accentuating inequalities.[68] The top teams have been able to achieve paramountcy by concentrating in their hands the game's revenues, investment, and professional business and playing skills.

Professionalization, of entrepreneurs and performers, from theatrical and music hall managers to modern sportsmen and women, has been another important influence behind the commercialization of leisure, and another force which, like the shift towards larger-scale enterprises, reflects broader trends within the economy. But any blanket thesis of the professionalization of leisure raises serious issues for the historian, thus questioning not only the degree to which leisure has been affected by commercialization, but also the extent to which it should be considered a 'normal' part of the economy as a whole.

A PECULIAR ECONOMICS

The paradox posed by professionalization is that the moment said by some to constitute the great leap forward in the commercialization of leisure, the late Victorian and Edwardian eras, also witnessed a remarkable resurgence of amateurism. The subject will be discussed at greater length in the chapter on class. The crucial point here is the contradictoriness of these developments. It is true that the amateur ethos was far from uncontested, and led to sharp differences between rugby and soccer, and the 'great schism' within rugby between the amateur and professional codes. But within the world of sport the dominant ethic, even within those recreations that accommodated a measure of professionalism, like cricket and soccer, was that of the amateur. This was the value system backed by the traditional ruling elite and the leading figures among the business and professional middle classes. Richard Holt and Tony Mason argue that amateurism reached 'its pinnacle of influence' in the 1950s, so that it was only from the 1960s, and then at varying rates depending upon the sport involved, that professionalization was finally let off the leash.[69] Even then it did not mean that amateurism disappeared. Many officials have continued to administer sport on an unpaid basis, and what has emerged is not the professionalization of sport *as a whole*, but simply the bifurcation of this sector of leisure into more defined professional and amateur camps.

The impact of the amateur ethic was to create an 'imperfect' and exceptional labour market. Those who produced the entertainment were expected to do so either for nothing or at an artificially low cost in terms of their labour. The imposition, until the 1960s, by the Football League of the maximum wage and the 'retain and transfer' system (limiting the players' capacity to initiate transfers, and allowing clubs to retain on their books footballers who were not playing and were not being paid) meant that there were severe restrictions on the players' capacity to sell their labour freely. Though the best paid professional footballers earned well above the average wage for a skilled worker (in 1914 the maximum wage was double the figure),[70] they received well below their market value given the huge crowds attending games. In effect, the players and officials subsidized the spectators, who enjoyed a bargain product. 'Shamateurism' (the receipt of remuneration while pretending this was not the case) and illegal payments, some in kind (reminiscent of the so-called pre-modern economy), were rife throughout sport.[71] W. G. Grace, 'the ultimate "shamateur" ', who at one point aired his concern that 'cricket might become too much of a business, like football', was notoriously on the make.[72] That sportsmen received a measure of reimbursement through such murky means only emphasized the imperfections in the market.

The balance of amateurism and professionalism varied at different times, and in any particular area of leisure. In the eighteenth century the theatre was far more professionalized than the concert world, where there was scope, in the proliferating music clubs, for the skilled gentleman to perform in an amateur capacity alongside paid musicians.[73] Though there was a strong trend towards professionalization in the orchestras of late eighteenth-century London, and amongst performers in the late Victorian music hall, those in the brass band movement happily mixed elements of paid with unpaid work, and Richard Hoggart found in the twentieth-century working men's club 'a great shadow-world of semi-professional entertainers, men and women who make a comfortable addition to their normal wages by regularly performing at club concerts'.[74] Hoggart goes on to describe how, 'Behind the paid stars of the concerts, and in special demand on "Free-and-Easy nights", are the individuals who can be relied on for a tune or a song, who are not paid by custom but are supplied with drinks, sometimes on the house, sometimes by members who "send one up", or "send one across".' Receiving payment in kind, they were probably like many pre-modern alehouse entertainers. The working men's club may be a dying breed, but music continues to be an important part of the club, pub, and party scene, much of it delivered by part-time DJs and scratch bands of young performers playing for small sums of money. Moreover, even if the line between the professional and amateur has been hardening, there appears little evidence to suggest that professionalization has reduced the extent of the voluntary (or non-remunerated) sector, which still flourishes, with many in the population continuing to make as well as consume leisure.[75] Indeed, professionalization – and more broadly commercialization – by generating services and role models, can stimulate amateur activity.

The persistence of the amateur ethos injected serious 'imperfections' into the labour market for leisure that undermined its purely commercial character. The *attitude* of professionalized labour itself may also have a similar consequence. The very strength of the amateur ethic socially and morally stigmatized those who demanded payment for performing leisure services. Moreover, because for the majority of the population leisure was voluntary, pleasurable, and unpaid, it was difficult for those for whom it was their work to treat it entirely as such, so that they were often willing to accept lower returns than they might have demanded in a 'real' job. Even in areas like catering, employees have found it hard to distinguish between work and leisure, and 'were convinced that they weren't really "working" for their pay packets at all'.[76] Peter Bailey has highlighted the problems in equating industrial and artistic labour;[77] in the latter the relationship between worker and product may be more intense and personalized, the anticipated non-monetary returns, such as community esteem or a glamorous image, higher, so that the emphasis is on job satisfaction and public success rather than financial reward. The individualism which often characterizes artistic labour, allied to the strategic difficulties in organizing an often dispersed workforce, has traditionally also led to low levels of unionization.[78] This depressed earnings levels compared with the industrial sector, and militated against the

high returns undoubtedly achieved by a few star performers rais-
ing the general level of income in their trade.

The 'peculiar' economics of leisure, the deviation from the
commercialized model, was not just a function of an abnormal
labour market. It is abundantly clear that in a number of areas of
leisure, entrepreneurs and investors paid less than close attention
to, and sometimes wilfully overlooked, the first rules of business,
profit-making and profit-maximization. This has been highlighted
in particular in the case of sport.[79] Wray Vamplew has shown
that horse racing was an inherently unprofitable pastime. Those
possessing the animals were often effectively competing for their
own money – in 1913 they contributed 63 per cent of the prize
money through entry fees – and 'the average owner could not
expect to cover his costs, let alone make money out of racing'.[80]
Keith Sandiford has observed that 'as a profit-making enterprise,
Victorian first-class cricket was a signal failure', and Tony Mason
argued of early twentieth-century football that 'if it was a business
it was a business of a special kind'. Dividends to shareholders were
forcibly limited to 5 per cent and 'directors were utility maximizers rather than profit maximizers'.[81] Though a great deal more
money flowed into football from the 1970s, and clubs were no
longer dependent on spectator revenue, it is still far from clear that
entrepreneurial attitudes had changed. The huge growth in media
and sponsorship income prompted the leading clubs to turn
themselves into public limited companies and invest in human
and physical capital in an effort to gain access to this new revenue
flow. This much made reasonable commercial sense. But despite
the growth in wealth, and the concentration of this in a newly
formed elite division, only one club in the English Premiership
was able to achieve a consistent level of profitability. The reason,
ironically enough given the position earlier in the century, was
over-investment in labour, with levels of transfer fees and wages
that were unjustified commercially given the returns available
from the sport. A report in 2002 discovered that clubs in the first

division of the English Football League had a wage-to-turnover ratio of 101 per cent so that 'the average club was in debt as soon as its wages were paid'.[82] This most commercialized of all sports was unable to meet the most basic criterion of a successful commercial enterprise, long-term profitability. Those owning and running clubs took far higher levels of risk than would be acceptable in other businesses, and were willing to place the prospect of on-the-field success above that of making money. In the language of the economic historian, they were utility- rather than profit-maximizers.

To what extent sport in this respect is typical of other areas of leisure, and has been so across time, is difficult to say. Today some of the financially most powerful and successful fields of business – tourism, film, and media spring to mind – are located in the broadly recreational sector, and it seems implausible to conceive of leisure entrepreneurs *en masse* forsaking the principles of profitability. But it may be that leisure stands at the more volatile and risky end of the business spectrum, with the products it trades in more subject to fluctuations in taste and fashion. John Walton has concluded that 'most' nineteenth-century seaside 'resorts offered grudging and limited rewards to most investors . . . the fortunes of the small family businesses which predominated at the seaside were fluctuating and usually precarious', and John Urry has observed the 'enormous vulnerability in the market' of contemporary small hotel and catering enterprises, with dramatic rates at which businesses failed or were replaced by new ones.[83] The lack of research into pre-modern recreational businesses makes it difficult to speculate on degrees of volatility.

Where anecdotal evidence survives it tends to relate to those whose careers were successful, like the London-based eighteenth-century theatre proprietor and actor–manager David Garrick.[84] But what of the mass of peripatetic theatre troupes and their managers travelling around the provinces, moving rapidly from one small venue to another, vulnerable both in their own movements and in that of their audiences to the vagaries of the elements, and having after 1737 to combat the potentially draconian restrictions imposed by the Theatre Act?[85] There seems no reason to assume that entrepreneurs of this type sought to be anything other than profitable, but the businesses that they operated and markets they serviced would have been structurally unstable. Moreover, even if the entrepreneurs involved were profit-seekers, they were not necessarily profit-maximizers. Most theatre managers had started their careers as itinerant players and the business and lifestyle associated with it was in their blood. In all probability they valued independence, camaraderie, the excitement of performance, and life on the road, over purely financial returns. Others who invested in paid entertainments were not profit orientated. The shareholders in the Assembly Rooms at York, opened in 1732, were limited to an investment of £25 or £50, and many did not bother to collect their dividends.[86] A sense of public duty and a desire for social kudos prompted such investments, as they also motivated the majority of those who subscribed to horse-race prizes in the period. It has been leisure's special capacity to provide investors and entrepreneurs with returns other than purely financial ones that has contributed so much to its peculiar economics.

One further factor that may have added to this state of economic deviance is that many leisure products are inherently anti-commercial. Much of the contemporary tourist trade is geared to finding destinations untainted by commercialism; the heritage industry often celebrates what it takes to be a pre-commercial past; and much of youth culture rejects the norms of the business world. Not that there is anything new in this. In the eighteenth century Lord Kames recommended cultivation of the fine arts as an antidote to the corrupting influence of commercialization and luxury.[87] Others, like Arthur Bedford, recognized that business practices had infected music in the period and proposed the propagation of 'ancient' music as a counter-commercial culture.[88] In the eighteenth and nineteenth centuries, visiting wild places and peoples became a growing theme of elite tourism, and the fine arts developed in ways that self-consciously rejected commercial and industrial forms and modes of mass production.[89] In such a light the high tide of amateurism that swept across British sport during the second half of the nineteenth century is perfectly understandable. When Victorian gentlemen and businessmen combined together to create the edifice that constituted the British sporting system they were making a product whose values were meant to be the antithesis of those represented by the world of commerce and industry. This did not, of course, mean that sport and leisure in general were immune to the forces of commercialization. These were far too strong to be restrained. But, as William Morris discovered at the time and many entrepreneurs found subsequently, it is perfectly possible to commercialize the anti-commercial.[90] What the anti-commercial dimension did give to the leisure economy was a distinctive profile that reflected the ambivalent position of leisure within a capitalist society.

The notion of a leisure economy has more than a hint of contradiction about it. Leisure is surely something undertaken when a person is not engaged in economic activity; indeed, it is something which potentially threatens economic efficiency. Historians have been keen to dispel these ideas by stressing the extent to which leisure contributes and conforms to the norms of the wider economy. The commercialization of leisure has been seen as the principal mechanism by which this has taken place. Differences of emphasis and opinion exist, however, as to when commercialization on a significant scale began, and even though few attempts have been made to push the threshold back before the late seventeenth century, it seems unlikely that leisure in some measure was not treated as a commodity throughout the early modern period, if not before. Taking a model of demand and supply that contains components common to the economy as a whole, it is possible to see how the volume of commercial leisure expanded, and did so in a phased fashion. However, it is also clear that certain aspects of leisure were at odds with and resistant to commercialization, so that the leisure economy acquired distinctive and exceptional characteristics. Some of these reinforced the notion that leisure and economic efficiency did not easily mix. This was one of the factors, as we shall see in the following chapter, which justified interference by the state in the pleasures of its citizens.

3

STATE

In the general preface to his *Observations on Popular Antiquities* (1777) John Brand launched a withering attack on those zealots who dismissed popular recreations and customs *en bloc* as immoral and unchristian:

> With regards to the rites, sports, &c. of the common people, I am aware, that the morose and bigotted part of mankind, without distinguishing between the right use and abuse of such entertainments, cavil at and malign them. Yet must such be told, that shows and sports have been countenanced by the best and wisest of states. . . . The common people, confined by daily labour, seem to require their proper intervals of relaxation; perhaps it is of the highest political utility to encourage innocent sports and games among them.[1]

What is striking about this passage is not the defence of the people's need for leisure, or even of pastimes whose origins lie in a superstitious and Catholic past; but the justification of recreations in terms of 'political utility' and 'states'. Moreover, Brand does not confine himself to generalized statements but specifies 'the *highest* political utility' and the '*best* and *wisest* of states'. There is an explicit

42

link in his mind between politics, the state, and leisure. Brand's claim, particularly in the case of the nation that, above all others in eighteenth-century Europe, prided itself upon its liberties and freedom from government interference, that the state has a role in authorizing and encouraging 'shows and sports' might appear surprising. Surely leisure, with its characteristics of freedom and choice, was the one area where the state left the people to their own devices. Though exceptional circumstances might require intervention, the idea that the state should have a *policy* towards leisure would seem odd. It could be argued that what has defined leisure, at least in Britain, has been its non-relationship with the state. This is the central issue which will be explored in the following chapter.

HANDS OFF OR HANDS ON?

There is a strong argument for the view that leisure was not an area which the state sought to control systematically and consistently. To talk in terms of a hands-off approach might be too strong, but relative to other matters of public policy, sports and games were historically low on governmental agendas. The underlying view was that the machinery of state should be preserved for matters of state. When in 1860 Lord Redesdale introduced into the House of Lords a bill to correct the abuse, as he saw it, of racing horses with absurdly low weights, there was a shocked response from the controlling body of the sport, the Jockey Club, not over the nature of the abuse, but over the resort to Parliament to correct it. The Earl of Derby presented a petition, supported by Lord Palmerston, deploring 'the interference of the legislature' in racing, which prompted Redesdale, after assurances from Derby, to withdraw his bill.[2]

Non-interference is an approach which many historians would see as the prevailing attitude of government towards leisure. Richard Holt contends that 'sport in Britain . . . has not historically been a matter for governments', and argues that in the twentieth century, 'The use of sport as an ideological tool was for the most part informal. Britain defined its political distinctiveness in part through the "small state", which left its people to get on with their own lives.'[3] Jeffrey Hill takes a similar view of the twentieth century, 'compared with the voluntary and commercial sectors, its [the state's] role has been slight and intermittent'.[4] Peter Bailey, discussing early and mid-Victorian England, notes that despite all the clamour of rational recreationalists, 'recreational reform failed to command any real priority with the legislators', and Alastair Durie observes of the promotion of Scottish tourism between 1789 and 1939, 'Though some legislation had a bearing . . . the British state remained aloof and uninterested except at the margin.'[5] The contrast with continental Europe, where the state played an important role in developing spas, was marked.[6] Though Stephen Jones felt that in inter-war Britain, 'the state made a greater impact on leisure than ever before', for the same period Ross McKibbin emphasized the 'passivity of the state', and Jack Williams that 'The nature of authority within cricket can be interpreted as an expression of the frame of mind which saw peculiarly English virtues in the tradition of an unwritten constitution and mistrusted a highly centralised authority.'[7]

After the Second World War, government came, with the general trend towards collectivism exemplified by the introduction of the Welfare State, to play more of a role in the control and delivery of leisure, leading to what Martin Polley has called 'the growth of the sport–state relationship'.[8] However, there were limits to how far intervention went. The sort of 'nationalization' policies advocated by Rowntree and Lavers in 1951, including placing the football pools and the brewing industry into public ownership, were never credible, and John Clarke and Chas Critcher have argued that in the 1960s, though 'Substantial in some respects, not least in the sums of money involved, the State's role [in providing leisure] was still residual and enabling.'[9] Moreover, the rise of Thatcherism reversed any trend towards intervention, so that Kenneth Roberts could observe in 1989,

> Of course, British governments have proscribed or discouraged particular pastimes. . . . Other leisure activities, especially sport and the traditional arts, have benefited enormously from state support. But all this has been achieved without any overarching leisure or cultural policies. . . . Keeping politics out of leisure is one of the few stances on which Britain retains a broad political consensus.[10]

When in 2004 Tony Blair ordered his culture secretary Tessa Jowell 'to produce an "ambitious and interventionist" fitness and sporting strategy', history and historians, never mind the escalating calorific consumption of his countrymen, would have seemed to be against him.[11] None the less, some commentators have detected a less hands-off role historically for the state. Peter Bailey, whilst acknowledging that 'untangling the role of the state in leisure formation is difficult', asserts that 'plainly *laissez faire* is a myth',[12] and Hugh Cunningham argues that though in the two centuries after 1750 'governments . . . always looked to market forces or to philanthropy as the preferred supplier, and themselves undertook that role most readily when the prestige or safety of the state was at stake. What is surprising is how frequent those occasions were. Increasingly from 1750 the way the people spent their leisure was licensed and framed by the state.'[13] Peter Clark and Rab Houston's view, that 'In contrast to the situation in England before the Civil War . . . the state had a limited role in reshaping the cultural image of British towns after 1700,' is as interesting in its hint as to the situation before 1642 as after.[14] Certainly, in Ronald Huttons's study of the ritual year between 1400 and 1700, the state, and political and religious conflict within it, played *the* crucial role in determining the 'rise and fall of merry England'.[15] Such observations suggest that the hands-off view of the state's role in leisure is not necessarily a historical given and deserves probing further.

Given the received view on non-intervention, one of the surprising features of even a cursory trawl through the past is the volume and character of legislation and orders relating in some manner to leisure. Many sports and pastimes, such as football in England (*c*.1314) and golf in Scotland (1457), first unambiguously enter the historical record in the medieval period because of orders regulating or banning them.[16] This may simply be a reflection of the fact that legal records survive better than other sources, but it leaves the impression of a significant degree of governmental intervention. The early modern centuries witnessed, at various times, strict regulation of drinking, hunting, and the theatre. Government regulation in England played a vital part in curtailing the surge in growth of alehouses that took place in the century before the Civil War, as well as in taming their image of unruliness and subversion, and there are signs of a similar crackdown in Ireland.[17] In 1208 King John had reserved falconry exclusively to the Crown, and since at least the late fourteenth century there had been laws to limit the right to hunt high-status game to elite groups, culminating in the Game Act of 1671, which forbade all persons to hunt game unless they possessed a freehold of £100 a year or a leasehold worth £150 a year. This was itself tightened up by further legislation during the eighteenth century.[18] Following 'a massive increase in the incidence of poaching' in the middle of the century, 'the establishment's response was', according to Tom Williamson, 'vicious', the Game Act of 1770 making poaching by night punishable by six months' imprisonment.[19]

The theatre was a particular target for state intervention and manipulation. During the reign of Henry VIII, and those of his Protestant offspring, a battery of Acts of Parliament were passed or proclamations issued which dealt directly or indirectly with public drama, censoring what could be performed and controlling the companies of players permitted to act. At the same time, the Crown, its officers, and its noble supporters promoted troupes and plays as instruments of Protestant propaganda.[20] From the 1580s the consensus of opinion among Protestant leaders over the use of the theatre collapsed, and this paved the way by the early seventeenth century for opposition, at the local government level, to permitting travelling players to perform, and eventually to the parliamentary ordinances and army theatre raids of the 1640s and 1650s.[21] The 'cultural revolution'[22] of Interregnum administrations may have been short lived, and the severe restrictions on recreational activity relaxed at the Restoration, but the later Stuart and early Hanoverian states were no more in the business of being permissive regimes than their predecessors, and when political and social necessities required, were capable of introducing potentially draconian legislation, such as the package of measures passed in the late 1730s severely restricting gaming, horse racing, and drama.[23]

The Theatre Regulation Act of 1843 ended the system by which the Crown licensed companies of actors, and the privileged position of the 'major' companies,[24] and it may be argued that from the nineteenth century the whole *ancien régime* edifice of state control of leisure was progressively dismantled. But censorship of the theatre remained until 1968, 'the savagery of game-preserving magistrates' continued into the early twentieth century,[25] control of drinking and drinking places remained throughout the nineteenth and twentieth centuries a feature of recreational policy,[26] and there is the curious case of betting. Like other areas of leisure, there was a long history, dating back at least to the fourteenth century, of restrictions on gambling and games associated with it. There is little evidence of a trend in the nineteenth century towards liberalization. Legislation in the 1850s and 1870s sought to close down betting premises and shops, and the Street Betting Act of 1906 turned the screw one notch tighter by clarifying and tidying up the earlier statutes and prohibiting entirely off-course cash betting. Despite massive evasion of the law it was not until 1960 that the Betting and Gaming Act legalized betting shops, though even then a range of petty restrictions remained – such as forbidding comfortable chairs, televisions, and refreshments – aimed at restricting access to shops and making them as unattractive as possible. In 1960 casinos were also made legal, though the Act of 1968 which established the Gaming Board gave it powers that made Britain one of the most tightly policed gaming regimes in the world. A state lottery had operated in Britain between 1694 (indeed, state lotteries date back to Elizabeth I's reign) and 1826, but it was not until 1994 that the government again permitted the introduction of a national lottery, the last of the European Union countries to do so.[27]

The history of the relationship between government and gambling must raise serious questions about how systematically the state operated a hands-off policy towards leisure. Central to the debate are three issues. First, there is the definition of leisure. Whereas it seems beyond doubt that sports or theatre are forms of recreation, hunting and poaching might be considered a means of food gathering, drinking a type of food consumption, and gambling a way, however financially misguided, of making money. Secondly, much of the legislation affecting leisure turns out to be of a non-specific or indirect character. Laws pertaining to religious practices and vagrancy, for example, could be used to control who and what was performed in the early modern theatre.[28] In the modern era the point is even more critical. There is no legislation *per se* to prevent an enthusiastic adult establishing a youth football side. None the less, at some point it is likely that the project would find itself enmeshed in the web of the law. Health and safety legislation would cover the premises used for changing, the surface for playing, and vehicles for transporting the team, and, given the age of those involved, there would be a general duty of care on the part of adult leaders, and a possibility of police vetting. If they needed to raise money this could be done by a raffle, though the operation of it would be governed by legislation, or by an application to Sport Lot. If the team wished to play on a competitive basis affiliation to the relevant national football association would probably follow.

The character of such a national organization raises the third and most crucial issue: What constitutes the state? The initial response might be to define it institutionally; the Crown, the government, and Parliament. However, there is also a case to be made that in practice the state is a multi-layered phenomenon, embracing at least three broad strata in society – central, local, and informal. The problem with adopting a narrow centralist definition is that it misses the true extent to which the state pervades people's lives. It may be ideologically comforting to imagine that this is not the case, a confirmation of a Briton's sense of his or her liberties, but the reality is otherwise. Moreover, it is in the interest of those who occupy the various layers of the state to reinforce the myth of non-intervention as it could be argued that the most effective state is precisely that which manages to convince its subjects that it is absent from their lives. However, it must also be recognized that too broad a definition of the state runs the risk of falling into a conspiratorial mode of analysis, and being simply insensitive to the pluralist and fragmented character of authority.

THE CENTRAL STATE

The various recreational laws and orders discussed earlier in this chapter show that the central state has throughout the last five centuries been willing to intervene in the people's leisure where it has seen fit. Generally this has been more in terms of controlling rather than promoting, playing a negative rather than a positive role. None the less, the importance of, say, royal patronage should not be underestimated. Early modern British monarchs, particularly the Tudors and Stuarts, operated courts that played, and were expected to play, a leading role in cultivating elite arts and pastimes such as music, theatre, masques, horse racing, golf, hunting, painting, and architecture. The innovatory and influential Inigo Jones, for example, designed sophisticated masques for James VI's and I's court, as well as drafting the plans (1619) for the Prince's (the future Charles I) Lodging at Newmarket.[29] The town's establishment as the headquarters of horse racing, and the evolution of the sport as a whole in the seventeenth century, owed much to Stuart patronage.[30] From the later seventeenth century the lead role of the Crown in cultural change was increasingly taken over by a coterie of aristocrats. However, this reflected not so much a decline in the influence of the central state as a reformulation of its character along more pluralistic lines.[31] Moreover, it would be misleading to write off the Crown's influence, as for example in the establishment of the Royal Academy of Music in 1719, to which George I gave £1000, the Royal Academy of Arts in 1768, and from the 1750s in the development of the gardens attached to the royal palace at Kew, what was in effect to become the national botanic garden.[32] George III's magnificent collection of books was passed on to the British Museum to form the King's Library, and the case has recently been made for the king as a major patron – of science, the fine arts, and especially architecture – of the Enlightenment.[33]

Royal influence could also take on a more subtle form. Spas and seaside resorts fell over themselves to cultivate royal associations. Princess Victoria opened, and agreed to give her name to, a new park at Bath in 1830; the tiny Victoria Spa at Bishopton outside Stratford-upon-Avon was opened in 1837 as part of the celebrations of the Princess's eighteenth birthday; and after she ascended the throne, Leamington Spa was quick to obtain in 1838 the prefix 'Royal' to add to its name (in 1897 it also went on to open Victoria Park to celebrate the queen's Diamond Jubilee).[34] Clubs and societies were equally keen to acquire royal imprimaturs. The Grand Caledonian Curling Club, established in the year of the queen's coronation, sought the patronage of Albert when he and Victoria visited Scotland in 1842, and were granted the right to use the 'Royal' prefix.[35] This was part of a much wider process, evident since the visits of Prince William of Gloucester and George IV, by which the monarchy was used in Scotland as an instrument to bind the country into the British polity.[36] The British state was a fluid geopolitical entity, its form changing with events such as the fall of Calais (1558, the last remnants of the Angevin Empire), the Acts of Union of England with Wales (1536, 1543), Scotland

(1707), and Ireland (1800), the expansion of the extra-European Empire between the seventeenth and early twentieth century, the formation of the Irish Free State in 1922, and in more recent years, decolonization and internal devolution. Victoria and Albert's enthusiastic conversion to Highland culture, as in their patronage of the Highland Games, and the warm response this engendered among the Scottish elite, helped bury the bitter memory of the onslaught on the Highland way of life following the 1745 rebellion, and lay the ghost of Jacobitism.[37] The central state thus moved in subtle ways to establish its integrity. Overt promotion (as opposed to the informal actions of the monarchy), and the substantial expenditure that this involved, was generally not the fashion of the nineteenth century. However, direct parliamentary subsidies for the arts began in 1816 with a grant for the purchase of the Elgin Marbles, and in 1824 for the founding of the National Gallery.[38] Moreover, even in a sport like horse racing, where the Jockey Club jealously guarded its control of the turf, the government, until the report of the Royal Commission on Horse Breeding in 1888, continued to fund race prizes in the form of King's and Queen's Plates, and in 1916 newly established the National Stud.[39]

THE LOCAL STATE

The promotional role of the state and its willingness to commit resources increased in the twentieth century, though much of this was distributed at the local level.[40] Historically the relationship between the central and local state has been a complex and changing one. The latter was not simply an extension of the former. The Tudor and early Stuart state is conventionally seen as engaged in a process of centralization. However, generally this was engineered not by direct intervention but through the promulgation of a proliferating body of policy to be implemented by local elites sanctioned by the Crown. The Civil Wars (1642–9) and then the 'Glorious Revolution' applied the brakes to this process, and though the rise of the 'fiscal–military state' after 1688 in some respects strengthened institutions at the centre, none the less for two centuries the local state flourished as the effective, and to a real degree independent, channel through which government was delivered to the majority of the people. What David Eastwood has called 'the apotheosis of English local government and provincial culture', and Richard Price the 'age of localism', was brought to an end during the later nineteenth century with a re-negotiation of the relationship between metropolitan centre and provincial periphery, which saw an expansion in government *in toto*, and a trend towards local government acting primarily as *agent* for an increasingly directive central government.[41] These forces have been accentuated by the growing dependence of local authorities upon central funding and by a tendency from the 1980s, initiated by the Thatcher administrations' attack on municipal government, to bypass local channels of governance altogether. It is probably too early to tell how far, if at all, Devolution has reversed the trend towards centralization.

Such an interpretation of central–local state relationships in the twentieth century does not sit easily with the hands-off interpretation of the state's policy towards leisure. None the less, it remains the case that for the majority of the period under review there was a large measure of local autonomy, primarily because the executive did not have the financial resources or administrative machinery to implement policy at the grass roots. This left justices of the peace, town councils, manor and church courts, parish vestries and the like a good deal of freedom to implement (or otherwise) central directives, make their own policy, and initiate crackdowns. Thus 'A campaign against gambling, especially with dice, appears to have been launched in a number of towns in the period 1410–25, from Basingstoke to Bradford', and in 1528 the 'town governors of Galway attempted to stop "apprentices or Irishmen" from gambling "at cards, dice, [or] tables [backgammon]" in shops or cellars by ordering that, if caught, the players should forfeit their stakes and the proprietor be fined twenty shillings'.[42] The attack in England on traditional festivity under the later Tudors and early Stuarts came not from 'the leaders of Church or state', but from local urban and rural elites influenced by evangelical Protestantism.[43] The decline of cock throwing in the eighteenth century was not the product of legislation, but due, according to the contemporary commentator Joseph Strutt, to 'The magistrates . . . [who] have for some years put a stop to this wicked custom . . . [so that] at present it is nearly, if not entirely, discontinued in every part of the kingdom.'[44] Even where legislation existed, its implementation depended ultimately upon the powers *in situ*. There were no state-controlled agencies to enforce the mid-eighteenth-century laws against gambling, the theatre, horse racing, and prize fighting, whose enactment depended upon magisterial co-operation.[45] The arrival of a professional police force in the 1820s strengthened the hands of those seeking to control recreational behaviour.[46] However, apart from the Irish Constabulary (established in 1822) and the Metropolitan Police Force (1829), control of the new forces remained in local hands, and as the response to the Betting Act of 1906 demonstrated – the policing of which was often perfunctory and ritualized and sometimes involved collusion – depended upon the sympathies of the 'men on the spot'.[47]

The legislation establishing local police forces was initially permissive (only becoming prescriptive in England and Wales in 1856, and Scotland in 1857), and this was also the case with much nineteenth-century recreational legislation. The Museums Act of 1845 and Museums and Libraries Act of 1850, for example, allowed sympathetic boroughs to charge a proportion of the rates to establish facilities, but the decision to do this was a local matter and could prove highly controversial, as was the case with the introduction of a public library in Birmingham and Bath.[48] Because of the rating implications, municipal financing of concerts proved similarly contentious, but was part of an attempt by progressive liberals to 'extend the scope of the local state' so as to widen public access to culture.[49] The Cinematographic Act of 1909 gave local authorities the power to license the showing of films in buildings of a certain size, and later this was extended to give effective control over the projection of any film. Using this and other relevant legislation, councils and magistrates were able to dictate what was seen and when.[50]

THE INFORMAL STATE

The local state was thus no poodle of its central counterpart, even if during the twentieth century the relationship tilted increasingly in favour of the national government (or with Devolution, governments). But it is wrong to see the relationship between local and central states, despite the existence of obvious tensions, as inherently antagonistic. The examples above largely point to complementary roles, the one enabling, the other implementing, within the broad machinery of government. To describe one as within the state and the other outside it misconstrues the underlying mutuality and unity of interests. This prompts a further question: Did the boundaries of the state stop here? The argument for the 'large state' is more debatable, but the case none the less deserves to be considered. Three types of 'non-governmental organizations' merit consideration; quangos, pressure groups, and voluntary organizations. The first of these is an invention of the modern era. Among the more prominent in relation to leisure are the British Board of Film Censors (established 1912), the British Broadcasting Corporation (founded 1922 as the British Broadcasting Company), the Racecourse Betting Control Board (established by Act of Parliament in 1928 to oversee the Tote), the Central Council of Physical Recreation (1935), the Arts Council (1946), the National Parks Commission (1949), the Sports Council (1965), and the nationally constituted heritage and tourist organizations and boards established in various parts of Britain since the Second World War. How far these organizations were part of the state is a matter of argument. That the Minister of Education and Science chaired the early meetings of the Sports Council, and took as his deputy his principal advisor from the Department, was probably unusual.[51] But Whitehall was often closely involved with the process by which quango membership was established. For example, of the 12 members of the Racecourse Betting Control Board, five places, including the chairman, were in the gift of ministers.[52] Moreover, those appointed to boards were generally part of the circulating elite known as 'the great and good', who, while not considering themselves in the pocket of the government, would share the broad values of the ruling class. The British Board of Film Censors was not even a public body, but one established by the film industry, yet such was its perceived closeness to the establishment that its 'judgements acquired a quasi-statutory force'.[53] The BBC epitomizes the problem of where politically to position the quango. On the one hand, it was not a straightforward agent of the government as were many state-controlled broadcasting networks overseas, and John Reith, its early Director-General, was nobody's stool-pigeon; on the other hand, it played a generally neutral or supportive role in relation to the state during moment's of national crisis, such as the General Strike or the Second World War, and the implications of doing otherwise, in terms of governmental pressure, were all too evident during the Falkland, Gulf, and Iraq Wars.[54]

Pressure groups, by definition, are separate from government and are either pressing for change to the *status quo* or seeking to sustain a *status quo* that is in danger of being eroded. From a recreational perspective their origins date back to the proto-Puritan reform campaigns mounted in Elizabeth's reign, though to talk of 'groups' at this stage may be misleading.[55] However, formal organization is evident in the Societies for the Reformation of Manners active in late seventeenth- and early eighteenth-century London and other English towns, which sought to reduce the level of vice in urban society by aiding and cajoling local officials to tighten the regulation and increase the prosecution, among other things, of prostitution, gaming, drinking, fairs, and Sabbath-breaking.[56] Their successors proliferated, particularly from the late eighteenth century, leading, for example, to organizations like the National

Vigilance Association and the Public Morality Council, which by the early twentieth century 'had developed excellent relations with the police' in the prosecution of prostitution and obscene literature, or the National Anti-Gambling League, an overtly propagandist organization founded in 1890, which played a crucial role in forcing through the Betting Act of 1906.[57] Groups of this type could undoubtedly be effective in influencing local and national government and some sought a formal relationship with the state by obtaining the patronage of the Crown, such as the Society for the Prevention of Cruelty to Animals, which was founded in 1824 and received its 'Royal' endorsement in 1840.

The notion that the RSPCA can be incorporated into the informal state raises the most problematic of all questions: To what extent should the voluntary sector as a whole be included within the boundaries of the state? Surely a line has to be drawn here? Jeffrey Hill has reminded us that 'Of all the sectors in which the British sports and leisure pursuits are to be found it is the voluntary . . . that is the most extensive and deeply embedded,' and Richard Holt has called British sport 'a vast voluntary enterprise'.[58] The great upsurge in the formation of clubs and societies – many associated with some form of leisure – after the Glorious Revolution, and exhaustively explored by Peter Clark,[59] formed the spring-board for the voluntary movement of the nineteenth and twentieth centuries. This early phase of growth was possible, Michael Schaich argues, because of 'the difference between the shape of the continental state and its British counterpart. . . . [T]he military–fiscal state in Britain withdrew from many areas of domestic policy which were left to voluntary initiatives on the ground. This self-restraint gave plenty of scope for the foundation of clubs and societies.'[60] In other words, the voluntary sector flourished in Britain because of the withdrawal of the state. The case is strengthened by the history of the established Church, an important controller and deliverer of leisure. Whereas in the sixteenth and seventeenth centuries it was indissolubly tied to the state, and acted as an organ of its policy, after the principle of

Toleration was accepted in 1689 the Church effectively joined the nonconformist sects as just one more voluntary organization.

The MCC (the governing body of English cricket) and the Football Association are clearly not the same political entity as the government. The gap in authority that exists between them is real and significant. However, it is possible to exaggerate the separation of state and society and to generate something of a British myth. The membership and particularly the leadership of many, though by no means all of the clubs and societies was drawn from the upper and middle classes. As the source of recruitment for a broad and pluralistic governing elite they shared a common set of values, especially over key issues such as law and order. This highlights a further point: that many of those who led the voluntary societies also occupied offices within central and local government, so that they moved effortlessly between the structures of the formal and informal state. In his study of English cricket between the wars, Jack Williams observes that 'First-class cricket was controlled by those who exercised power in so much of English political and social life,' pointing to an almost seamless continuum between the statutory and the voluntary sectors.[61] The committee of the MCC in the 1920s and 1930s was packed with former Eton and Harrow pupils, peers, serving or ex-Members of Parliament, government ministers, and colonial administrators, and the Jockey Club, from its origins in the 1750s possessing a strong representation in the House of Lords, could be said, even in the mid-twentieth century, to possess 'virtually complete coverage of the elites that governed British society'.[62] This was the English trick, to suggest a separation of powers where none in reality existed. Some large-scale associations often mimicked the structures of the state, and their governing councils adopted a self-consciously national perspective. In a body like the National Trust, probably the largest recreational organization in Britain with over two million members by the late twentieth century, there is a palpable sense of bearing the responsibility for protecting the nation's heritage, and of possessing the authority to do this. Formally constituted in 1895, its provisional council included the Prime Minister, the Provost of Eton, the Master of Trinity College Cambridge, and representatives of the Royal Academy of Arts and the Royal Botanic Society, and several members of the aristocracy, and it met for the first time in the London home of its president, the Duke of Westminster. With the passage of the National Trust Act in 1907, which gave the Trust the right to pass its own by-laws, and crucially made its lands inalienable (except by approval of Parliament), it acted in proxy for a state astute enough to realize the benefits in delegating its powers.[63] Paradoxically the Trust was founded at a time when the classic age of the voluntary society was over, and according to Robert Morris, 'ambitions within state institutions met realizations of weakness on the part of the promoters of voluntary societies, creating part of the environment for growth in the scope and depth of the social actions of the state'.[64]

THE MOTIVES OF THE STATE

The thesis presented in this chapter is that the influence of the state in leisure was greater than is generally understood to be the case. Why should it have involved itself so much in a field where, on the face of it, there was little need to intervene? There were three areas in particular, fundamental to the operation of the state, which leisure impinged upon; image, economy, and security and order.[65] Every state must create an image of its own destiny and superiority with which to justify its authority and engender deference. While the Crown remained the central player in the political process, much of this image building would be focused on the monarch and the court. Leisure, in the broadest sense, was a critical medium through which royalty represented and defined itself. There was a long tradition which associated high-status hunting with the monarchy. The wide spaces commanded, the prestige of the quarry, the licence to kill, and the deeply ritualized character of the 'pastime' exuded power. William I designated extensive tracts – by Henry II's reign this may have extended to

30 per cent of the country – of his newly conquered land as royal forests in which hunting, primarily for deer and boar, was confined to the king, and there were savage penalties for infringing the laws. Though these came under attack in Magna Carta (1215) leading to the issue of a separate Forest Charter in 1217, hunting rights were extended no further than the nobility.[66] Tudor and early Stuart monarchs were heavily committed to the sport. Henry VIII invested substantial sums in hunting lodges and Elizabeth was still actively involved in her late forties in large-scale highly ritualized hunts (involving her in the *coup de théâtre*, the slitting of the hart's throat), carefully calculated to contribute to the cult of Gloriana.[67] The modern royal family's commitment to blood sports, revivified by Victoria and Albert's promotion of the pseudo-medieval sporting culture of the Scottish Highlands,[68] can only be understood in the context of the long-standing links between hunting and the image of monarchy. However, by the early seventeenth century hunting's contribution to the royal sporting image was being added to and modified by horse racing, with the Stuart monarchs playing a prominent role at Newmarket and Ascot in the development of the sport,[69] an involvement that the modern house of Windsor also shares. Racing better fitted the more civilized image of kingship evolving during the early modern period. Above all, the Renaissance prince and his court were expected to demonstrate the monarch's civility by the patronage, and where possible practice, of the arts, such as music, drama, dancing, painting, and architecture. Early modern monarchs generally invested heavily in these areas, aware of the subtle but powerful way in which the arts contributed to the charisma of authority.

During the early modern period the state underwent three key changes which altered the relationship between leisure and image; the consolidation of the various parts of the British polity, the emergence of an overseas empire, and from the late seventeenth century the decline in the power of the Crown. It was the nation and the mythical personage of Britannia that now became the focus of attention, and though the monarchy remained an important symbolic force, it was as the representative of the reconfigured state rather than as its *raison d'être*, a point encapsulated in the introduction of the Civil List under William and Mary. The role played by leisure in constructing the image of the state now became more problematic. The cycle of exhibitions initiated by the Great Exhibition at the Crystal Palace in 1851 constituted one way of putting on a show for the people, and to this could be added the occasional state funeral, but as the fiasco of the Millennium Dome demonstrated a century and a half later, invest-ment in this sort of grandiose public entertainment, whatever attempts were made to frame it in serious terms, could rebound on the government's image. With persistent British anxieties, dating back at least to the seventeenth century, about the threat of an overbearing state, it was politic for the formal state to play a low-key role in advertising its presence, and leave responsibility, in leisure and the arts, for cultivating the national image to the agen-cies of the informal state, supported by modest government grants. Occasionally twentieth-century governments came under pressure to act more directly to protect the national interest, such as saving the British film industry from collapsing under American competition,[70] and preventing football hooligans or a poor perform-ance at the Olympic Games damaging the country's self-esteem and international reputation. But any action in these areas was essentially negative rather than positive, reinforcing the point that there was little mileage for the modern central state in Britain, unlike its pre-modern predecessor, in investing directly in leisure for the purpose of image making.

The position of the urban local state was rather different. Guilds, corporations, and councils historically invested a good deal in promoting the civic image on which their authority rested. Much of this investment took a form which mixed ceremony and enter-tainment in a seamless ensemble. Pre-Reformation guilds, for example, staged and financed the great processions on occasions such as Corpus Christi and Whitsun, when the civic body was symbolically and really presented to the public, who would enjoy the theatre of the formal ceremony and that of the so-called Miracle Plays, delivered at intervals from portable stages embedded in the cavalcade.[71] The Reformation put an end to the religious guilds and Miracle Plays, but civic ceremony continued, geared to its dual role of representing the municipal state and entertaining its subjects. In the more substantial towns, many of them newly incorporated, mayor-making became the central public ritual, as at London, where the midsummer shows were downgraded in favour of the extraordinarily elaborate Lord Mayor's Show.[72] Such events invested the new mayor and his corporation with legitimacy and authority by ceremonializing the transfer of office. However, they were also occasions of festivity and pleasure, not only for the well-off participants, who would feast and drink extravagantly, but also for the 'plebs', whose enjoyment would be catered for by the introduction of unashamedly popularist features. In eighteenth-century Norwich the procession included a dragon, which 'gave great diversion to the common people'.[73] The interests of central and local state intersected in celebrations mounted in towns to mark national events, such as royal coronations and anniversaries, and thanksgivings for military victories, during which alcoholic refreshments might be provided for both civic big-wigs and the *hoi polloi*.[74]

Investment in civic recreational facilities was under way by the eighteenth century, but the later nineteenth century saw what, in the context of Bristol, Helen Meller has called a 'civic cultural renaissance' and a 'municipalization of the main cultural institutions'.[75] With the building of libraries, museums, art galleries, parks, swimming baths and such like, cities, whose cultural reputations had been tainted by the impact of industrialization, embarked on projects of civic boosterism, or what today would be called image-repositioning and place promotion.[76] This not only raised the profile of an urban council in its relations with external political bodies, but also strengthened its moral authority within the town itself. For communities like Merthyr Tydfil, which had scarcely had time to establish a truly urban identity during its meteoric rise to prominence as the steel capital of Wales, there was felt by the later Victorian period to be an urgent need to invest in cultural infrastructure to generate a civic and civilized image.[77]

Spending on leisure was not only about image building. Economic benefits were also a major consideration. This was the second motive behind the state's involvement in leisure. There have been two major concerns here, macro- and micro-policy. The state has registered an enduring anxiety about the willingness of the common people to work. Left to their own devices, and freed from the pressures of poverty, it was feared that ordinary workers would choose pleasure before toil, the so-called 'leisure preference'.[78] Such attitudes not only threatened the supply of labour for employers and the overall efficiency of the economy, but also risked escalating the welfare bill as a consequence of breadwinners failing to care for their families. Poor relief was a key factor in the equation, since if it was made too accessible, or set at too generous a level, it would encourage workers to exercise the leisure preference. Wage, social, and recreational policy thus intersected in a triangular relationship, and government had a responsibility to keep a wary eye on the supply of leisure, and where necessary act to prune this back. So in 1740, after a period of rising real incomes in the general population and a growth in commercialized leisure, severe restrictions were imposed on popular horse racing. According to the Act passed in that year, 'the great number of races for small plates, prizes, or sums of money, have contributed very much to the encouragement of idleness, to the impoverishment of many of the meaner sort of the subjects of this kingdom'.[79] For employers during the early Industrial Revolution the leisure preference manifested itself among the labour force not so much in an unwillingness to work, as in the irregularity of attendance, occasioned in part by the continuing impact of the festive calendar with its wakes and fairs. It was felt that restricting and suppressing these through national legislation or local orders was one way of removing temptation and producing a more diligent workforce.[80] The state's dogged resistance to popular gambling was in part due to the anxiety that it would erode working-class incomes and throw more families onto poor relief. There was also the fear that any culture that encouraged a something-for-nothing attitude, and was premised upon chance rather than a just reward, would undermine the work ethic. Gambling was part of the complex problem that faced governments between the First and Second World Wars, when there was a concern that the shorter hours, higher wages, and widening range of commercial entertainments enjoyed by some workers might encourage the exercise of the leisure preference, whereas the mass unemployment and enforced leisure (supported by unemployment payments) faced by other workers might similarly reduce the will to work.[81]

However, it would be a mistake to assume that the state's attitude to the economic implications of leisure was wholly or even predominantly negative. The basic human need for periods of relaxation after hard labour had long been recognized. One of the justifications that the puritan Philip Stubbes gave in 1583 for Sabbath observance was that 'every Christian man might repose himself from corporal labour, to the end that they might the better sustain to travails of the week to ensue', and in 1789 Brand, in the passage which opened this chapter, acknowledged that 'the common people, confined by daily labour, seem to require their proper intervals of relaxation'.[82] A recreated workforce was a healthier, happier, and therefore more efficient one. Many employers were well aware of this – supplying harvest dinners, arranging day trips to the seaside, and sponsoring sports teams and brass bands – but the formal and informal state needed to provide a broad framework of support. Fears about the physical, mental, and genetic deterioration of the workforce as a consequence of urbanization and industrialization – particularly acute and visible from the late nineteenth century with the growth of large urban conurbations, and a welter of social investigation reports – underpinned the state's reaction to health and social policy, and encouraged the provision of appropriate, and discouragement of inappropriate, recreations. There was another major economic reason why the state should support leisure: quite simply, it made money. Whatever the arguments about the extent, timing, or nature of the commercialization of leisure, it is clear that from at least the late seventeenth century leisure was increasingly big business, capable of generating considerable wealth and employment. Though attempts to restrict commercial pastimes might discourage idleness among some workers, among those put out of work they would simply enforce it. The state was thus engaged constantly in balancing out the perceived social and moral gains of restricting 'unsuitable' forms of pleasure, and the losses in employment, wealth generation, and tax revenue resulting from imposing such restrictions. There was pressure on governments, particularly during periods of 'moral panic' – such as the Gin Crisis of the early eighteenth century or the temperance campaigns of the Victorian era – to legislate to reduce alcohol consumption. But acquiescence risked putting agricultural labourers, farmers, maltsters, brewers, distillers, publicans, and gin-shop and beerhouse proprietors out of work. The dilemma continues today with the public debates over imposing restrictions on smoking and fox hunting. The state thus needed to assess carefully the economic as well as social implications of intervening to restrict the market for commercial leisure.

Positive promotion of leisure for economic reasons did not carry these risks, but central government has historically shown a reluctance to go down this road. However, in the twentieth century a recognition of the direct and indirect returns for the economy of supporting recreations – especially sports events, the arts, tourism, and the national heritage – has prised significant resources out of the central state, though often these are distributed through local authorities and quangos. The local state has in fact long understood the economic value of investing in leisure facilities. The corporation in early Georgian York provided funds to make and maintain public walks; to support the Assembly Rooms, music society, and horse races; and to upgrade elements of the urban infrastructure, such as the road network and street lighting, which supported the city's recreational services. Councillors were quite explicit in their motives for doing this; in providing a race prize in 1708 it was declared that 'the making of a yearly horse-race . . . may be of advantage and profit to the . . . city', and a payment to support the music society in 1739 made clear the rationale behind such investment, 'it conduces to bring company to the city who spend money and advance trade'.[83] This was a time when towns were increasingly being used and marketed as places of health and leisure, and a new breed of urban centre devoted to this was emerging, the inland and coastal watering-place. John Walton has argued that local government in the seaside resorts was slow initially to invest in facilities, because of ratepayer resistance, but that during the last third of the nineteenth century there was 'a revolution in municipal government in the larger resorts' as the pro-investment lobbies, particularly the holiday and building industries, gained the upper hand.[84] Penarth in South Wales was not one of the larger resorts, and the presiding influence over its late Victorian and Edwardian growth was Lord Windsor, on whose property much of the fashionable new town was located, and his agent Robert Forrest. However, in 1875 a local board was established, and over time it took on more and more of the responsibility for maintaining and investing in the recreational facilities. So, for example, when during the 1920s the resort was facing serious competition and its recreational infrastructure was deteriorating, the council introduced an ambitious programme of investment which included the purchase of the pier (from the private consortium which had originally opened it in 1895) and its redevelopment, the centre-piece of which was the construction of a spectacular Art Deco pavilion, and the substantial upgrading of the Esplanade, partially using monies channelled from the central state through the Unemployment Grants Scheme.[85] Public investment in leisure was not just an issue confined to resorts or even towns. As tourism grew, as heritage became an increasingly marketable commodity, and as industrial degeneration set in after the Second World War, so the local state and regionally based quangos acquired a growing function in place-promotion and economic regeneration through investment in culture and leisure.

The economic motive was important, but it was politics more than any other factor that motivated the state to intervene, usually negatively, in the people's pleasures. In particular, the maintenance of public order and national security were fundamental. Leisure played an important part in this because of its special capacity to express conflict in a symbolic rather than real fashion. Thus it could be argued that medieval kings permitted and eventually encouraged tournaments, and early modern monarchs tolerated poaching raids among the aristocracy and gentry, because such 'pastimes', aggressive though they were, released the competitive tensions within the elite, and prevented more serious outbreaks of violence.[86] The notion of the Renaissance court, at which rival potentates and factions jockeyed for the attention of the prince using the civilizing currency of culture, was based on a similar principle. Monarchs and states have also historically deployed 'bread and circuses' to divert the mass of the people from their disempowered and impoverished condition. Thus the promotion of sport, and particularly football (England and Scotland) and rugby (Wales), has been portrayed as a sort of safety valve, releasing pent up tensions and channelling energies away from politically subversive directions.[87]

A critical problem in treating leisure as a force for stability is its potentially dangerous character. The notions of leisure and licence are intimately associated. Recreations provide an opportunity for suspending the rules of everyday life. Norm-breaking is acceptable so long as it is understood that the event in question takes place within closely defined spatial and temporal boundaries, is largely symbolic in character, and does not intrude into the 'real' world and provoke actual violence and/or a challenge to the dominant social and political order. Though generally these rules are observed, occasionally so intense are the forces generated that the boundaries that enclose the leisure experience are breached and chaos is released into everyday life. It was for this reason that the state has felt the need to monitor recreational practice closely and where necessary intervene to prevent the threat of social break-down. It was fears about the capacity of alcohol to dissolve the bonds of deference, and of alehouses and pubs to accommodate sub-cultures outside the control of the ruling order, that led to the careful regulation of drink and drinking establishments through-out our period. Some sports were seen as particularly prone to inducing disorder. Racing attracted elements from what was per-ceived as the social riff-raff and criminal world, and at meetings outside elite control this could lead to violent disturbances. Thus in 1879 legislation was introduced to prevent several metropolitan meetings, especially those on the fringe of the capital, organized by local publicans and bookmakers.[88] Since the earliest references to football in the medieval era the game has been seen as a potential social flashpoint, and the treatment of football violence became for late twentieth-century administrations a test of their ability to govern.[89] Young males have been considered an especially unsta-ble group, most likely to press licence beyond acceptable limits, and their pastimes have been closely monitored.

The state has been particularly inclined to intervene in leisure practices where the resulting disorder was perceived to have a political motivation, and there was a direct challenge to the ruling establishment. The problem in large measure arises from the fact that riot and recreation are parallel forms of behaviour, the one easily capable of merging into the other.[90] There is evidence of leisure and its locations being used as a cover for politicized and seditious activity. A riot in support of Christmas at Canterbury in 1647 'helped to usher in the Second Civil War', and Charles II and James II considered coffee houses to be sites of 'the most seditious, indecent and scandalous discourses' and repeatedly attempted to curtail their activities.[91] After the alteration of the calendar in 1752 plebeian elements in England continued to stage games on old

May Day as an anti-Hanoverian gesture.[92] Camp-ball and football matches were employed in England as a camouflage for enclosure riots.[93] From 1649, Interregnum regimes banned racing throughout Britain, and an order of 1655 recorded 'how great a concourse of People do usually frequent . . . [race] Meetings, and the evil use made thereof by such ill-disposed Persons as watch for opportunities to raise New Troubles'.[94] From the seventeenth century hurling in Ireland was seen as a cover for seditious activity (a *camán*, or hurling stick, draped in black was carried by some of those attending Parnell's funeral in 1891), including Whiteboy agrarian protest and Ribbonism, a catholic pro-nationalist movement. William Wilde wrote in 1852 that to counteract this,

> hurlings and football playing, which generally took place on Sundays or holidays, were strictly interdicted, but the ire of the authorities was chiefly directed against calies and dances. When information was obtained with respect to the locality of one of these, thither the magistrate, with his *posse comitatus*, repaired, broke in to the assembly, dispersed the merry-makers, spilled the whisky, danced on the fiddle, and carried off to the nearest blockhole, or guard room, the owner of the house.[95]

In Wales the *ceffyl pren* or wooden horse was the centre-piece of the carnivalesque ritual punishment imposed by the community on moral transgressors. It was also 'undoubtedly the "role model" which inspired and groomed Rebecca' during the anti-turnpike riots in South-west Wales in the 1830s and 1840s, and led local magistrates and the newly established professional police force to launch a campaign to suppress its practice.[96]

The state was responsible for external as well as internal security, and leisure policy had its part to play in meeting this duty. During the medieval period citizens were required to engage in regular archery training and one of the motives for banning games like cockfighting, camp-ball and football was that they were felt to sap the fighting energies of the male population and divert them from practice in the shooting butts.[97] The Statute of Kilkenny (1367), imposed on the Anglo-Norman community in Ireland, asserted that

> whereas a land, which is at war, requires that every person do render himself able to defend himself, it is ordained . . . that the commons . . . who are in divers marches of war, use not . . . hurling, with great clubs at ball upon the ground, from which great evils and maims have arisen, to the weakening of the defence of the said land . . . but that they apply and accustom themselves to use and draw bows and throw lances . . . whereby the Irish enemies may be better checked.[98]

Until the development of the petrol engine, horses were a vital cog in the military machine, so that from the early modern period the Crown's and state's support of horse racing could be interpreted as a mechanism to improve the nation's breeding stock.[99] Concern about the condition of the rank and file of the forces, especially after the Boer War, led in the late nineteenth and early twentieth centuries to the introduction of physical training and sports into the teaching programme of the recently founded state school system. However, the commitment to this was mitigated by anxieties about the appropriateness of sports as opposed to drill for working-class youth, and, as Richard Holt has pointed out, by the British emphasis upon the navy rather than the army as its defensive shield.[100] Sport was thought by some to encourage the soft life and to channel energies away from serious concerns in a way that was unacceptable during periods of national emergency. In the First World War this led to considerable pressure on the sporting authorities, such as the Jockey Club, to suspend the normal calendar of sporting events, but by the Second World War the state was taking a much less negative stance, aware of the substantial benefits for civilian and military morale of continuing, as far as possible, the regular programme of recreations.[101]

A DIVIDED STATE

The thrust of the argument in this chapter has been to emphasize the reach of the state in matters of leisure. However, the flaws in the structure of the governmental machine, and the diffuse sources of power that propelled it, generated inefficiencies and contradictions that prevented the development of a monolithic and omnipotent state. The gaps that existed between the central, local, and informal strata provided considerable potential for friction. The battle between the Greater London Council and the Thatcher government was one manifestation of this. Though it ended in a victory for the central state and the abolition of the GLC in 1986 (and the transference of the South Bank's arts complex to an unelected South Bank Board), a major reason for this was pressure for change from London's Conservative boroughs – that is, fissures within the local state itself.[102] Central–local frictions have been seen as the cause of the conflict that underpinned the issue (in 1618) and re-issue (1633) of the so-called *Book of Sports* by James I and Charles I. The reign of Elizabeth had seen a progressive erosion of the festive calendar, and the sports associated with it, by locally-based evangelical Protestant elites.[103] The early Stuarts' declarations on sport were an attempt to restore the legitimacy of traditional forms of leisure, but were also part of the wider struggle for power within the state that was eventually, but not inevitably, to lead to its fracturing and reconfiguration during the years of the Civil Wars, Republic, and Restoration.

The conflict over leisure policy in the early seventeenth century cannot simply be reduced to one of central–local tensions. As Robert Dover's attempt to revive the Cotswold Games in about 1612 (on the property of Sir Baptist Hicks, who had close connections with the court of James I) demonstrates, there was plenty of local support amongst the gentry for traditional leisure.[104] At stake were issues of ideology and the distribution of power that regularly divided those who occupied the different layers of government. During the seventeenth century, as a result of the explosive events of the 1640s and 1650s, there emerged profound divisions of belief within the elite between those who supported a unitary state and those who favoured a pluralist one, which were to take party form as separate Tory and Whig camps emerged during the latter part of the century. The Tories conceived of the state as a single chain of authority flowing from a divinely appointed monarch to the parish gentry, and saw leisure as one part of the deferential cement that held together that political order. For the Whigs, the Crown's authority was ultimately conditional on its proper exercise, and this involved a tacit recognition that power was more broadly based and multi-centred, opening up the potential – though it is unlikely that this was the intention – for greater cultural (including religious and recreational) plurality. Characterizing the fissures within the governing elite in these party terms is inevitably crude and misleading, but it does account for much of the traditional Tory gentry's resistance to recreational 'reform' – such as the Sabbatarian campaigns and the attack on blood sports – in the later eighteenth and nineteenth centuries. The Tories saw crusades to reform popular recreations as partisan and divisive, a consequence of pressure-group politics, and as a threat to the traditional concept of the paternalistic local community on which their power rested.[105] Not that divisions were entirely along party lines. As Edward Thompson pointed out, 'attempts to interfere with the leisure of the people were thrown out of the House of Commons, on slender majorities made up of one part *laissez faire* inertia, one part Foxite defence of the liberty of the subject, and one part traditional Tory tolerance for "bread and circuses" and dislike for Methodistical "fanaticism".'[106]

In the eighteenth century, recreational events such as cricket matches and race meetings were used by the political parties as recruiting grounds and/or occasions for bonding.[107] This may not have reflected any ideological content to the pastime itself, though the Tory contribution to the development of the idea of 'ancient' music seems to have sprung from the feeling that traditional music embodied Anglican royalist sentiments,[108] but it reinforced the public image of a divided elite and state. Nor could the unity of the local ruling order have been enhanced by its handling of the Victorian music hall, where competing business interests, religious and moral pressure groups, and Tories and temperance Liberals fought, from within and without councils and benches of magistrates, to determine municipal strategy.[109] Local recreational policy must have been as much a product of conflict as of consensus,[110] and widening electoral rights, though extending the need to represent popular interests, simply institutionalized the tensions that existed. The British state has never presented a unified front. Even organizations on its margins, whose aim is to promote a single issue or recreation, have found it difficult to speak with one voice. The ruling bodies in rugby and football have emerged out of a series of schisms and divisions, while the structure of modern football in England – with the Football Association, the Football League, and the Premiership, not to mention the individual fiefdoms of the leading clubs – parallels the pluralism and internal tensions of the state itself. Even an organization like the National Trust, committed to the one task of securing the nation's heritage, on occasions has been deeply divided over its own internal governance, and over issues such as blood sports, and deciding which heritages to promote, coasts or country houses, popular or polite.[111]

The fragmented character of the British state, alongside the internal ideological tensions it harboured, prevented it from ever exercising a hegemonic influence over leisure. Some would contend that this was never its intention, and that recreation was one area where the state operated a hands-off policy of benign detachment. This was the British way of doing things. The people should be left unhindered to make their own pleasures. There is some truth in this position, but there is also more than a whiff of myth-making. John Brand's bonding together of recreations with the wisdom of states and 'political utility' suggests that an alternative hypothesis is worth considering: that historically the state has concertedly, if more negatively than positively, intervened in leisure policy; that it has been able to do so precisely because its multi-layered character – central, local, and informal – allowed its reach to penetrate so far; and that it intervened because leisure played such an important role in matters of image, economy, and order and security, which were fundamental to its operation. Moreover, if hegemony was not achieved, this was a result not so much of intention as of the contradictions within the workings of the state itself.

4

CLASS

In 1736 Francis Drake, writing of the York race meeting, complained that 'the attraction of this, at the best but barbarous diversion, not only draws in the country people in vast crowds, but the gentry, nay even the clergy and prime nobility are mixed amongst them. Stars, ribbons, and garters here lose their lustre strangely, when the noble peer is dressed like his groom.'[1] Such social promiscuity was anathema to him. It would have been a view shared by many of his contemporaries. One of the motives behind the Horse Racing Act of 1740 was to reduce a popular invasion of what was considered a high-status recreational activity. This recognized the importance of leisure in shaping the social structure, and was a reminder that, for the state, maintaining political stability was a matter not simply of preventing physical disturbances, but also of protecting the integrity of the social order. Society was constructed around a series of hierarchically arranged categories and layers. Allowing these to dissolve into each other was the highroad to chaos. But what exactly was and is the social order, and to what extent did leisure reflect or structure that social order? This chapter will address these questions from three perspectives. First, it will discuss the notion of a social order or structure in general terms. Secondly, it will attempt to identify specific strata or categories.

Thirdly, it will debate how viable such strata- or category-based descriptions of society are.

THE SOCIAL ORDER

Just as there are many ways of cutting a cake so there are multiple options in slicing a society. This chapter is predominantly concerned with those which involve an element of inequality based upon differential possessions of wealth, status, and power, where these are not determined by age or genetic factors of gender and race. Conventionally such inequalities would be embraced by the notion of class. However, the use of the 'c' word is highly problematic. It carries with it a cultural baggage that is impossible to unload. First, it is bound up with a set of theoretical frameworks, especially that associated with Marx, and a periodicity, especially the Industrial Revolution, that makes its use difficult outside these contexts. Secondly, it, more than any other concept, has been subject to the vagaries of historiographical fashion.[2] It is tempting to occupy some Olympian seat of detachment and pretend that it is possible to separate the fad from the facts in what historians have written, and thereby arrive at some 'truth'. But the writing of leisure history has been so inextricably bound up with the history of the concept of class that no such process of disentanglement is possible. It matters hugely not just from what ideological standpoint a historian is writing, but also when he or she is writing.[3]

Class was the concept which galvanized the academic study of social history in the decades after the Second World War. Key figures in setting the agenda were Richard Hoggart, Raymond Williams, Edward Thompson, Asa Briggs, and Harold Perkin. All had something to say about leisure, but it was not their principal concern. Though leisure history as a sub-discipline came onto the scene rather later, it was born when the idea that class was the motor of history was in full flood. Consequently almost all the work that established the subject in the 1970s and 1980s was built around the notion of class and allied issues such as social control, and it has continued to be a powerful influence. Hugh Cunningham's 1980 study of *Leisure in the Industrial Revolution* was in many respects a revisionist text, but the central idea which underpinned the debate it engaged in was clear enough from the blurb on its rear cover, 'this book is a study of what different classes of society understood by leisure and how they enjoyed it', and the title of Peter Bailey's 1978 exploration of *Leisure and Class in Victorian England* speaks for itself. As a sub-discipline of a sub-discipline, the academic history of sport has followed a similar trajectory, with Richard Holt's seminal study of *Sport and the British* (1989) declaring that 'The way changing class structures and urban experience have moulded sport has been the central concern of this book.'[4]

If the 'long' nineteenth century has set the agenda in terms of leisure history, class has also strongly informed work on the twentieth century, such as Ross McKibbin's study of the inter-war period, *Classes and Cultures* (1998), and the sociologists John Clarke and Chas Critcher's *The Devil Makes Work: Leisure in Capitalist Britain* (1985), with its trenchant claim that 'Class . . . stubbornly refuses to be buried. Each announcement of its death has, so far, been premature.'[5] The relatively few historians working on leisure in the pre-modern period rarely deployed the full-blown language of class, which was considered inappropriate for a 'pre-industrial' society. However, the most influential model used to describe recreational relationships, the so-called bi-polar model, reflected in the work of Edward Thompson and Peter Burke, and juxtaposing popular and elite, plebeian and patrician cultures, and little and great traditions, was underpinned by the broad notion of social class.[6]

During the 1980s intellectual fashions began to change and class began to lose its cachet as a master concept. This reflected the waning influence of Marxist theory and the emergence of cultural studies and postmodernism, which challenged both 'the old assurance of a formative link between social structure and culture',[7] and the appropriateness of grand modes of explanation or 'meta-narratives'. Historians of different complexions recognized that a sea-change in thinking had occurred. Robert Morris (1997) acknowledged that 'social class has lost its privileged position in the narrative of British social history', while John Golby and William Purdue, who in the first edition (1984) of their text on popular culture in England from 1750 to 1900 had swum against the tide and asserted that 'the characteristics of the culture and ideology of late nineteenth century society were not the prerogative of any one class nor dictated by the interests of any class', could, by the second edition in 1999, declare with some satisfaction that though 'class terminology remains inevitable in any description of a modern society or its culture . . . there can be little doubt that it has been dethroned from its privileged position'.[8] The bi-polar model of popular and elite cultures suffered a similar demotion, faced with powerful criticism from historians of early modern England such as Ronald Hutton, Jonathan Barry, Tim Harris and Adam Fox.[9]

Fundamental to the critique of class have been two points. First, important a factor as class may be, it is no more significant than a range of other collective identities such as gender, race, and community. The case was put forcibly by two historians whose subject of study, late nineteenth- and early twentieth-century industrial South Wales, has often been represented as the archetypal class-based society: Andy Croll pleaded for 'class . . . [to] be seen as just one – albeit vitally important – identity amongst others' and Martin Johnes argued that 'the experience of soccer suggests that class was not a dominant concept. . . . It was not the only window through which workers looked at life.'[10] Secondly, cultural forms, and this includes leisure, are not rooted to particular socio-structural formations. As David Hall has contended, 'artefacts of culture cannot be automatically distributed among the social groups or classes that make up society', and Barry Reay warned, 'common cultural values spill across tidy social demarcations'.[11]

The rapidly changing historiographical context undoubtedly complicates an understanding of the relationship between the social order and leisure. There is no simple answer to the problem other than to recognize that such complexities are fundamental to the historical enterprise. It is useful, however, to consider a little further what is meant by the social order. David Cannadine has suggested that during the period 1700–2000 it was viewed in three different ways: as a hierarchy, ladder, or 'seamless web', with no major barriers between the various strata; as 'triadic . . . with upper, middle and lower collective groups'; and as 'dichotomous', with a fundamental division between 'us' and 'them'.[12] Most leisure historians, to the extent that they are concerned with social structure, deploy one or other of these three models. The first, for example, can easily be recognized in Mike Huggins's view that nineteenth-century horse racing was characterized by the 'vertical ties' that operated in traditional society; the second, in Tony Mason's analysis of sport and recreation between 1900 and 1914 in terms of a three-class society; and the third, in Robert Malcolmson's view that during the early nineteenth century 'a solid barrier had developed between the culture of gentility and the culture of the people'.[13] Cannadine embraces all three models under the umbrella of class, though conventionally only the second and third models, and perhaps only the triadic version, would be recognized as a genuinely class-based society. He also feels that throughout the period 1700–2000 all three models were continuously part of the public perception of the social order, and rejects the notion that class came into existence at some point around 1800.[14] In fact it is tempting to argue, and this will be the approach adopted here, that there is nothing magical about 1700, and that there are good grounds for taking the three-model approach back at least another two centuries. This is not to argue that the specific formulation that the models took, or their relative weighting in public perception, remained unchanged. It is simply to say that all three have maintained at the very least a latent presence in British society over the last half-millennium.

Models are one thing. But the social order is more than simply a representation. It is built upon concrete differences in the distribution of wealth, status, and power that impact directly, if sometimes unconsciously, upon the way people perceive and experience their lives. Recreations were one of many arenas in which class differences could be expressed. What made leisure special was its saturation in the three qualities of symbol, play, and otherness. The articulation of social distinctions is potentially a dangerous exercise, capable of instigating conflict and breakdown. Confining expressions of social difference to symbolic and playful forms has the benefit of externalizing these differences but keeping the tensions generated at one remove from the 'real' world. Carnival and allied forms of inversion behaviour are cases in point. Momentarily the social order is turned upside down. Because this occurs in the 'unreal' context of recreational time and space, it has the effect of reinforcing the social order when 'real' time and space are re-entered. It is tantamount to inoculating the social body with a small dose of a dangerous pathogen, safe in the knowledge that it is too small to risk infection but large enough to build up the body's defences against a future hostile attack on a larger scale. Carnival is a form not only of play, but also, like many recreational experiences, of otherness. This creates contexts in which feelings are accentuated and heightened, and a latent social order energized.

Leisure was, therefore, an important arena in which to play out the social order. In the following sections it is proposed that we explore how social structure and leisure interacted, taking as a starting point the triadic model of class. However, the intention is not necessarily to privilege this model over the other two. This is simply the most convenient way to accommodate the three key elements in the social order that operated across the years 1500–2000; an upper, lower, and middling element.

THE UPPER CLASS

During the five centuries explored in this study it is plausible to argue for the presence of a continuous, but not unchanging, upper stratum in the social order. To what extent this constituted a class before the late eighteenth century is a matter of debate. Peter Laslett considers it the only class, 'the only body of persons capable of concerted action over the whole area of society' in the 'one-class society' that he feels constituted pre-industrial England.[15] This 'class' can also be referred to as an elite, or as *the* elite, because of the extent to which it concentrated wealth, status, and power in a very few hands. In pre-modern Britain there was one social boundary that counted for more than any other, that between the gentleman (and gentlewoman) and the rest. It is this division, at the heart of the bi-polar model, which historians conventionally refer to when using the terms 'elite' and 'popular', and 'patrician' and 'plebeian'. Though this distinction was crucial, there was no clear-cut definition for contemporaries of what constituted a gentleman. None the less, it was not the possession *per se* of wealth and power, or even of inherited titles, that made a gentleman a gentleman. The critical factor was how the self was presented. What was at stake was a subtle but fundamental point. The expenditure of money or the exercise of power can induce, or force, one human being to do the bidding of another, but this will not of itself instil the respect, deference, and charisma of authority that underpins a viable social order. For this wealth and power have to be transformed into forms of cultural capital which mask the crude forces behind them and bestow qualities of intrinsic superiority that enjoy a broad measure of acceptance in society.

Leisure is a form of cultural capital in its own right and also provides the context in which other forms can be deployed. In his *Theory of the Leisure Class* (1899), Thorsten Veblen defined his notion of an upper class largely in terms of 'conspicuous leisure' and 'conspicuous consumption'. By the former he meant an 'abstention from productive work', the 'non-productive consumption of time', or more bluntly, 'a waste of time and effort'. A 'code of status' was adopted which 'shows most plainly its incompatibility with all vulgarly productive work. A divine assurance and an imperious complaisance, as of one habituated to require subservience and to take no thought for the morrow, is the birthright and the criterion of the gentleman at his best . . . before which the base-born commoner delights to stoop and yield.'[16] Veblen was overdoing the point. The upper class were never as dissociated from economic production or wasteful of time as he implies, but his account contains more than a grain of truth. Keith Thomas has argued that 'The attitude to work held by the upper classes throughout the Middle Ages and into the early modern period is not difficult to chart. A contempt for manual labour permeates aesthetic, educational, scientific and religious assumptions until very modern times,' while Hugh Cunningham feels that the key facet of Veblen's theory is its emphasis upon the 'conspicuous', upon the public display of leisure in order to elicit the appropriate response from the rest of society.[17] The wealth of the upper class, and the means by which it obtained it, created an opportunity for continuous, conspicuous, and expensive leisure that was not available to the vast majority of society.[18]

It was no doubt an awareness of this which a character in George Powell's 'Cornish Comedy' (c.1696) had in mind when he posed the question 'What is a gentleman without his recreations?' His answer, however, makes clear that it was not just the mere practice of leisure, but also the type of recreations enjoyed which was important: 'Hawks, hounds, setting-dogs, and cocks, with their appurtenances, are the true marks of a country gentleman.'[19] What factors determined the character of a gentleman's recreations? Of undoubted importance was the requirement for a substantial expenditure of money and time since this was precisely what the productive orders could not afford. Holidaying exemplified this more than any other pastime, and the Grand Tour was the example *par excellence.* A tour of Europe could typically take two, three, or more years (though the length declined between the seventeenth and nineteenth centuries), and the costs incurred were not only those of travel and accommodation, but also souvenir collecting on the most expansive and expensive scale.[20] Nor did tourists necessarily travel light. When John Cecil, fifth Earl of Exeter, set off on his fourth expedition to the Continent in 1699, eager to pack Burghley House with prestigious *objets d'art*, there were twenty-four in his party, including his wife, two sons, maidservants, a tutor, steward, cook, butler, and farrier to service the twenty-nine horses and three carriages.[21] However, the choice of recreations was not simply about expense and time. Also vital was the character of the pastimes themselves. Here we see two facets of gentility that do not always sit easily together; the physical and the mental, or the iron fist and the velvet glove.

It was no accident that when the character in Powell's play had to specify the games the gentry played he should have turned to animal sports and particularly hunting. Nicholas Cox opened his *Gentleman's Recreation* (1677) with the ringing declaration that 'Hunting is a Game and Recreation commendable not only for *Kings*, Princes, and the Nobility, but likewise for private Gentlemen.'[22] Through the medieval and early modern periods, kings, nobility, and gentry jealously guarded their exclusive right to engage in certain forms of hunting, particularly deer hunting and falconry, continually issuing directives and passing legislation to enforce this. In the eighteenth and nineteenth centuries the organization, quarry, and location of hunting may have changed – fox hunting rose to prominence, grouse and deer shooting appropriated huge swathes of the Scottish Highlands, and hunting exotic big game became a feature of the imperial project – but the centrality of the sport as a marker of prestige remained unshaken.[23] In part the reason was simply a matter of history. Medieval kings, nobles, and knights had defined themselves as hunters and it was natural that those who sought to be their heirs should copy the practices and conventions of their predecessors, for much the same reason that the cult of medieval chivalry captured the imagination of the Victorian gentleman.[24] But it is also hard to avoid the conclusion that there was something in the nature of hunting itself which appealed to a ruling class. Power was one element; the licence to pursue and kill a quarry, sometimes in such large numbers – improvements in firearm technology ensured that game bags got bigger and bigger[25] – and such a ritualized manner that any food-gathering function, and in the case of lions and foxes this was clearly not the case, was of only secondary significance. Roger Manning also sees in hunting a symbolic substitute for military prowess, a way of investing the gentry with the kudos of warfare, central to the knightly image, without having to engage in actual hostilities.[26] In South-west Wales 'an aura of chivalry and valour, formerly experienced in battle, was transferred from the battlefield to the hunt meet. When the "Tivyside" hunt was revived in 1825, Lewes of Llysnewydd was described as a Chevalier Bayard *"sans peure et sans reproche."* '[27]

Alongside power, and intimately associated with it, land was a critical element in hunting. Up until the twentieth century the possession of a major landed estate was virtually a prerequisite for membership of the upper class. Hunting, because it was a sport which usually required large areas of land to pursue its objectives, was perfectly suited to highlight the elite's role as large landowners. The early modern Crown and aristocracy jealously guarded their forests and deer parks as hunting preserves; the nineteenth-century fox hunts parcelled out great swathes of the English countryside between them; and substantial portions of the Scottish Highlands were, during the nineteenth century, remodelled into vast grouse moors and deer forests. In 1883, 16 per cent of the crofting counties was given over to deer stalking, and by 1911 this had risen to 34 per cent, at which point around 3.5 million acres in Scotland were occupied by deer forests.[28] The other obvious feature of hunting was the presence of animals, with which the upper class had a special if deeply ambivalent relationship. An obvious attachment, displayed in the strength of sporting and animal art, and the way family and animal portraits jostled for space in the country house, derived in part from the value of animals as surrogates.[29] But also vital, and horse racing exemplified this more than any other area, was the capacity animals provided for sophisticated breeding programmes.[30] The upper class liked to think of itself as a genetic order, a class whose power was justified by the continuing concentration within itself of society's superior genes.

Animal breeding generated a parallel sphere in which to indulge in this belief and develop theories about it. Moreover, to the extent that better breeding produced better performance among the chosen animals, so it justified the aristocracy's own breeding programmes and claims to superiority.

The elite's relationship with animals was often an affectionate one, but this did not disguise the fact that it was also one of power. The animals were not free. They faithfully did their masters' and mistresses' bidding. Where they were free, as was the case of game, they were shot, or killed by other animals acting as surrogates for their masters. This all proclaimed the dominion of man over beast in the natural order and by implication of patricians over plebeians in the social order. However, it left the upper class exposed to the charge that they were brutalized by their close contact with animals. By the eighteenth century the boorish fox-hunting gentleman had become a stock figure of fun.[31] This reflected the acute pressure on the gentleman to demonstrate not only his physical but also his mental superiority, a requirement that had grown during the Renaissance and reached a crescendo during the Enlightenment, with its emphasis upon the primacy of reason.[32] If hunting represented the iron fist of gentility, then the arts provided the velvet glove. It was here that mental and intellectual attributes could be cultivated and displayed through mediums such as architecture, gardening, painting, sculpture, literature, and music. To take the case of the last of these. Art music, with its sophisticated structures and complex interplay of intellect and emotion, theory and practice, provided an ideal aesthetic environment in which to refine the mind and, particularly when associated with dancing, the body.[33] But art music, or as it has become known, 'classical' music, has also tracked the fault lines in the social order, since appreciation of it became a litmus test of a person's taste and therefore class. Through adopting a 'classical' mode of music the elite in eighteenth-century Scotland gathered themselves into exclusive clubs like the aristocratic Edinburgh Musical Society, and found an 'expression of . . . community with the educated classes of England, Holland, France, Germany and Italy'.[34] In later eighteenth-century England the aristocracy created a world of high-status concert music, defined by its social exclusivity and adoption of 'ancient' styles of music, so that the hierarchies of class and taste converged and 'the new framework of musical classics reinforced social status and political power in a brilliant and successful manner'. From the early nineteenth century 'the idea that the greatest music belonged to England's social élite . . . was to be a basic principle of musical life'.[35] Throughout the period from 1500 to the present day the elite used sport and the arts to define and justify its position in the social order. Over time the size of the elite and range of pastimes expanded, and this required the development of new organizational structures and calendars. To the medieval poles of court and castle/country house were added a range of sophisticated urban venues, exclusive clubs, and a social calendar that moulded those involved into a community and gave them a sense of caste identity.

THE WORKING CLASS

If it is possible to identify the continuous presence of an upper class since 1500, can the same be said of a lower class? Whereas the former only embraced a tiny minority of the population, making it feasible for them to operate as a cohesive group, the latter encompassed the vast majority of a population whose numbers grew from under 3 million inhabitants in 1500 to over 50 million by 2000. The exercise might seem hopelessly flawed, especially if leisure is the subject of study, since – if Veblen is to be followed – the elite concentrated recreational resources in their own hands. Yet contemporaries and historians have consistently felt able to locate a lower level in the social order – labelled in various ways, for example as the common people, the mobility, the plebs, the populace, the rabble, the masses, the lower orders, the lower classes, the labouring people, the working class, and the workers – and have felt able to identify a particular type of recreational life for this group. The classic modern account of working-class culture is Richard Hoggart's *Uses of Literacy* (1957), based heavily upon personal memories of his upbringing in the industrial north before the Second World War. He deliberately omits the 'self-improving minorities' to focus on the essential working class, emphasizing the enveloping, coherent, and visceral nature of its culture: 'To live in the working-classes is even now to belong to an all-pervading culture, one in some ways as formal and stylized as any that is attributed to, say, the upper classes.'[36] For Hoggart the basic features were clear enough: home, parents, and neighbourhood; a sense of 'them' and 'us', and among the latter a 'group warmth'; a rough, raucous, earthy, concrete, anti-intellectual, instinctive world of heavy drinking and sports; oral communication, tradition, and superstition; and pleasure in the gaudy and effusive, 'an untidy, messy, baroque, but on the whole drably baroque, world'.[37] The qualities he describes find a close resonance with other accounts of the culture and pastimes of the common people across the centuries.

Shaping the character of working-class leisure for the majority of the period under review were the constraints imposed by low incomes and poverty. Though over the long term industrialization raised income levels and commercialization pushed down prices, they were both part of an economic process which lifted the relative poverty line, so that not to be able to visit the cinema or a football match in the inter-war years might categorize an individual among the poor, as today might the inability to purchase a portable compact disc player or a pair of branded trainers. In the Tudor and early Stuart period it was demographic growth, declining real incomes, and rising poverty which stimulated the growth of the alehouse, and created an institution that reflected the limited means of its clientele, many of whom were travellers or subsistence migrants; providing cheap and basic food, drink, accommodation, games, and sex.[38] Andrew Davies's study of leisure in Salford and Manchester in the early twentieth century makes it clear that poverty – and this was not confined to those at the bottom of the occupational ladder, but could include skilled workers – seriously restricted access, especially for women, to the growing range of 'mass' leisure products.[39] The pressures of poverty, and the anxiety that it would probably affect an individual at some points in their life, does much to account for what many historians see as a central feature of popular/working-class leisure: its articulation and reinforcement of neighbourhood and community ties. Investing in the community was a practical way of safeguarding against the risk of falling seriously into poverty, providing a support network that could be called upon when times proved difficult. Edward Thompson has emphasized the 'rituals of mutuality' within northern working-class communities in the early nineteenth century, and Raymond Williams sees the 'crucial distinction' between working-class and bourgeois culture as that 'between alternative ideas of the nature of social relationships', the former 'collective and mutual', the latter 'individualist'.[40] In nineteenth-century Wales there existed a range of customs – such as the *cyfarfod cymorth* (assistance meeting), the *cwrw bach* (small beer), and the *pastai* (pasty or pie) – whose aim was to raise money for a member of the community facing hardship. Entertainment was an integral part of these occasions. The *cyfarfod cymorth* at Llangollen, according to an account of 1822, involved a number of young women giving a day's free work knitting or spinning to help a poor neighbour, 'and towards the close of the day, when their task was ended, dancing and singing were usually introduced, and the evening spent with glee and conviviality'.[41]

Mutuality and community may have underpinned working people's leisure, but this did not mean that when they played they played softly. 'Working-class society was deeply competitive,'[42] so that fierce rivalries characterized much leisure activity, whether it be football, fishing, or brass bands (to which the notion of contesting was central).[43] Heavy drinking and rowdiness have also been frequently associated with the lower orders, and though the accusations of drunkenness and violence were regularly deployed as a tool to stigmatize the common people, there is little reason to doubt that generous corporate and public consumption of alcohol and high levels of inter-personal and inter-communal violence were woven closely into the fabric of (at least male) popular leisure. From this perspective working-class pastimes might be seen as the surviving vestiges of a pre-rational, pre-Enlightenment culture, characterized not only by roughness,[44] but also by a deep conservatism, an emphasis upon oral and visual modes of communication rather than literacy, and a naive dependence upon luck, fate, and magical forms of explanation. The latter frame of mind could be seen to manifest itself most strikingly in a working-class passion for gambling, from betting on horse races, brass band contests, angling competitions, cricket matches, animal contests and human fights, to football pools, bingo, and fruit machines. However, precisely what mind set gambling characterizes remains unclear. On the one hand, the element of chance and participants' resort to 'irrational' devices to influence the outcome, all seem to hark back to a world of magic and astrology. On the other hand, as Ross McKibbin has shown, gambling, such as betting on horse racing or doing the pools, could involve the application of considerable intellectual skills (particularly in studying 'form') and perfectly rational decision making in choosing which animal or team to back.[45] Moreover, treating magic as a non-rational mode of thought and behaviour is highly problematic, particularly in the context of early modern society where it was so widely accepted and formed such an important part of the operation of everyday life.

THE MIDDLE CLASS

The existence of upper and lower strata in the social order begs the question of what, if anything, lay in between. The bi-polar model would suggest there was nothing, whereas the triadic version posits a middling stratum. Implicit in much discussion of the social order, though it is rarely represented in these simple terms, has been the notion that up until about 1800 it was either the patrician/plebeian model that operated or that of a seamless hierarchy, and that it was only with the onset of industrialization that a true middle sector emerged and introduced a genuine version of the triadic model. This view is now untenable, at least in its crude form. A powerful case has been made for a rapidly expanding middling order in the century or so after 1660.[46] Moreover, as the processes of commercialization and industrialization are pushed further and further backwards chronologically, and more and more economically independent individuals are discovered (particularly in towns) who are neither patrician nor plebeian, so it becomes difficult to conceive that there was a time after 1500, and probably well before, when there was not something that could be described as a 'middling sort of people'.[47] This does not exclude the possibility of the middling order growing in size and self-consciousness. However, 'the rise of the middle class', like commercialization, is a phenomenon frequently described by historians of very different periods. Jonathan Clark has argued, 'It may or may not be that this scenario applies to *one* . . . period; it is highly implausible that it applies to them *all*.'[48] The middle class cannot always be rising. A point must be reached at which it either achieves a state of equilibrium in relation to the other classes, or it simply engulfs them and produces a single-class society.

Unlike the lower orders, the middling sort were not generally constrained by poverty, but had sufficient disposable income to give them viable options in the world of commercial leisure. But here we come up against a central problem. The values conventionally associated with the middle stratum – hard work, thrift, capital accumulation, saving, moral rectitude, sobriety, respectability, and religious commitment – are not obviously conducive to spending money or time on leisure. However, it would be wrong to assume that the possession of such values necessarily prompted an antipathy to leisure. First, there appear to be periods when the middling types were either more or less pleasure orientated. It could be argued that whereas an ethic of work and saving predominated during the Reformation and the Industrial Revolution, a tendency towards consumption and pleasure was prevalent in the century or so after the Restoration and from the mid- to late Victorian period onwards (Gary Cross would place the change a little later, from *c.*1900).[49] To borrow a financial metaphor, after periods of capital accumulation investors took their profits. As Michael Thompson has argued, 'the culture of the late Victorian middle classes . . . shed the husk of earnestness and self-righteousness and embraced the notion of fun. . . . The mantle of moral rectitude, sanctimonious piety, and austere recreations lugubriously endured, had shrunk until it no longer fitted any but the lower middle class.'[50]

Secondly, making money was one thing, but in the pursuit of social position it was of little use unless converted into status. Leisure was crucial in this process, providing the arenas in which cultural consumption and display took place. So, for example, fashionable spas and seaside towns often possessed sophisticated shopping quarters, together with venues such as theatres and assembly rooms in which the purchases acquired could be flaunted. Thirdly, it was possible to spend and play, but to do so in ways which reinforced rather than undermined respectable values. In the eighteenth century the sacred oratorio, pioneered by Handel, combined the excitement and opportunity for social display offered by opera, with the spirituality of a church service, and charity balls, plays, and concerts were used to inject occasions of pleasure with a moral purpose.[51] During the nineteenth century a form of painting and connoisseurship developed which emphasized the role of art as a moral text and which through the production of highly finished canvases, celebrated the work ethic. Art thus became 'a key element in the affirmation of a middle-class identity that was distinct from the leisured existence of the aristocracy'.[52] Moreover, from the mid-Victorian period a regime of 'rational recreations' emerged, including the new more regulated forms of sport, which conceived of leisure as a vehicle for character building and self-improvement.[53] Fourthly, the hard-worked business and professional man could always justify recreation on health grounds, as a way of improving his physical fitness and reducing the stress of a demanding job.[54] This provided the moral rational for the bourgeois penchant for holiday-making. From the late eighteenth century John Towner feels that the middle class began to constitute the majority of those undertaking the Grand Tour, and John Walton argues that even as late as the Edwardian era 'the mainstay of the . . . seaside resort was a broad band of middle class demand'.[55] The health motive might, of course, simply be a convenient mask for a less worthy desire simply to have a good time, and Mike Huggins argues that a cult of bourgeois hedonism ran alongside that of respectability, as evidenced, for example, by the heavy middle-class involvement in horse racing.[56]

The middle class could never entirely free itself from the stigma of work and money making. The smell of trade clung to the businessman despite every effort to disguise it. This was why the bourgeoisie fought so tenaciously to create and protect the amateur ethos in sport. Middle-class leisure must be seen to be utterly uncontaminated by lucre. Only thus could the bourgeoisie be truly seen to be a part of the Veblenian leisure class. At the same time the amateur code also erected a powerful barrier between the middle- and working-class sportsman, since the latter could not afford to waste any economic opportunity to exploit his physical skills. This barrier was reinforced by the middle-class aestheticization and cerebralization of sport. The amateur cricketer would pay as much attention to how he made his runs, as to how many he made. Physical effort and brute force were eschewed in favour of elegance and timing, and the best shots were those which displayed the least trace of work and effort. The middle class created a counter world of leisure, an 'other' space, underpinned by a set of norms the very opposite of those which operated in the world of business. The emphasis upon aesthetics and mind also helped protect bourgeois sport from the criticism that it was brutish, and strengthened the social divide promoted in the Enlightenment between man the thinker and man the animal. Pierre Bourdieu has drawn a distinction between working-class wrestling, with its nudity and rough bodily contact, and petty-bourgeois aikido, where contact is 'ephemeral and distanced', a triumph of mind over body.[57] Chess and the recently revived real tennis offer similarly cerebral pastimes.[58] Traditionally aikido has been a non-competitive activity,[59] and this chimes historically with a middle-class tendency to prioritize sociability, especially as embodied in the notion of the club, over competitiveness in sport. This recognized the value of leisure as a mechanism for business and status networking. But it may also be seen as a compensation for the inherently individualistic, competitive, and isolated lifestyle of the bourgeoisie, particularly once the flight to the suburbs had begun. Moreover, it provided a counterpoise to, and a divider from, the aggressive and openly competitive character of working-class sport, itself, ironically, an escape from the corporate and communal norms that underpinned the daily existence of most working people.[60]

The discussion above has explored the relationship between leisure and the social order by identifying separate categories of experience that relate to three broad strata in society: upper, lower, and middle. It is argued that there is a measure of continuity across the period 1500–2000. However, this position should not be pressed too far. Neither the social order, its constituent parts, or the way people perceived these was static. An upper order, defined by its ownership of land, survived a remarkably long time, but by 1900 the history of its 'decline and fall' was well under way.[61] To what extent this constituted the end of the upper order *per se* – an order capable of drawing on the cultural symbols of its predecessor – is quite another matter. It is arguable that the working class, as it is generally characterized and often caricatured, has a defined history. Forged through the dual processes of industrialization and urbanization, and concentrated in geographical pockets, it reached its apogee in the years before the Second World War. The surest sign that its days were passing was when in the 1950s and 1960s historians like Edward Thompson and literary critics like Richard Hoggart began to write about it, and television soaps began to turn it into a part of the heritage industry. However, this does not mean that a lower order did not exist before c.1750, or after c.1950, and that it did not share characteristics with the classic formulation of the working class. The most illusive of all the orders is that of the middling sort. In a state of apparently constant expansion, it seems capable of achieving the Marxist goal of a classless society, not by being destroyed by the proletariat in the final stage of a class revolution, but by itself gobbling up all the other classes and their cultures. The great country houses, for example, have been appropriated by an instrument of collective bourgeois control, the National Trust; and the football terrace, the recreational heartland of the male working class, has since at least the 1970s been colonized by middle-class 'post-fans' and voyeurs.[62] Without accepting this crude history it is possible to conceive that the middling order has become proportionally larger, wealthier, and politically stronger over time. However, this has not necessarily weakened the triadic model of the social order, as the higher echelons of the middling sort have regularly been absorbed into the ruling elite. The function of many of the pastimes of the upper class, such as assemblies in the eighteenth century, concerts in the early nineteenth century, sport and the seasonal round in the Victorian era, and hunting in the twentieth century, was to provide mechanisms for drawing eligible new members into the elite and relegating those no longer able to sustain their position.[63]

FRAGMENTED CLASSES

The argument so far has been that class was a fundamental feature of the social order, and that leisure played a vital role in expressing and moulding class distinctions. There are powerful arguments, which have grown stronger in recent years, against such a class-based interpretation of leisure. Three broad critiques have been developed: that the three (or two, if the bi-polar model is adopted) classes were not homogeneous but sometimes deeply fragmented; that cultural forms can and often did transcend strict socio-structural categories; and that class is not a master category, but simply one type of identity among many others.

The members of the ruling class were often bitterly divided amongst themselves. The competition for power and status that engrossed those who possessed these assets in largest quantities, and had most to gain and most to lose in pursuit of them, led to conflict and division. Richard Wilson and Alan Mackley have demonstrated how 'Emulation and rivalry were powerful motives in country house building', as the gentry strove to outdo each other in what for most 'was certainly the biggest item of expenditure in their lives'. The early modern gentry deployed violent poaching raids as a type of 'political theatre', to articulate inter-family and inter-factional rivalries within the ruling order, and inter-personal feuds were an endemic feature of fox hunting in the nineteenth century.[64] How far the use of leisure in this way fragmented the upper class as a *class* is difficult to say. It was perfectly possible for families and factions to slug it out with each other and yet retain a sense of being part of the same social group. What would be significant would be for these conflicts to have emerged from sociological divisions, such as big landowner versus small landowner, and business plutocrat versus landed gentleman. On occasions such divisions may have created tensions and fed ideological and religious differences, but it is difficult to demonstrate that this was a consistently important feature. Moreover, there is evidence that culture and recreational contexts were used to mitigate social and political tensions, as in the case of the eighteenth-century spa, where powerful norms operated to encourage a corporate and highly sociable lifestyle.[65]

Competition for status was not something confined to the upper class. Inter-family and inter-communal rivalries were rife among the working class, whose members had an acute sense of their own internal social hierarchy. In early modern England 'the lower orders were not merely an undifferentiated and amorphous agglomeration'.[66] Famously Robert Roberts opens his reminiscences of Salford,

> No view of the English working class in the first quarter of
> this [the twentieth] century would be accurate if that class were
> shown merely as a great amalgam of artisan and labouring
> groups united by a common aim and culture. Life in reality was
> much more complex. Socially the unskilled workers and their
> families, who made up about 50 per cent of the population in
> our industrial cities, varied as much from the manual élite as did
> people in middle station from the aristocracy.[67]

A division frequently cited by historians is that between unskilled
and skilled workers, and it was from the latter group that in the
Victorian era professional cricketers, those playing and watching
professional football, and the membership of brass bands were
largely drawn.[68] Another fissure often described is that between
the respectable and the rough.[69] However, this can be overdone.[70]
Working people were able to adopt a variety of seemingly contradictory cultural forms and roles, in Peter Bailey's words both
'thinking and drinking',[71] so that, for example, the seemingly
respectable choral culture of late nineteenth-century Wales was
often accompanied by unbecomingly boisterous behaviour on
the part of performers and spectators, prompting one Rhondda
commentator to observe, 'the eisteddfod will soon vie with football and the prize ring for disorderly scenes and rowdyism'.[72]
Some historians, such as Stephen Jones, have also doubted that
there was a gulf between the leisure of the so-called labour elite
and the rest, and Wray Vamplew has eschewed locating the
Victorian professional sportsman 'within the ranks of the labour
aristocracy'.[73]

The sheer size of the lower order militated against homogeneity.
The same point could be made about the middling sort, particularly
if the thesis of expansion is accepted. Additionally, those in
the middle faced two rather than one social border, increasing

the potential for overlap and fragmentation. Indeed, where the borders lay between the middling, lower, and upper orders was problematic and ill-defined. Early modern contemporaries recognized a distinction between a yeoman and a husbandman, but it would be dangerous to assume that it represented an absolute boundary between a lower and middle order. Were shopkeepers necessarily of the middling order? The case of the eighteenth-century Sussex grocer Thomas Turner is often cited as an example of someone who ran his own business, was highly literate and a parish official, yet engaged in heavy public drinking and was often inebriated, visited the local fairs, and seemingly had close contact with the common people of his village.[74] Turner might best be described as socially amphibious, and his experiences were probably not untypical of those on the margins of the middling stratum. In such circumstances it is difficult to argue at a practical level for a tightly coherent order. When David Cannadine writes that 'there was no such thing as *the* late Victorian and Edwardian middle class: it was far too protean, varied and amorphous for that', the same point could be made for most periods.[75]

The divisions that existed could vary according to location, such as town or country, or even different types of town. In seaside resorts and heritage towns, for example, there could be serious tensions between indigenous business interests, keen to exploit the location as an economic asset, and exogenous residents, many retired, eager to restrict the volume and nature of development and keep rates low.[76] The most important divisions which have emerged, a product of long-term trends within the economy, are those between a professional and a business-managerial order, and between an *haute* and *petite bourgeoisie*. Leisure is vital because it is a form of cultural capital, and it is investment in and control of this type of capital, as opposed to merely financial capital, which differentiated the social groups. In the eighteenth century, as a new phase of professionalization was entered upon, it was crucial to those who aspired to professional status to invest in high-status and sophisticated architecture, art, and pastimes, to distinguish themselves from other elements in the middle class.

During the 1830s and 1840s, whereas the liberal professions in London patronized classical concerts, the business elite attended ones with a less refined content.[77] In late Victorian Britain 'the middle class was effectively split between gentrified occupations . . . and the rank and file of factory managers or retailers',[78] and it was this social fissure that contributed to the schisms between soccer and rugby, and between rugby union and rugby league.[79] The professional middle class treated sport as a form of pure cultural capital, and fought hard to ensure that it was uncontaminated by money, whereas the managerial middle class were willing to treat sport as an example of mixed capital. The growth in cultural capital in the twentieth century made possible and reflected further fractionalization within the middle class, so that it is no longer a question simply of cultural versus financial capital, but of different forms of cultural capital ranged against each other. The spread of 'modern' serial music (a method of composition based on a fixed arrangement of elements, most commonly the 12 notes of the equal tempered chromatic scale) in Britain after the Second World War, against all forces of market demand, owed much to the capture of the cultural levers of the informal state – the BBC, the educational institutions, and the arts quangos – by a small elite of taste setters, internationalist in outlook, who were determined to undermine the insular, tonal, traditional, and commercial musical establishment.[80] The growing complexity in the forms of cultural capital, and the way in which they are manipulated, suggests an increasingly fragmented and protean middle class, spawning new sub-groups such as the so-called service class, and characterized by a widening range of lifestyles.[81]

One of the reasons that the professions and *haute bourgeoisie* placed so much emphasis upon cultural capital was because it was this that the upper class had deployed so effectively for centuries to assert their superior status. It may have been impossible for all but a tiny minority to have the resources to purchase a great landed estate, but it was not difficult for the well-off middle class to acquire some of the cultural trappings of society's traditional leaders and mix socially with them in recreational contexts.[82] This points to the second basic argument against a class-based analysis of leisure; cultural forms, even if they originate in a specific social order, can transcend it. It is evidenced in the sharing of recreations not only by the upper middle class and gentry, but also, a point frequently made by historians of nineteenth- and early twentieth-century leisure, by the working class and lower middle class, in fields such as music hall, choral music, dancing, football, gambling, and popular literature.[83] In the bi-polar model the elite/popular barrier was no less permeable than that between the classes in the triadic model. Andrew Gurr has emphasized that 'play-going was popular at all levels of society in Tudor England', and Lawrence Klein contends that the culture of politeness in the eighteenth century was easily accessible to those below the elite, either directly or vicariously through printed manuals.[84] A buoyant market in fashionable second-hand clothing allowed further contact, for those unable to afford the pristine articles, with the world of the polite.[85] Certain groups within the lower orders were particularly receptive to, or had especially good access to high-status leisure; servants, apprentices, and those who produced the recreational goods consumed by their superiors.

A key factor that underpins much of the argument about the capacity of cultural forms to move freely through the social structure is the diffusion thesis, in which cultural goods are introduced in the upper echelons of society and, over time, filter down the social structure. In this model of cultural change the engine is social emulation and the assumption is that it is present, to some degree, at all levels of society. Countless examples are cited by historians. In the medieval period there were tournaments and chess, and in the early modern era, hunting, morris dancing, and luxury foodstuffs like sugar, tea, coffee and tobacco, all of which travelled a good way down the social order.[86] Since the late eighteenth century a similar process of social diffusion has been detected in sports ranging from curling and quoits to rugby and golf.[87] Probably the most striking example of top–down diffusion is holidaying away from home. John Walton argues that 'emulation and social competition were the most important triggers of resort expansion', with the 'seaside holiday habit' percolating 'downwards through the increasingly complex social strata of the first industrial nation', and the later twentieth-century explosion in overseas travel suggests a middle and working class, empowered by growing wealth, aping a pattern of leisure that originated in the aristocratic Grand Tour.[88]

In recent years the diffusion thesis has faced something of a critical assault.[89] The principal objection has been to the notion that culture flows from top to bottom, that 'mass follows class'.[90] From their documented origins some sports are practised by more than one class,[91] and many instances can be cited where popular pastimes have been appropriated by superior social groups. The self-conscious rediscovery by educated society of 'folk' culture is evident from at least the eighteenth century,[92] and folk song fertilized the English classical musical renaissance in the early twentieth century.[93] Various sports – such as archery, tennis, cricket, and fox hunting – which at one time appear to have been commonplace, have risen up the social structure to become symbols of elite leisure.[94] In the early sixteenth century Robin Hood plays 'seem to have begun at parish level and travelled upwards in society to the royal court', while the middle-class Victorian reinvention of Christmas involved refurbishing a popular custom.[95] The 1939 *Mass Observation* volume, by T. Harrison and C. Madge, expressed the view that the dissemination of the dance known as the 'Lambeth Walk', 'quite reverses the more usual cultural current which flows from the upper class *down* to the working class',[96] but it was not as unusual as the investigators might have thought. Music hall and cinema-going were initially predominantly working-class pastimes before attracting middle-class audiences, and the introduction of the ITV channel provided middle-class television viewers with access to popular idioms unavailable under the Reithian BBC.[97]

It is not difficult to show that cultural forms have travelled up as well as down the social structure. Indeed, it is probably best to think in terms not of movement in either one direction or the other, but of constant 'interaction', 'interchange', and 'cross-currents'.[98] In itself such a process does not negate the role of cultural diffusion in eroding class categories. If anything, a two-way is more effective than a one-way process in dissolving social boundaries. But some of the criticisms of the diffusion thesis do point in a different direction. Without denying an element of cross-fertilization, some historians are keen to emphasize the capacity of specific classes to generate their own culture. Susan Barton and Richard Holt have stressed the degree of working-class agency in the shaping of modern holidays and sport.[99] Several historians have challenged the middle- and upper-class role in the development of modern football, arguing, in Adrian Harvey's words, that the 'game . . . would have developed as a rationalized sport in the latter half of the nineteenth century had there been no public school model whatsoever'.[100] Even in the case of rugby the public school was only one motor of change. Leeds Athletic was started in 1864 with an advertisement placed by a clerk at the city's North Eastern Railway goods depot, and 'the phenomenal pace at which rugby spread through the valleys [of South Wales] is the most eloquent testimony to the self-generating power of popular culture'.[101] John Lowerson has not only questioned the top–down model of cultural diffusion but argued that in the case of middle-class sports any movement tended to be lateral rather than vertical.[102] From about the 1820s there were initiatives, largely driven by a middle class anxious about the socially and politically divisive and degenerative impact of industrialization and urbanization, to harmonize social relations and improve the working class by encouraging them to participate in 'rational recreations'. Potentially a powerful tool of diffusion and social cohesion, the exercise ultimately foundered because working-class culture resisted penetration and control from outside, and the middle class was unwilling to fully fund the initiatives involved and sacrifice the exclusivity of its own leisure pursuits.[103]

A SHARED CULTURE?

Diffusion thus had a limited impact in breaking down social barriers. It has in particular to be remembered that when a form of leisure forged in one zone of the social order enters another, its meaning can be transformed. However, it may be a mistake to think in terms of all culture being created at particular points in the social structure, or belonging originally to a specific class. Might there not be a shared culture, the property of everyone? Though this would not preclude the existence of socially exclusive cultures, it would mitigate their divisive effects. From the British perspective such a shared culture may have exerted a particularly potent influence, given that the nation escaped the modern political revolutions experienced on the Continent.

Much of the research into pre-modern society is premised upon, or seeks to establish, the character of a shared culture. An especially influential cultural model has been that constructed by Peter Burke, though it must be stressed that his focus is on Europe. Drawing upon the anthropological concept of the 'small' and 'great' traditions he argues for the existence of a common set of customs, beliefs, and practices, owned by all. Running alongside an exclusive culture possessed only by the elite, the shared culture constituted a common bond that held together the two groups. Burke goes on to propose that during the early modern period there was a progressive 'withdrawal from popular culture' by the upper classes, though the timing of this varied from place to place – in England from the later Tudor period, in Scotland not until the eighteenth century – so that what was once a corporate culture was now, by default, one exclusive to the lower orders.[104] The argument received persuasive support from Henry Bourne, when in 1725 he introduced and justified his study of the 'antiquities of the common people' with the comment that 'the following sheets are a few of that vast number of *ceremonies* and *opinions*, which are held by the common people; such as they solely, or generally observe. For though some of them have been of national, and others perhaps of universal observance, yet at present they would have little or no being, if not observed among the vulgar.'[105]

Though many historians would now reject the bi-polar cultural model there is widespread acceptance that there did exist in the early modern period a set of recreational practices and ceremonies accessible to, and participated in, if not necessarily in the same way, by the whole of society. Moreover, many would also question whether any sustained process of elite withdrawal had occurred in Britain by the late seventeenth century.[106] At what point – and it may be a mistake to try and identify a particular date – the upper and middling orders in general found participation in traditional pastimes unacceptable is a matter of debate. What is critical is that such pastimes, as a consequence of the rise of a polite and improving commercial culture, and the gathering impact of the Enlightenment, became deeply unfashionable. Engagement with 'popular' culture ran the risk of being stigmatized as socially inferior. That said, many among the gentry were wedded to the vision of an organic paternalist society and were unwilling to jettison recreations which they enjoyed. In some parts of Britain, such as Wales, elite participation may have lingered longer.[107] In Ireland gentry patronage of popular pastimes continued for much of the eighteenth century, and though 'the crisis of the 1790s marked the end of an era in the relations between élite and popular cultures', and there was a 'sinking social centre of gravity of participation in popular culture', it was still common in the early nineteenth century for the corporation to dine on Fair Green during Dublin's Donnybrook Fair, and for the Lord Lieutenant to visit on occasions.[108]

Popular culture was far from the static phenomenon portrayed by antiquarians like Henry Bourne. The common people were engaged in a long-term process of selective retention *and* rejection. They jettisoned those parts of traditional culture which no longer suited their notion of an urbanizing industrial society, and, as their wealth increased, they created and absorbed new forms of cultural practice, some drawn from the polite and improving culture of their superiors. This established the context, under the impact of commercialization, for the development of a new type of shared, or as it is often referred to, 'mass' culture. John Golby and William Purdue see by the late nineteenth century the 'emergence of a more national leisure culture in which mass spectator sports and the entertainments industry had the effect of homogenising many regional and social distinctions'.[109] Similar types of argument are made for the inter-war and post-war periods, Richard Hoggart asserting in 1957, 'We are becoming culturally classless.'[110] The principal engines in the forging of a modern 'classless' culture, it is argued, have been sport, holidays, popular music and fiction, and the media, access to which has been facilitated by a relentless process of commercialization and globalization. Royalty, aristocracy, professionals, and workers are now, it is claimed, all watching the same football matches, listening to the same pop groups, watching the same block-buster films and TV soaps, and visiting the same continental resorts as each other. Music hall provided a prototype for the new model of popular culture, 'a widely shared social and symbolic resource . . . increasingly colonised by emergent cultural industries . . . not coterminous with any single class',[111] when in the later nineteenth century it began to lose its predominantly, though never exclusively, working-class image and clientele, and began to cater for a growing middle-class audience.[112] It is also claimed that certain sports – such as curling, cricket, fox hunting, and horse racing – have for long periods operated on a pan-class basis, articulating the vertical ties that it is argued held together pre-modern society.[113] As Robert Roberts argues of Salford, 'Racing held the rabid interest of millions. It bound the labourer with a cap-touching loyalty to the aristocrat. There were those who would back only King Edward's, Lord Derby's or Lord Rosebery's horses. Winning, they felt for a brief moment a glow of unity with the greatest in the land.'[114] Some sports, though they were exclusive in England, have been claimed to possess a wide social following in other parts of Britain, such as rugby union in Wales and golf in Scotland.[115]

The argument that between 1500 and 2000 there existed, in various forms, a core culture available to all classes, capable of bridging the various strata in the social order, carries some force. None the less, we should be wary about over-emphasizing the degree to which a shared culture moderated social divisions. One problem is the tendency to sentimentalize and mythologize the egalitarian element. The evidence, for example, for golf as a pan-class sport in Scotland is open to question.[116] But the most serious criticism of the shared-culture thesis is that though it is true that different elements in the social order often engaged in the same pastimes, they frequently did so in very dissimilar ways, which tended to accentuate rather than mitigate differences of class. Barry Reay has argued of early modern culture in England that 'observations about shared cultures will only get us so far', 'it is not enough . . . simply to locate patrician and plebeian in the same place; one has to determine what they were doing in that place, what their respective roles were, whether they participated on equal terms'.[117] Horse racing was riddled with social distinctions. The ownership of the major assets and control of the sport were concentrated in a very small number of hands. Early on, different types of events and meetings catered for different social classes; and though over the long term there was probably a tendency towards rationalization and concentration, with race-goers attending the same large meetings and betting on the same horses, on the course spatial segregation separated the nobs from the riff-raff.[118] The upper and middle classes' passionate espousal of a sport's ethic in the later nineteenth century, together with the growing resources and time among the working class, to invest in sport, provided the potential for social mixing. However, much of this opportunity was wasted by the creation of exclusive elite pastimes. Moreover, where activities were shared, as in football and cricket, power was largely concentrated in the hands of the well off, rigid social distinctions were maintained, and upper, middle, and working classes experienced the recreations in markedly different ways.[119] The amateur–professional divide was critical.

Though accentuated in the later Victorian years, it had a long pedigree in the field of leisure. For example, in the eighteenth century it was possible for gentlemen and women to perform in theatricals and play instruments, and even for gentlemen to play alongside professional musicians; but the occasions must be essentially private (or in the case of men and music, at worst semi-public) affairs, and there was to be no hint of payment. Appearance on the commercial stage was particularly dangerous for women.[120] Thus the amateur and the professional actor and musician might effectively do the same thing, but they were seen to experience it in fundamentally different ways that were socially determined. For one it was perceived to be an act of labour undertaken for remuneration, for the other it was a purely aesthetic experience; for one it was an exercise in manual dexterity, for the other a mental process drawing upon the superior qualities of the mind.

Leisure pursuits, therefore, may be shared, but invariably they were shared in very different ways that reflected inequalities in wealth, power, and status.[121] Victorians might visit the theatre together, but playhouses were physically divided into boxes, pit, and gallery, with separate entrances for different sections of the audience, so that 'one of the most striking things about the Victorian theatre is its faithful reflection of social class'. This reflected a long tradition of spatial segregation that can be traced back to the playhouses of Shakespeare's London.[122] When the middle class started to attend the music hall in substantial numbers in the 1890s, seating arrangements helped to preserve the distinctions of social class.[123] The arrival of cinema might have been expected to have ironed out some of the differences found in traditional performing venues, but the evidence is that though, during the inter-war years, the middle class joined the working class to make this a mass pastime, the two classes attended different cinemas, in different locations with different prices, and experienced the occasions in different ways. The working class preferred American films, the middle class British ones; the working class enjoyed the sociability of the pastime whereas the middle class focused more on the film itself.[124] Cinema is a warning against the easy assumption that the development of 'mass' forms of commercial entertainment in the twentieth century necessarily dissolved class distinctions. Whether or not a common national and even global leisure culture now exists, differences in wealth, status, and power will ensure that access to, and reception of, this culture will vary according to a person's position in the social order.

It will vary, and has historically also varied, according to a range of other factors, such as age, gender, ethnicity, religion and locality. The strongest argument against a reading of leisure focused predominantly upon the social order is that class is only one among a range of identities that influence the way people recreate themselves. The de-prioritization of class, evident in so much of recent research, has emerged not just negatively from disillusionment with the Marxist interpretation of social change, but also positively from a growing recognition of the importance, in shaping the human condition, of identities other than class. These will be explored in the following chapter. However, the point of such an exercise is not so much to dethrone the significance of class and the social order – which, it will be clear, this author feels have been of great significance – as to broaden and enrich the influences which bear upon how people have behaved historically.

5

IDENTITIES

SELF- AND COLLECTIVE IDENTITIES

It may be tautological, but it is important to affirm that identity is central to what people are. So powerful is the need for *an* identity, so deep the concern that this may be compromised by equivocation, that there is a tendency to think in singular rather than plural terms. Yet identities are multiple and often contradictory. One schoolboy Manchester City supporter felt he could not legitimately mourn after the Munich aircraft tragedy of 1958, in which several of the Manchester United team died, because his club loyalties cut across his local ones.[1] Many spectators watching international tournaments will undergo similar ambivalent experiences (though they may be careful to conceal it) as their club heroes appear in the shirts of a foreign team. Identities also intersect, as, for example, in the case of class and gender. Both working- and middle-class males participated in the late Victorian boom in sport, but women's experience was very different, with the bourgeois female able to carve out a niche in the new structure, albeit a restricted one, whereas her working-class counterpart was very largely excluded from the transformation under way.[2] It is misleading then to place identities into tightly sealed boxes.

None the less, for convenience's sake three separate categories are explored in the following discussion. This chapter will address biological or pseudo-biological identities (gender, age, and ethnicity) and organizational ones (family, club, and community); the following chapter ones of place. The overlap between these categories is obvious enough. Family is treated here as a form of organization, but it clearly has a biological input; parishes as places, but they are also organizations. This reinforces the point that identities are plastic and fluid.

All the forms discussed are collective identities. This raises a dilemma, at least in the context of modern western culture, where so much emphasis is now placed upon self-identity. Among the women interviewed by Tia DeNora in her study *Music in Everyday Life*, 'Nearly all . . . were explicit about music's role as an ordering device at the personal level, as a means for creating, enhancing, sustaining and changing subjective, cognitive, bodily and self-conceptual states.' One of Ben Malbon's interviewees for his investigation of clubbing mused, 'I think I like to believe that when I'm on an E I have no defences whatsoever, so in many ways I would say that the person I am when I'm on an E is the "real me" right.' The sociologist Joffre Dumazedier would 'prefer to reserve the word leisure for the time whose content is oriented towards self-fulfilment as an ultimate end'.[3] Yet is the self a separate category of identity? As well as being a woman, black, young, and a Londoner, is a person also a self?

The answer to these questions may in part be historical. In the early modern period, Protestant theology, allied to rising levels of literacy, created a context in which scrutinizing the self became a pastime in itself. Diary-keeping was one manifestation of this, as also were new forms of reading directed at individual consumption, notably the novel, a literary genre designed to fill lonely hours of private leisure.[4] The growing value attached to sentiment in the mid-eighteenth century, a reaction to the emphasis placed, by politeness, on the exterior rather than interior persona, paved the way for the intensive focus on the self which characterized the romantic movement of the early nineteenth century.[5] The cult of the heroic artist, finding the self through struggle with an unsympathetic outside world, became a cultural *leitmotiv* of the modern age. This process was reinforced by what has been seen as another feature of modernity, a trend towards privatization in the ownership of property, family relations, and general lifestyle, including leisure.[6] Some have associated this with the growing strength of the middle class and its ideals. The outcome can be seen in the contrast, and sometimes acute tension, between individual and corporate forms of identity. In sport this is reflected in the difference between individual and team-based games, and in the latter, relates to the potential conflict between personal and collective aspirations. John Urry has detected two types of 'tourist gaze', the 'romantic' form, as exemplified in visiting mountainous areas like the Lake District, 'in which the emphasis is upon solitude, privacy and a personal, semi-spiritual relationship with the object of the gaze', and the 'collective' form, in which holidaying is a gregarious activity transacted in places of mass pleasure like seaside resorts.[7]

The pursuit of a self-identity may thus be a historical phenomenon, something which the modern age places much more emphasis upon than did previous eras. It remains unclear, however, to what extent it constitutes a true form of identity. The very notion of the self may be little more than a carefully contrived, primarily middle-class form of collective identity. Those visiting the Lake District to indulge in the 'romantic gaze', though they may see this as an exercise in self-discovery, will in practice be pursuing an activity shared at any one moment by thousands of their compatriots. Indeed, recreational walking is often an overtly social activity. Many working-class walkers have enjoyed hiking *en masse* in areas like the Pennines and Lake District, and for middle-class rambling clubs, whose origins date back at least to the late nineteenth century, the social element has always been important.[8] Locations of what are conceived of as exceptional physical beauty or historic interest also offer visitors a form of place identity, a site with which they can develop a special – but rarely unique, given the number of other visitors – relationship. Sometimes this involves succumbing to the perceived superior force of nature or the past, losing or negating the self in an external phenomenon. This raises a critical issue in the pursuit and construction of self- and collective identities, the extent to which this involves some element of what may be called surrogacy. Much of the appeal of sport involves close bonding with an animal, athlete, or team, though this is often done remotely. This process will be discussed more extensively in the final section of this chapter. So fierce can the attachment be that those so 'possessed' may feel that the link reveals their hidden self-potential, buried beneath their humdrum lives. However, this does not negate the fact that being a fan is essentially an act of surrogacy, and a collective one given that millions may share a similar sense of bonding and self-revelation. It may be, then, that at best the self is a combination of library and sorting office that acquires, accommodates, and negotiates all the collective identities that inhabit a persona.

Paradoxically, bonding invariably also involves rejection. To associate with one collective identity will frequently require renunciation of another. It is not possible to support both of Glasgow's major football clubs, Celtic and Rangers. The two are defined against each other and bonding is as much about forsaking one as about favouring the other. Many identities turn upon the axis of attraction and repulsion. This can engender powerful antipathies so that conflict and violence often accompany recreational activities. In the early seventeenth century Richard Carew recorded how players returned home from inter-parochial Cornish hurling matches 'as from a pitched battle, with bloody pates, bones broken and out of joint, and such bruises as serve to shorten their days', and Samuel Bamford noted of the teams that attended the rush carts sent by rival hamlets to the wakes in early nineteenth-century Middleton (Lancashire), 'it was very extraordinary indeed if a quarrel did not take place amongst some of them, and half-a-dozen battles were not foughten before the wakes ended'.[9] Yet in both cases it was understood that there were limits to the conflict.

Real as the bruises were, the violence was largely ritualistic and its impact was intended to be confined to the occasion itself. As Carew said, 'yet all is good play, and never attorney nor coroner troubled for the matter'. The reference to 'play' indicates why leisure was so important. In forging effective identities, high levels of conflict needed to be generated which in everyday life would have seriously threatened the overall stability of society. However, when these were transacted through the safe medium of play, with its underlying norm that the energies released were to be confined to the event itself, then the risk of any overspill of violence into 'real' life was substantially reduced. The presence of conflict in identity creation reminds us that identities are relational phenomena and depend upon the presence of some 'other' against which the principal object can be defined. The centrality of the 'other' to leisure, therefore, gave it a particularly important role in making identities. So the European Grand Tour helped define what it was to be British, travel to the 'Orient' what it was to be Western, and a visit to Africa what it was to be white and civilized.[10]

GENDER

Biology and genetics play their part in determining identities, but in the three considered here – gender, age, and ethnicity – the emphasis will be upon socio-cultural as opposed to physiological factors. In considering sexual identities there are two central definitional problems. First, Claire Langhamer has argued that 'our historical understanding has been limited by researchers' preoccupations with a "male" model of leisure'. There is a tendency to 'focus upon "institutional", commercial, or organized, out-of-doors, leisure "activity" ', rather than the more 'informal realm of family, street and neighbourhood', where women's recreational activity is likely to be concentrated.[11] The result is the relative invisibility of women's leisure. This is compounded by the sharp physical and temporal distinction between male work and leisure as compared with the fluidity of women's position. Secondly, people are conventionally defined sexually in strictly bi-polar terms, as either male or female. This assumes that an individual cannot possess more than one sexual identity or display multiple gender characteristics. It also ignores the problem of how to define these characteristics, and how that definition might vary according to a range of non-gendered factors, such as class and status. Richard Holt, for example, has argued that 'The working class imbued sport with a masculine value-system of their own which differed markedly from the manly Christian ideal' of the middle class.[12] Alexandra Shepard has also noted of early modern England, that 'hierarchies of age, social status, and marital status were deeply ingrained, interacting with gender hierarchies to produce a complex multidimensional map of power relations which by no means privileged all men or subordinated all women'.[13] The mix of sociocultural identities varied from person to person, as each exercised choice over the gender identities they wished to adopt. However, this was dependent upon the resources available to them. Better-off women, for example, especially those of independent means, possessed more room for manoeuvre, and were more able to 'trespass' into male-defined areas of leisure – such as sport, arts patronage, tourism, writing, and gambling – than their poorer sisters. As the recreational symbols of masculinity and femininity became increasingly commodified so the issue of economic access for both sexes became more acute.

The plurality of identities was further accentuated by an individual's location on the heterosexual/bi-sexual/homosexual spectrum, and the varying historical and social opportunities to express these identities. It is argued of England that 'there was early modern homosexual behaviour but not early modern homosexuality' and that 'the idea of homosexuality as an identity had no meaning in the seventeenth century'. However, by the early eighteenth century it is claimed that a distinctive molly subculture based on clubs and alehouses had emerged in London through which an identity could be articulated.[14] The existence of such sub-cultures is crucial to the generation of identity. Hence the importance in the twentieth century of recreational contexts and events, or niches within wider events, aimed specifically at allowing the homosexual community to assert its separateness. The Gay Games founded in 1982, and held every four years, was by 1994 attracting 11,000 athletes from 44 countries, though the first four games were held in the USA or Canada, suggesting that its influence was felt predominantly in North America.[15] In the later twentieth century several British seaside resorts targeted the gay market, developing an array of specialist accommodation, clubs, and events.[16]

Though, in practice, individuals and groups have pursued a variety of sexual identities, recreations have usually been constructed to service specific gender constituencies, and as such have been aimed at simplifying rather than complicating the sexual identity of those who participated. The predominantly male character of modern sport is clear enough.[17] Some of this can be attributed to the cult of manliness, forged in the Victorian public school,[18] but it is difficult to see this as the engine behind the masculinized nature of working-class football and rugby league, or the 'dominantly male' character of Gaelic games.[19] Nor can the cult of manliness, or for that matter the biological factors which are often taken to underpin the male association with sport,[20] account for the fact that probably the largest and most male-dominated of all participation sports in the twentieth century was angling. By the late 1970s there were 3,380,000 anglers in England and Wales, and a further 345,000 in Scotland. A survey in 1980 found that 88 per cent of these were men, and that 15 per cent of the male population over the age of 12 fished regularly.[21] The gendered character of the sport may lie not so much in its content as in its context – the sustained period of escape it allows, relatively free from spectator scrutiny, for father and sons from the female-dominated domestic sphere. Similar arguments could also be made for the potting shed, the allotment, and the pigeon loft.

One of the attractions of working-class fishing was its clubable and 'pubable' character. These two institutions have traditionally possessed a strong masculine profile. Peter Clark has shown how the club and society, whose numbers proliferated from the late seventeenth century, were part of a 'male-dominated associational world', and in this respect drew upon the tradition of the medieval guilds, responsible for the delivery of much public and private leisure, in which women 'were excluded from office . . . and, unless widows, rarely attended craft meetings or banquets'.[22] Clubs and societies frequently met in alehouses, taverns, pubs, and inns, where, under the narcotic influence of heavy doses of tobacco and alcohol – there was a long association between pub, sport, and drink[23] – male bonding might reach transcendental levels. Wives and widows often played an important role in running early modern alehouses in England and Ireland, and women certainly visited these establishments, especially for purposes of courtship. However, the clear majority of victuallers and customers were men, and women were constantly deterred from using drinking places because of the stigma of prostitution, so that despite a trend towards refinement in the Hanoverian period, 'the social world of the alehouse remained predominantly male'.[24] This continued to be the case for much of the nineteenth and twentieth centuries. In late Victorian Scotland women were increasingly excluded from pubs as drinkers and barmaids; in early twentieth-century Salford the pubs, some of which banned women or exiled them to a special lounge, were the hub of male working-class networks; and in their post-Second World War survey of leisure in England, Rowntree and Lavers found that the proportion of women who never drank alcohol (40.1 per cent) was twice as high as that of men (21.5 per cent), and that 'A large proportion, probably a majority, of women of all classes of society never enter public houses.'[25]

Science and technology have often provided the basis of male recreational culture. Early modern science was an almost exclusively male pastime, with the Royal Society, founded in 1660, effectively a gentleman's club.[26] In the nineteenth and twentieth centuries technological developments have tended to reinforce the male orientation of sport, and allowed men to carve out a distinctive niche in the world of music, through, for example, the electric guitar and the developments in hi-fi sound reproduction.[27] Many of these technologies provide access to sources of physical energy and act as symbols of a wider power – the male obsession with amplifier output is a case in point – and this is even more evident in the case of the motor car, which has proved to be a highly gendered territory. Even in the late 1970s twice as many men (68 per cent) held driving licences as women (30 per cent).[28]

Not that this went uncontested. Women have driven cars since their introduction, albeit in the early years at the risk of being labelled 'dangerous' or masculine, and they have regularly engaged in so-called male sports such as cricket, football, and golf. Women's football was growing before and after the First World War, with teams based around factories and businesses, but the decision by the Football Association in 1921 to deem the game 'unsuitable' for women and to ban them from playing on the pitches of FA and League affiliates, a requirement only rescinded in 1971, 'had a profound effect on women's football culture in England'. Rising levels of participation from the 1960s, allied to changes in the legal and social framework that forced the football authorities to reverse their opposition, have given women's football a boost, but limited commercial and spectator support, and continuing perceptions of football as a male preserve, have ensured only slow progress in Britain.[29] The position of women in golf has always been stronger and the opportunities for gender mixing much greater, but this depended upon accepting segregationist practices and inferior roles that still riddle the sport.[30] Yachting is a sport where any 'physical deficit' between the sexes is of relatively little importance, yet the general growth in confidence of middle-class women after the First World War 'did little more than briefly shake the foundations of the accepted principle that yacht clubs were a male preserve into which women were sometimes "allowed" on sufferance and in no sense as equals'.[31] Though women's participation as players and officials in 'men's sports' was restricted, their role as spectators was subject to fewer constraints, and the growth in televised sport and the opportunities for gambling, such as the football pools, has expanded significantly their 'passive' involvement.[32]

Leisure with a predominantly female input has been less well researched than male recreations. This is in part due to the definitional problem. Historically the central motifs in women's leisure have been home and family. Thus practical activities – such as sewing, knitting, embroidery, cooking, and gardening – which support domestic life, and where the line between work and leisure is unclear, have often contained a strong but concealed recreational element. The same may also be said for the rich networks of informal socializing, characterized pejoratively as chatting and gossiping, which are home and neighbourhood based and offer a counterpoise to the male camaraderie of club and pub.[33] In Wales the *noson neu* was an informal gathering of neighbours, usually on moonlit evenings, to knit together, 'a means of combining work and pleasure in a sociable evening spent on the hearth'.[34] The charitable role adopted, effectively as a pastime, by better-off women, though it took them out of the home, was often concerned with reinforcing the domestic ethos for the objects of their philanthropy.[35]

Consumption is an area closely associated with women and embodies similar ambivalences. It drew those engaged in it away from the household, but was primarily about servicing the home; it was a form of work, yet because it involved exercising choice and visiting markets, shops, and towns, it also provided scope for leisure and pleasure. This was particularly the case for well-off women for whom the 'consumer revolution' of the eighteenth century widened the range and sophistication of products available, and who according to Amanda Vickery 'jealously guarded their role as family consumers'.[36] The same case has been argued for the development of the late Victorian and Edwardian department store, which gave middle-class women access to the streets of London's West End without the fear of being stigmatized as a prostitute, and created a context in which, Erika Rappaport has argued, 'women's emancipation and consumer pleasures had merged to a certain degree'.[37] The association between the much debated rise of the 'new woman' in the 1890s, the feminist movement, and the widening opportunities for female consumption is a tempting if ambivalent one to explore.[38] In the twentieth century such opportunities have enhanced the recreational returns on shopping for women, though it is far from clear that this has done much to reduce the broadly domestic orientation of their purchases, or enhanced their power in the home.[39]

Certain pastimes new to the twentieth century – such as the cinema, bingo, and aerobics – which are either exclusive to women, or of which they are the primary users, have drawn them away from the purely domestic arena. An older recreation, dancing, also placed women in the public sphere. Up until the eighteenth century it is argued that men participated equally in dance, but, concerned at its increasingly feminized image, they became uneasy about engaging in the activity.[40] The legacy showed itself in the world of popular commercial dancing, which grew rapidly in the early twentieth century, with the new emphasis upon rhythm rather than steps, and the opening of the big Palais ballrooms such as that at Hammersmith (London) in 1919 and the one at Fountainbridge (Edinburgh) the following year.[41] *Mass Observation* recorded that at a large-scale open-air dance in London in 1938, 'Sample counts of the couples dancing showed that there were about equal numbers of man-and-girl and girl-and-girl couples; one or two man-and-man couples were observed,' while among the interviewees approached by Rowntree and Lavers (1951) was a Miss F, who declared 'I think dancing is the best form of pleasure there is. I like dancing with other girls just as well as with boys,' whose sentiments contrasted with Mr M, 'I don't care for the palais. . . . I'm not all that keen on dancing really, but if there's plenty of beer it's all right. It's a good place for picking up a girl.'[42] For women dance was a pastime in its own right, through which they could assert their feminine identity, for men it was a means to an end.

Dancing was, of course, also a means to an end for women, and historically that end was more often than not marriage. One of the principal functions of public assemblies, which emerged as a central feature of fashionable urban culture in the early eighteenth century, was that of an elite marriage market.[43] For women this led back to the domestic sphere, which acted as a persistent constraint on the recreational opportunities open to them.[44] At the practical level, caring for home and family rested primarily with women, and whatever resources of time and money they commanded had to be directed first of all towards meeting their domestic responsibilities. For women in or close to poverty this could leave little scope for anything that resembled formal leisure, particularly once the brief flowering of adolescence and courtship had passed, and marriage and motherhood was entered upon.[45] Practical considerations apart, there were also socially determined limits on women's access to public spaces, and anxiety that certain activities were inherently unfeminine and/or might threaten their reproductive and maternal functions. There was, for example, a debate in late Victorian and Edwardian Britain over whether sport enhanced or detracted from the role of child-bearing.[46] These constraints, serious as they were, did not necessarily confine women to exclusively female recreations. There was a substantial grey area of activities which both sexes engaged in. Any pastime involving the selection of a mate and courtship was necessarily a shared one. Many of the events in the traditional festive calendar, such as May Day, offered moments of relaxation when personal relationships could be explored and developed.[47]

Better-off women faced considerable restrictions on who and how they courted, on what spaces they entered, and on how they deported themselves. None the less, wealth and time provided the opportunities to participate in a wider range of recreations than their poorer sisters. The Grand Tour was an initiation ritual for young elite males, but men also undertook the tours with their wives and there was, during the eighteenth century, a growing breed of women touring independently, at home and abroad, whose personal records reveal a different take on the tourist experience: 'Whereas men's travel accounts are preoccupied with conquest, connoisseurship and domestication of the wild, women's narratives record more diverse experiences concerned with individual growth, independence and health.'[48] Women formed the mainstay of those undertaking Thomas Cook's continental package tours in the nineteenth century, and he was careful to assure them of their safety, and the opportunities for developing friendships.[49] Tourism provided a means for women to escape either the pressures to marry or the consequences of a bad match. The same also applied to the fashionable spa and seaside resorts. Though these were marriage markets, they had a strong female profile and offered wealthy spinsters and widows a conducive environment in which to forge a feminized lifestyle.[50]

Reading was a pastime shared by the literate among both sexes, and formal education was increasingly available to middle- and upper-class women. During the eighteenth and nineteenth centuries they came to form a key sector in an expanding market, much of which was geared towards leisured reading and the female consumer, who through reading had the opportunity, as Kate Flint has argued, to 'assert her sense of selfhood, and to know that she was not alone in doing so'.[51] The potential for this was strengthened by the fact that print was one area of commercial cultural production where it was possible for women to contribute to the nature of the product as authors. Reading was an activity almost tailor-made for the home, and it may be that popular levels of female literacy have, since the Reformation if not before, been much higher than is revealed by signature evidence.[52] During the twentieth century women from all areas of society were huge consumers of popular literature, much of it directed specifically at them, and women have also been at least as influential as men as users of the new, electronic, home-based media such as radio – with a 'feminized' Light Programme and its successor, Radio 2 – and television.[53]

Sport may be predominantly male territory, but there have always been areas of female participation. In the medieval and early modern period hunting provided an arena for initiation into manhood, but falconry and hawking offered a niche for elite women to engage actively in blood sports.[54] In the early nineteenth century during the fox-hunting season, Melton Mowbray and Market Harborough hosted informal sets of 'well-born hard riders' that constituted 'a horse-centred continuation of the all-male social life of Library at Eton or rooms in Christ Church or Trinity'. However, from the middle of the century women were increasingly admitted to the field, and not just the hunt balls, and this presaged a process whereby during the twentieth century equine sports, other than horse racing, became increasingly feminized, fuelled in part, in Raymond Carr's words, by 'middle-class snobbery and the inexplicable passion for horses in adolescent girls'.[55] In the late nineteenth century better-off women were able, to a degree, to participate in the sporting revolution, in some non-team activities – such as archery, lawn tennis, croquet, cycling, and rambling – playing a prominent part, mixing with the other sex, and contributing to the image of the 'new woman'.[56]

If there was one pastime more than any other which occupied the grey zone not dominated by a single gender it was music. Well-off women and men were both heavily involved as amateurs in Georgian musical life as players and audiences.[57] Christmas carol-singing and wassailing were especially associated with young women in the seventeenth century, mixed church choirs were introduced into Scotland in the eighteenth century, and though the male voice choir has acquired an iconic status in the musical culture of the nineteenth-century industrial districts, mixed choirs or single-sex women's choirs were present even in these areas.[58] Music hall attracted mixed audiences, mothers might even bring their young children with them (as they might to the popular theatre), and female performers could exert as powerful a presence on the stage as their male counterparts.[59] However, though music was shared territory between men and women there was endless scope for playing different roles. Eighteenth-century musical instruments, education and performance were highly gendered;[60] until the 1930s, brass bands were almost exclusively (the Salvation Army was a notable exception) a male domain,[61] as has been musical composition in general;[62] and the modern popular music scene, though appealing equally to both sexes, has generated a wide variety of gendered musics and performing contexts, such as boy bands, girl bands, 'cock' rock, 'chick' music, and teenybop.[63]

Leisure has thus been a powerful arena for the moulding and expressing of sexual identities. Not that the boundaries between male and female leisure have been fixed historically. It is argued that since the 1960s there has been a domestication of male leisure, with a shift from pub and club to the home, from corporate pastimes like football to private ones such as TV, DIY, and car maintenance, and from male peer groups to family and children.[64] Sport is often taken to be a recreation which is biologically male orientated, with its emphasis upon strength, competition, and combat. However, historically the extent of female participation in physical sports remains unclear. There is evidence of medieval and early modern women engaging in a wide variety of sports, such as smock racing (where a smock was the prize), ice-skating, curling, archery, angling, falconry, hawking, football, cricket, rowing, swimming, and prize fighting.[65] Some of the instances may have been recorded because they were unusual, but there are enough examples to suggest that it was an important element in women's leisure, and one that did not run contrary to the creation of feminine identities. Curling matches, for example, would take place between married and unmarried women, at one and the same time asserting both a common and a divided femininity. It seems likely, as Keith Sandiford and Katherine McCrone have argued of cricket,[66] that during the early nineteenth century sport became increasingly masculinized, so that any subsequent re-feminization from the late Victorian period constituted simply a return to a pre-modern norm.

ETHNICITY

Ethnicity is a problematic identity, not only because it is difficult to find any genetic basis to race, other than simple physical characteristics such as skin colour, but also because what constitutes an ethnic group is unclear. For the purpose of the discussion here, the various 'races' of the British Isles will be treated largely as place identities. This leaves relatively small pockets of so-called ethnic groups – in Georgian London, for example, there were perhaps 20,000 Jews and between 5,000 and 10,000 blacks[67] – until the large-scale immigration after the Second World War from areas of the Commonwealth and former empire, such as the West Indies, western Africa, and the Indian sub-continent, which turned Britain, or at least parts of it, into a genuinely multi-ethnic society.[68] However, the historically small presence of ethnic minorities does not mean that race has been, until recent times, an insignificant factor in generating identities. Expanding contacts between Europe and the wider world since 1500, and particularly the growth of a British overseas empire since the seventeenth century, necessarily changed the cultural framework within which Britain operated. Two principal types of response can be detected. First, other races became a way of negatively defining what it was to be white and British. There is a long tradition, dating back at least to the eighteenth century, of poor Jews, Irish, and blacks appearing as professional fighters.[69] This reinforced their image as physical, primitive, and savage peoples. More importantly, it allowed the majority population to celebrate their own identities as children of the Enlightenment – rational, progressive, and civilized. Tipsters – shady figures in racing – were sometimes referred to as 'blacks', such as 'the Black Tipster' or 'Prince Monolulu'. Children blackened their faces during some traditional festivals, as, for example, in parts of early twentieth-century Manchester and Salford when on May Day boys formed 'nigger troupes', imitating the 'nigger minstrels' that were a stock-in-trade of the music hall.[70] No wonder then that when real blacks arrived in large numbers in the

1950s they discovered that their skin colour attracted such a bemused and hostile response.

But there was a second and much less negative response on the part of native whites to ethnicity, and this, reflected to some degree in the music hall minstrels, was one of fascination with the 'other'. There has been a long-term eagerness to explore multifarious aspects of 'ethnic' cultures, including foodstuffs, horticulture, architecture, clothes, drugs, and music. In the last case white popular music and dance were transformed in the twentieth century by the introduction of Afro-American, Afro-Caribbean, and Asian influences.[71] One of the appeals of 'ethnic' cultures has been the possibility of recovering a pre-lapsarian identity, now lost in dominant western cultures with the march of civilization and commercialization. Among Britain's indigenous cultures the Celtic 'fringe' has served this role, but it is a function also fulfilled since at least the emergence of the cult of the noble savage during the Enlightenment by contact with non-European societies.[72] Though fascination with the 'other' and the exotic embodies a more sympathetic response to ethnicity than is obvious in outright racism, it remains problematic to what extent it modifies the nature of this response. The noble savage will always be a savage, the 'other' always a yardstick to measure how far civilization has progressed. Cultural absorption can also be extraordinarily superficial. There is little evidence that the current culinary fashion for Indian foods and restaurants has done much to mitigate racial stereotypes. Moreover, as long as ethnicity is defined as something possessed by other cultures and not one's own – in the way, for example, World Music is categorized as any other type of music apart from that of mainstream western popular culture – then its primary function will be to reinforce rather than reconfigure the identities of those in the majority population.

For ethnic minorities resident in Britain the appeal of ethnic 'otherness' must appear perplexing, not to say offensive and disadvantaging. They must feel excluded, for example, from a tourist industry geared to selling exotic destinations to white bodies with the aim of converting these into brown ones.[73] This highlights a fundamental problem facing modern Britain: how to cope with a multi-ethnic society. While the presence of ethnic minorities remained very small and highly localized they were generally not perceived as a threat to British identity. But with the influxes of the 1950s and 1960s – though the numbers involved were tiny in relation to the overall population – the white majority's perception of the situation changed. Immigration bred a fear of loss of identity which in its turn generated hostility. At the same time immigrants and their descendants had to come to terms with the radical changes in their own sense of identity prompted by relocation and the prejudice of the indigenous white population. The result has been a process of unequal and highly fraught negotiation, within and between majority and minority populations, which has produced a mixture of inclusion and exclusion.

Sport, so critical in fashioning identities, demonstrated the complexity of the process. Many recreations, such as golf and tennis, remained largely white preserves, though this may reflect as much pressures of class as of race. Coloured sportsmen made more impact on cricket, but racial barriers have been erected by both communities. Migration from the Indian sub-continent into north-east Lancashire in the 1960s led to the formation of separate Asian teams – in the case of Nelson, playing in their own leagues, and at Bolton being confined to a lower stratum of the existing league system.[74] Contrariwise, some sports have witnessed 'over-representation' of coloured players. Though banned from fighting for British titles until 1947, even if born in Britain, by the 1980s about a third of professional boxers were of Afro-Caribbean background (a group that comprised only 2 per cent of the overall population), and a quarter of Football League players were black.[75] None the less, football management, and power in sport in general, has remained a white preserve. Racial stereotyping is also reflected in so-called stacking, by which black athletes are over-represented in certain positions within sports: sprinters rather than long-distance runners in athletics, forwards rather than mid-fielders and goalkeepers in soccer, wingers – in the 1993–4 season two-thirds of black rugby union players in the Heineken League, the premier competition in Wales, were wingers – rather than centre three-quarters, stand-offs, and scrum half-backs in rugby.[76] Such roles reinforced the notion of coloured athletes as explosive and aggressive, but questioned their stamina and capacity to organize and manage. This strengthened the white male's sense of a separate identity and superiority. However, coloured players, as members of club and international sides, are also integral to the identities of the white males who comprise the vast majority of spectators and supporters of those teams. A sense of ambivalence is no doubt felt by players and spectators among the ethnic minorities as they struggle to reconcile their local, national, and ethnic loyalties. This reflects the wider reality that Britons, whatever their colour, possess multiple, and sometimes conflicting identities. The complexity of human nature in this respect was something which the 'Tebbit Test' – demanding as it did that those who lived in England had a patriotic duty to support the national cricket team – missed entirely.[77]

AGE

Immigrants are likely to experience different feelings about identity from those of their children born in Britain and to some extent ethnicity can be perceived as a generational rather than a racial issue. This raises the question of how far age, a biologically determined but socially constructed factor, constitutes a form of identity. Several sociologists, such as Rhona and Robert Rapoport have emphasized the importance of the life-cycle in governing people's recreational experience, and historians have recognized the significance of different life phases in the practice of leisure. Claire Langhamer, for example, organizes her study of women's leisure between 1920 and 1960 around this principle.[78] But age *per se* has not deeply influenced historical studies of leisure. Where there is an emphasis it tends to be upon youth. Old age has received little attention.[79] In all probability the distinctive feature of the elderly's leisure experience is the limitations – economic, social, political, and cultural as much as physical – placed upon it.[80] Though the emergence of mass enforced retirement should in theory have increased older people's leisure time, in practice the opposite effect may have occurred, since what was once defined and experienced as leisure time through the presence of work now becomes simply ordinary time. None the less, improved health care, the introduction of pension arrangements, and the re-orientation of the leisure industry to meet the growing market provided by the grey pound have mitigated some of the constraints on old age. It is important to recognize also that the old are a highly variegated group, of very different economic circumstances, ages, and physical capacities. Even if it could be demonstrated that the elderly as a whole constituted a new leisure class, there remains the problem of how this relates to identity. Greater access to holidays or community-based clubs can bring the benefits these provide in terms of sociability, but it may do little more than counteract the structural isolation of later life. Moreover, old age as such is not today an identity which most of those who qualify for it would seek to cultivate.

Was the position different at some point in the past? Keith Thomas has argued that 'In early modern England the prevailing ideal was gerontocratic: the young were to serve and the old were to rule.' Among the young, 'the sixteenth and seventeenth centuries are conspicuous for a sustained drive to subordinate persons in their teens and early twenties and to delay their equal participation in the adult world'. However, it is clear that the very old were also marginalized, and Thomas has warned that it is 'wrong to regard the depreciation of old age as a recent affair'.[81] The constraints operating on old age were not that dissimilar to those today. It is the middle aged who emerge from this analysis in the optimal position, though this seems even less likely than old age to constitute a category of identity. None the less, it is probable that people would behave and dress in a manner which conveyed the impression that they were neither too young nor too old to occupy the middle spectrum at which status and power came into play. That meant being *actively* involved in leisure, purchasing and consuming recreational goods, and engaging in some form of sporting activity. But it also required conveying an appropriate mixture of gravity and experience, and avoiding the excesses of the young.

It is youth that has attracted by far the majority of research. Within the category a distinction has been drawn between childhood and adolescence, and the critical questions have been to what extent, and if so at what times, either spawned a separate culture or sub-culture. There is the further distinction, as Hugh Cunningham puts it in respect of childhood, though it could equally apply to adolescence, 'between children as human beings and childhood as a shifting set of ideas'.[82] One influential line of argument is that in medieval society adulthood and childhood were merged together. 'In 1600,' writes Philippe Ariès, 'the specialization of games and pastimes did not extend beyond infancy; after the age of three or four it decreased and disappeared. From then on the child played the same games as the adult, either with other children or with adults.'[83] It was only in the later part of the early modern period that hard concepts of childhood began to crystallize. Ariès sees the seventeenth century as the turning point, as adults began to withdraw from a common pool of recreations, so that these became by definition children's games. Other commentators would point to the eighteenth century for the emergence, in J. H. Plumb's words, of 'the new world of children', characterized by the development of specialist children's educational services, literature, and toys. This was followed during the romantic era by the celebration of childhood as a more pristine and even as a superior state to adulthood.[84]

The history of adolescence has received less specific attention. That some profound process of change was under way in this sphere underpins the widely accepted view that the years after the Second World War[85] – though some historians would point to the inter-war years, when young people were patronizing cinemas and dance halls in heavy numbers,[86] and even the late nineteenth century, at the very least, laying the foundations[87] – saw the emergence in the West of a distinctive youth culture. This was focused broadly on those in their teens and twenties, was fuelled by escalating spending power within these age groups, was articulated primarily by the deployment of recreational goods such as music, dance, and sport, and was characterized by a rejection of adult modes of behaviour and mores. Such attempts to locate chronologically the rise of both the idea and the experience of childhood, adolescence, and youth culture have proved controversial. Many medieval and early modern historians reject the 'folkloric theory' that there were no contemporary concepts of childhood and adolescence.[88] The evidence from leisure would tend to support the notion that the young did things differently from adults. In the medieval period there were games played especially by the young, and Strutt was able to include a specific section of his 1801 study of leisure on children's pastimes.[89] In the customs of the festive calendar it is clear that the young had collective roles to play, as in ritualized begging at Shrovetide and Hallowe'en, the games and sports held at village wakes, and in the dancing and games that attended May festivities. William Wilde describes how on May Eve in nineteenth-century Ireland the children resorted to 'small plays and various rural games', including 'threading my grandmother's needle: in which . . . the boys and girls join hands and dance a sort of serpentine figure up and down the roads, sometime for a mile in extent', and on the night of May Day itself 'crowds collected round the may pole, with the boys and girls dancing in a ring until a late hour, before the king and queen'.[90]

It is clear that the young have long engaged in recreations that were largely exclusive to them. Indeed, it is highly probable that sports and physical recreations have persistently been weighted towards youth, though this should not be assumed uncritically to be the case, even in energetic activities. Late eighteenth-century pedestrianism, which involved covering long gruelling distances, was associated predominantly with experienced middle-aged athletes.[91] Did this necessarily lead to a sense of separate identity? Iona and Peter Opie implied as such when, in their monumental study of the 'thriving unselfconscious culture' of schoolchildren, they argued that 'the school-child's verses are not intended for adult ears. In fact part of their fun is the thought . . . that adults know nothing about them'.[92] The Opies had the advantage of talking to children. However, historical sources about childhood are almost exclusively derived from adults (even the Opies' data is filtered through grown up minds). These sources may express concern about inappropriate influences on young people and unacceptable patterns of behaviour, concerns that are premised upon the notion of a youth problem, as defined by adults. Autobiographical reminiscences, such as those of Samuel Bamford, are an important source, but the perspective is that of the older self, often keen to re-create the notion of an innocent and idyllic pre-adult phase. In all these accounts there is a tendency for adults to construct a child identity, but how far this conforms to children's lived experience is an open question. It is probable that young people's eyes would be on the ultimate prize – success in the grown-up world of money, status, and power – and that they deployed their childhood in learning to be successful adults rather than constructing a separate identity that would have little use in the long term. Accounts make clear that many of the activities associated with the young are part of a wider recreational context that embraced multiple age groups, limiting its potential to create a youth identity. Henry Bourne, for example, describes how on Midsummer's Eve 'it is usual . . . for both old and young to meet together, and be merry over a large fire, which is made in the open street. Over this they frequently leap and play at various games, such as running, wrestling, dancing, &c. But this is generally the exercise of the younger sort; for the old ones, for the most part, sit by as spectators, and enjoy themselves and their bottle.'[93] Young and old do different things, but these are part of a shared celebration of community rather than of generational identity. Even where children engaged in activities on their own – such as when Bamford describes 'the rambles I took with . . . [the] gang on our holiday afternoons'[94] – their identification was with the group, not a general category of youth.

Adolescence is the phase most likely to give rise to a youth culture. This is the time at which the greatest potential exists for the creation of an age-specific culture as a vehicle to facilitate the transition from childhood to adulthood. Though it is tempting to perceive adolescence, and the troublesome teenager, as modern phenomena, they have a long history. Alexandra Shepard has noted in the early modern period a 'camaraderie of misrule' among young men, and argued that the 'collective consumption of excessive quantities of alcohol was an intrinsic part of male youth culture and the rites of passage into manhood'. This is a point Peter Clark reinforces in his description of the alehouse as 'a natural alternative centre for young unmarried people, some of whom may have felt an enhanced sense of social or group identity by the mid seventeenth century'.[95] Gervase Rosser records how in medieval 'towns young men, in particular, tended to gang together', sometimes joining guilds of 'bachelors', and Barbara Hanawalt has discovered in medieval London a distinctive set of adolescent games, together with a penchant among young men for frequenting taverns, though she also warns that 'No full-fledged youth subculture in which peers were the chief influence on an adolescent's life existed in the Middle Ages.'[96] Hanawalt's distinction is an important one. However boisterous and unruly the practices engaged in, the chief influence on medieval adolescents' games and lifestyle was that of adults. Youth was a preparation for adulthood, not an end in itself.

It was the link between youth and adulthood, the notion that adolescence was a rite of passage, which youth culture after the Second World War appeared to have severed. Youth was no longer simply a staging-post on the journey to maturity but had become a destination in its own right, 'a self-contained domain that functioned according to its own generational laws' at odds with those of the adult establishment.[97] As such, youth spawned a culture and identity of its own.[98] However, the distinctiveness, homogeneity, and novelty of this phenomenon are open to debate. First, some commentators prefer the notion of a sub-culture (or sub-cultures) so as to emphasize the continuing connection with the majority culture. Arthur Marwick, for example, challenges the notion 'that there was a "youth culture" which ever became completely independent of, or alternative to, the larger culture involving parents, educational institutions, commercial companies, technology and the mass media'.[99] Secondly, we need to strip out the violence that is often seen as a characteristic of 'youth culture'. Historically there was nothing particularly new in this, though it may have seemed so, after the comparatively disciplined environment engendered by two world wars. Nor was there anything novel about the camaraderie and gang orientation of groups like mods and rockers. Adolescents had always coalesced into peer groups that were at one and the same time fiercely defensive and aggressive. Thirdly, it has to be asked: How radical in practice were the ideas, how dissociated from those of adults, of the 'new' youth? For example, more liberal mores on sexual relations may have developed, compared with those of the pre-war generation, but it is far from clear that basic attitudes to gender relations changed among the young. Fourthly, 'youth culture' was defined by the perceptions of adults, and the fears that lay behind these, as much as by the actions of young people themselves. Moreover, the 'folk devils' and 'moral panics' that characterized aspects of the adult response,[100] and gave youth culture much of its edge, were not a new phenomenon. After a riot on May Day 1517 the king exhorted the relevant London authorities to address the problem of the 'wild, undiscrete Parsones named to be menes apprentices and menes servauntes of this Citie'; a gang of young gentlemen 'who have lately erected themselves into a Nocturnal Fraternity, under the Title of *The Mohock Club* . . . from a Sort of *Cannibals* in *India*' were reported to be terrorizing early eighteenth-century London; and in the 1880s there was widespread concern about street gambling among the young and about the level of juvenile drinking and delinquency.[101] Fifthly, it is arguable that even if a distinctive youth culture did emerge in the middle of the twentieth century, by the latter part of the century it, and its associated identity, had been absorbed into the mainstream of commercial adult culture. Nowadays a youth identity is as likely to be sought by people in the middle as in the earlier phases of their life.

FAMILY, COMMUNITY, AND CLUB

Of all the collective identities people possess, potentially the most powerful is that of the family. They are exposed to its influence from birth, and imprisoned in its orbit during the formative years of life; it would be surprising if it did not comprise a critical piece of the jig-saw that makes up a person's identity. The family was the subject of much of the new social history that emerged from the 1960s. In general the research, a large part of it focused on the early modern period, stressed the centrality of the nuclear family (parents and children) and household. Some would see this as a structural feature of British society, stretching back to the medieval period, whereas others detect a long-term trend away from larger collective units, in particular the community and the extended family (kin, parents, and children), towards the nuclear family.[102] For those who take the dynamic view of change there is evidence in leisure of the shift towards a more privatized and home-oriented lifestyle. The Stuart puritan family's rejection of traditional popular recreations, though it was justified in moral and religious terms, may be seen as a withdrawal from the community, the focus of much of old-style popular culture, into the sanctum of the private household. Georgian fashionable urban culture drew the elite out of their country houses into wider social settings and encouraged the development of a public sphere. However, despite the overtly adult orientation of the new culture it appears that parents took their offspring, sometimes at a surprisingly young age, with them. The implication is that children were there to observe and learn the mores of the adult world so that they could operate successfully within it, when the moment of release arrived (in women, known as 'coming out'), and in particular, secure an advantageous marriage. Leisure was thus directed towards reproducing families.[103]

One theme regularly rehearsed by historians of the Victorian period is the shift, particularly among the middle class, from public to private sphere, community-orientated to home-based leisure.[104] This was exemplified in the rise of the Victorian version of Christmas, for which Dickens's *Christmas Carol* (1843) was an important catalyst, and which in Wales 'changed gradually from an intensely social occasion in which all the community took part to one of family celebration in the seclusion of private houses'.[105] Ronald Hutton considers this as part of a longer-term sequence of changes in which, after the Reformation, the parish and great household were replaced by the local community as 'the principal unit of celebration', which in its turn, 'During the past 150 years . . . has been replaced, almost universally, by the family.'[106] The rise of the formal seaside holiday, and its development into a product of mass consumption, can be seen as part of this process – in John Walton's words, 'an ideal device for upholding the ideal of the domesticated nuclear family'[107] – drawing people away from locally based community leisure. John Benson detects a growing trend in the twentieth century for young people to holiday with their parents, and the annual vacation has become defined in many households as domestic space, the moment in the year when the *ideal* of the family, for much of the time submerged beneath the business of ordinary living, is allowed, under the influence of play and a sense of otherness, to blossom.[108] The modern drift towards domestication has been reinforced by the fashions for gardening and DIY, the rise in owner-occupier households, and the emergence of home-based electronic media.[109]

It hardly needs saying that this analysis should be treated with caution. There is a major problem in equating the family and the home. Most people live in private dwellings, but far from all occupy the archetypal nuclear household of parents and children. An ageing society has increased the proportion of people living as couples or singly, a trend accentuated by the historically high rates of divorce and partner separation, which have also contributed to the growing number of single-parent households. All this is indicative of tensions within families, though not necessarily more so than in the past, which makes any notion of a model family problematic. For a 'dysfunctional' family, leisure taken together, particularly on occasions defined as 'family time', such as Christmas and annual holidays, is likely to expose tensions, and precipitate dissolution, rather than increase bonding. That said, the family *ideal* is a powerful one, embedded at the heart of British culture, and regardless of the realities of inter-personal relations the family remains a critical site of identity.

A similar line of argument can be developed for the community. Internal tensions can often be acute, but the *ideal* remains extraordinarily potent. J. A. Mangan has argued of the Victorian and Edwardian public school, a total institution that constituted a form of closed community, that 'communal solidarity was achieved by deliberately created internal diversity' through inter-house sporting competitions.[110] Internal rivalry, though it generated potentially damaging conflict, also defined the opposing parties as members of a shared social system. Inter-parochial, -occupational, and -zonal conflicts were not uncommon in British towns, and were sometimes institutionalized in ritual form, as when the parishes of St Peter's and All Saints competed in the Derby Shrovetide football match. At Ludlow on Shrove Tuesday 'a Rope . . . is given out of the window of the Market House as the clock strikes four; when a large body of the inhabitants divided into two parties, one contending for Castle Street and Broad Street Wards, and the other for Old Street and Corve Street Wards, commence an arduous struggle'.[111] Out of conflict came a sense of communal unity and identity.

The festive calendar provided regular opportunities for affirming the bonds between households and bringing the community alive. Certain material forms – for example, the maypole, May-bush, bonfire, and rush cart – demanded a corporate effort in their preparation as well as acting as symbols of the community. On festive occasions, and these would include the completion of great communal tasks such as harvest and sheep shearing, there was considerable emphasis upon the corporate consumption of food and drink. Church-ales, formally an opportunity to raise money for the parish church, constituted a formidable exercise in collective feeding. Carew describes how in late Tudor Cornwall a collection was made among parishioners of provisions for the Whitsun church-ale, 'upon which holidays the neighbours meet at the church-house and there merrily feed on their own victuals, contributing some petty portion to the stock, which by many smalls groweth to a meetly greatness'.[112] The implicit notion that underpinned the custom, that each individual could through pooling their resources acquire a strength ('a meetly greatness') far greater than their individual contribution, symbolized and reinforced the community *ideal.*

Carew states that any contributions to the church-ale were bestowed 'voluntarily', but it seems unlikely that this was entirely the case. There were powerful expectations that townspeople and villagers would contribute, and failure to do so would carry the threat of stigma and exclusion. Coercive begging was a common feature of the festive calendar. During this the community asserted its right to access the resources of its members and in theory redistribute from the well-off to the needy. It also enforced its prerogative to invade the domestic and private sphere, as with the *Mari Lwyd* (Grey Mare) custom of South Wales, in which a horse's skull draped in a white sheet which concealed its male operator, went from home to home demanding entry, and once admitted ran amok, snapping at the girls before consuming the food and drink that had been prepared for it.[113] Coercion was glaringly obvious during the collective shaming rituals known as 'charivari', 'skimmingtons', 'rough music', and (in Wales) the *ceffyl pren*, when during an explosion of discordant sound and mock festivity the community bared its teeth, invaded the private lives of its targets, and enforced the moral code of the majority against such acts as infidelity, 'deviant' sexual behaviour, and wife and husband beating.[114]

What of the widely held thesis that in the modern era the community has declined at the expense of home and family? The dwindling significance of the traditional festive calendar would seem to suggest so. The increase in the scale of living units as a consequence of urbanization would appear to have made it impossible for people to operate effectively at the communal level. However, before relegating the community to history some caution should be exercised. First, we must avoid romanticizing the *ideal* of the community in the past. It could be a pretty nasty beast, and internal tensions were capable of blowing it apart, as during the witch trials of the late Tudor and early Stuart years, or the conflicts of the Civil Wars period. Secondly, large towns were not a creation of the modern era. London already had half a million inhabitants by 1700. Nor was size a barrier to the formation of sub-communities or neighbourhoods. Wilde describes how in Dublin, with around 200,000 people in the early nineteenth century, each neighbourhood erected its own May-bush and bonfire around which 'the entire population of the district collected'.[115] Industrialization and urban expansion, far from weakening social ties, created the need to build new communities, importing, modifying, and rejuvenating old recreational forms and rituals to achieve this end.[116] In the textile towns of Lancashire the traditional wakes week transmuted into the annual seaside holiday, prompting Robert Poole and John Walton to argue that 'the seaside visit . . . could become an expression of urban and neighbourhood identity as streets, pubs and religious organizations figured prominently among excursion-promoting bodies, and neighbours joined forces to stay at boarding-houses kept by people from their own home town'.[117] The nineteenth-century urban pub, often located on a corner or road junction, became the hub of a street-based neighbourhood, inheriting the pivotal communal role of the early modern alehouse.[118] Over the short and medium term, industrialization and urbanization may have strengthened rather than weakened communal forces, throwing together large numbers of people, often engaged in the same employment, in tightly packed living units such as courts and terraces. These are the sort of 'communities' written about by Robert Roberts in his portrait of early twentieth-century Salford, or Michael Young and Peter Willmott in their survey of London's East End in the early 1950s.[119]

The death of the community is therefore a concept we should be wary of. The issue is complicated in particular by two related developments. First, the rise of clubs and societies, whose numbers proliferated from the late seventeenth century, and most of which either concerned the delivery of recreations or used leisure as a means of cultivating sociability.[120] It was a flexible solution to the problem posed by urbanization, where the formal unit of settlement became too big to accommodate a face-to-face community. Infinitely variable in size, composition, and function, easy to construct, reformulate, and dismantle, clubs and societies allowed towns to build their own associational system to counteract the potential for anomie posed by urbanization. In one sense this process did constitute a fragmentation of the community *ideal*, and it was more heavily deployed by the middle than the working class, and decidedly more so by men than women. But similar points could also be made about the medieval and early modern guild. Moreover, it is clear that some clubs were closely related to community structures, particularly in the case of football clubs, choral societies, and brass bands, whose appeal and influence derived directly from their roots in a particular locality.[121]

The second development was the emergence of the 'virtual' community. All organizations are to some extent imagined, but in this case the critical issue is the relative mental and physical distance that exists between the members. One of the earliest examples was provided by the rise of the newspaper and journal, which took off after the lapse of the Licensing Act in 1695. The readership would have no direct contact with each other, but by regular subscription they became part of 'communities of taste and knowledge',[122] to which they could contribute with letters, poems, and essays.[123] Several early periodicals created an imagined club, the conversation and opinions of which they purported to be relaying.[124] Over the long term the media, and electronic forms of communication such as the internet, have spawned a plethora of virtual communities, some of which stretch across the world. Television has brought the virtual community into the home and invites its audiences not only to watch the same programmes as millions of others, but also to share the trials and tribulations of the characters in soap operas – such as *Coronation Street, EastEnders*, and *Neighbours* – which seek to re-create street- or neighbourhood-based urban communities. The media have also been responsible for turning the leading sporting clubs, notably those associated with soccer, into global virtual communities, the majority of whose fans have never seen them play in the flesh, or even visited the geographical location from which they originally emerged.

SURROGACY

That young men in Japan can bond so closely with a football team in Manchester, or with an archetypal white Anglo-Saxon male player from the East End of London, reveals a great deal about the relationship between leisure and identity. It demonstrates the centrality of what may be called 'surrogacy' – the capacity of one being to live through another. Surrogacy is at the heart of identity creation. Heroes and stars make us what we are, and have a long association with leisure. The popular literature of the early modern period, available in the so-called chapbooks, was full of medieval chivalric romances, with castings headed by larger-than-life characters who came invariably from superior social stock, like Guy of Warwick, Bevis of Hampton, King Arthur, St George, and Robin Hood.[125] In the later early modern period three important changes occurred to the nature of the hero. First, actors and musicians, who had been largely seen as the mediums for the characters or parts they played, began to emerge as stars in their own right, with their private lives subject to public scrutiny. It is likely that the employment of foreign singers – Handel visited Italy specifically to recruit new stars, and foregrounded their presence in his operas – had the exotic appeal of overseas footballers today.[126] Secondly, we witness the appearance of the first national sporting heroes, such as the swordsman and cudgel-player James Figg, the cricketer William Beldham, and the boxers Jack Broughton, Daniel Mendoza, and Tom Cribb.[127] Thirdly, the new breed of heroes was contemporary, professional, secular, and of relatively ordinary stock. These changes made the process of surrogacy that much more immediate and effective. These were living and breathing figures, whose careers were not impossibly beyond the dreams of common people.

Critical to the rise of the modern hero were commercialization and the media. Money made it possible for the contemporary star without inherited wealth to make a living and cut an appropriately impressive image. The later Victorian cult of the amateur to some degree suppressed these tendencies in sport, but not in the music hall and the theatre. However, in sports with a large public following professionalism, mixtures of professionalism and amateurism, and if this failed, liberal doses of 'shamateurism' guaranteed a continuing flow of contemporary stars. In the longer run, huge transfers of wealth into the pockets of film, music, and sports personalities, allied to a recognition – early in the case of the cinema, later in the case of most sports – among employers of the commercial value in promoting them as stars, has allowed modern heroes to adorn themselves with the material trappings that enhance their appeal to a consumer society in which the possession and display of goods is central to identity creation. This is now widely recognized in the sports industry, where athletes are used to promote not only sports equipment and dress but a wide range of other fashion products, from mobile phones to children's clothing. In the eighteenth century Mendoza was the object of a product line in plaques and mugs, and this no doubt helped the ceramics industry.[128] But it was also valuable publicity, and from the eighteenth century the media were to play a critical role in making and promoting recreational heroes. John Lowerson has argued that it was the 'printed word which created the aura of heroism' that surrounded legendary cricketers like W. G. Grace, C. B. Fry, and 'Ranji', and newspapers, magazines, boys' and girls' comics, biographies and autobiographies have played a vital role in crafting the heroic persona.[129] Printed media have for long carried visual images, but the arrival of film, television, video, and DVD generated a far more immediate, intimate, and dynamic range of media for placing hero and audience directly in contact with each other. Electronic forms of communication also extended the dimensions of the audience, paving the way for the global hero.[130]

If commercialization and the media tend to universalize the hero, it should not be forgotten that he or she often possessed qualities with which particular constituencies could identify. It was their *local* rather than *global* associations that attracted the rapt attentions of Geordies to the rower Harry Clasper (d. 1870) and the Irish community in South Wales to the boxer 'peerless' Jim Driscoll (d. 1925), both of whom were the subject of funerals in which crowds lined the streets of Newcastle-upon-Tyne and Cardiff respectively.[131] Evan (b. 1869) and David (b. 1867) James were the 'Merlins of Welsh rugby'; half-backs for Swansea and labourers in the copper works, they were local heroes whose small size, inventiveness, and trickery embodied qualities of carnival and resistance that appealed to Welsh working-class sentiment. The fiery, impulsive, and aggressive approach of the Scottish footballer Dennis Law radiated 'an ancient tradition of raiding across the English border, of lightning strikes against a bigger and less mobile neighbour', all of which contrasted with the persona of Bobby Charlton, 'the quintessential understated English sporting hero'.[132] Such heroes were also quintessentially male, and sportsmen have long provided vicarious models of masculinity. Film stars serve a similar purpose, though any notion of simple sexual stereotypes must be treated with caution. George Formby hardly possessed the archetypal male physique and personality of the

Hollywood star, but his 'well-honed persona: as a small, rather gormless, bashful, ukelele-playing representative of the ordinary man who, despite overwhelming odds, always wins his girl' provided a quasi-hero for the sexual – it was well known that he was dominated by his wife – and social underdog.[133]

Formby was in a long line of impish, inverted male heroes – the music hall star Dan Leno is an obvious predecessor, and Norman Wisdom continued the tradition – and it is arguable that the anti-hero is as much a part of the heroic model as its more orthodox counterpart. This was in part because the anti-hero helped define the heroic norm, but also because he or she may embody demotic and subversive qualities with which an audience could identify. Punch and Judy puppet shows were well established by the early modern period and Punch constituted an ambivalent figure, capable of combating a shrewish wife and the devil, but also of deploying gratuitous violence against women and children.[134] Fools were a feature of much popular ritual. The procession at mayor-making in early eighteenth-century Norwich included 'a man or two in painted canvas coats and ridiculous red and yellow cloth caps, adorned with cats' tails and small bells, [who] went up and down to clear the way: their weapons were only small wands'. More sinister was the fool who attended the May boys and morris dancers in early nineteenth-century Connaught and Munster, wearing

> a sort of loose garment covered with many-coloured shreds and patches of cloth and rags tacked to it; a large, brimless hat, with the front of it formed into a hideous mask, came down over his head; a row of projecting pieces of sticks made to resemble teeth surrounded the mouth. . . . In his hand he carried a long wattle, to which an inflated bladder was attached, and a very formidable weapon it was, particularly against the women and children.[135]

The Satanic overtones are clear enough and are a common feature of the anti-hero. When the *Observer* monthly sports magazine included an interview with Roy Keane, its cover photograph showed the footballer staring demotically at the camera, holding a bird's skull and beak in his hand, under which was the headline 'A MAN POSSESSED'. This was the counter-thrust to the saintly images now adopted by some sports stars. David Beckham carries a tattooed angel on his back, 'whose arms reach out in a crucified posture along his shoulder blades', and this possibly accounts for the fact that he is prone to taking up a crucifix-like stance after scoring a goal.[136] Here, in the modern football match, there is an obvious echo of the medieval miracle play, except that it is not simply a matter of black against white, Satan versus saint. There is something blasphemous and Dionysiac about Beckham's appropriation of Christian imagery. Both he and Keane – as do many pop, film, and sports stars – mix the hero and anti-hero (after an English/Welsh qualifier match for the 2006 World Cup a newspaper headline proclaimed 'The beauty and the beast in Beckham')[137] in a potent psycho-montage that greatly enhances their appeal to the complex and contradictory aspirations and fantasies of their publics.

One form of surrogacy in leisure involves living through animals. They have been employed in competitive sports, but also acquired as objects of display and companions. Their recreational use has historically been subject to two interrelated trends, both gathering pace in the eighteenth century: a shift away from violent animal sports, and a swing towards pet-keeping. Both reflect a growing empathy for animals – or, more correctly, certain types of animals – part of a developing self-conscious interest in the natural world.[138] But what underpinned the increasingly sentimental attitude towards the animal kingdom was industrialization and urbanization, which drew more and more people away from direct contact with agriculture and the associated rearing, deployment, and killing of animals.

Why should animals be so widely used in leisure? They could serve as status and class markers, and to assert a distinctive self- or corporate identity. Tending pets or taking part in competitions involving animals can also require a range of highly specialized skills, which could take time to acquire and add to a person's public esteem. However, much the same could be argued of collecting, maintaining, and racing motor cars and motorbikes. What was it about animals that made them special? Critical is the fact they are living and sentient beings, that they can express feelings which appear to approximate to human pleasure and pain, and that they can die. Here was something that no machine or inanimate object could replicate. It underpinned the often intensely close relationships between person and animal. This pertained even where the animal might meet a violent death in the interests of its master. Cockfighting was a bloody and brutal affair, but that did not prevent the owners of the birds caring for their animals and developing a close bond of affection for them. John Brand, for a period a curate in eighteenth-century Newcastle, recalls visiting the death bed of a Northumbrian collier:

> to my great astonishment I was interrupted by the crowing of a game cock, hung in the bag over his head; to this exultation an immediate answer was given by another cock concealed in a closet, to whom the first replied, and instantly the last rejoined. . . . It had been, it should seem, industriously hung there for the sake of company. – He had thus an opportunity of casting, at an object he dearly loved in the days of his health and strength.[139]

The potential for bonding might account for the use of animals by humans in leisure contexts, but that simply begs the question: Why not either perform oneself or bond with another human being? Three key reasons can be suggested. First, it has proved possible historically to expose animals to levels of suffering and risk of injury and death that would generally be unacceptable in the case of humans. Secondly, in acting as human surrogates, animals could compete in a manner that, were their masters to do the same, would be a serious risk to social and political stability. Thirdly, compared with humans, most animals can be easily manipulated, trained, and commanded.[140] Animals have limited rights, and these are all bestowed by humans. How and when they perform, how they are kept, the rewards they receive, their contact with other beings, all are determined by their human masters. In a society which outlawed serfdom and then slavery, and in which service and notions of deference were declining, animals provided a continuing and legitimate forum for the exercise of power over other living beings.

6

PLACE

In 1920 a statue of Griffith Rhys Jones, paid for by public subscription, was unveiled in Victoria Square, Aberdare. Jones, who had died almost a quarter of a century earlier, was better known as the great choral conductor 'Caradog', who was born at Trecynon near to Aberdare, lived and conducted in the area for much of his life, and led the South Wales Choral Union (in which the core was drawn from the choirs of Aberdare and the Cynon Valley) to their famous victories in the Challenge Cup at Crystal Palace in 1872 and 1873.[1] Erecting the memorial was not just a means of commemorating a person and a cultural achievement, it was also a way of celebrating a *place*. Local heroes are icons of place, and bonding with a location is one of the key means of establishing personal identity. That heroes are often recreational ones is an indication of the important part leisure plays in this process. The following chapter will explore two types of place identities, the locality/region and the nation.

LOCALITY AND REGION

Patterns of leisure have differed considerably from locality to locality, and region to region of Britain, and have been vital in shaping place identities. In the case of traditional customs and recreations, though there were common types and forms, there was endless scope for subtle variations on these.[2] On Plough Monday in Hull and Grimsby, for example, a ship was drawn through the streets rather than the usual plough, an assertion of the towns' maritime rather than agricultural identities.[3] In the Cotswolds, a predominantly pastoral economy, Plough Monday does not figure at all, and Bob Bushaway has shown how the 'customary calendar' was 'perceived of as local'.[4] Regional variation is a theme that repeats itself across Britain.[5] Cockfighting was found throughout Scotland, but took place on Fastern E'en (Shrove Tuesday) in the Lowlands, as in England, and on Candlemas (2 February) in the Highlands and Islands. Maypoles were more common in the south of Wales, and the *cangen haf* (summer branch), carried from house to house mainly on May Day, in the north-east of the country, and the excesses of the 'merry wake' evident in Ireland's three other provinces were missing from early modern Munster.[6]

The existence historically of distinct local and regional recreational cultures owes much to differing environmental, economic, and social conditions. David Underdown has argued that in Stuart Wiltshire, football, an overtly team game, and festive culture in general were strongest in the nucleated villages of the southern chalk downlands, whereas bat-and-ball games like stoolball and trap-ball, with their more individualistic emphasis, were most popular in the relatively scattered settlements of the northern wood–pasture cheese-producing region. It was also the 'forest counties' of the south-east of England that formed the cradle of modern cricket.[7] The burgeoning industrial districts of late Victorian South Wales, the Midlands, the North, and the narrow belt of land in the western and eastern Scottish Lowlands – where there was a need to weld substantial numbers of immigrants into a new community, and factories or mines encouraged an intensely corporate lifestyle – were fertile territory for team-based pastimes such as choral singing, brass bands, soccer, and rugby. Club cricket also proved popular in some of these areas, but significantly it was run on a competitive, semi-professional basis that the more rural and gentrified areas of the south were keen to eschew.[8] It was also the industrialized and urbanized north-west of England, with its relatively high wages, that pioneered the gregarious working-class seaside holiday in the late nineteenth century.[9]

The kaleidoscopic nature of cultural variation provided the foundation for the construction of local and regional identities. However, some of the fiercest loyalties were generated at the micro-spatial level, where there would be least potential for differences of cultural practice. For the mass of people the most powerful place identities have been constructed around the street, neighbourhood, parish, and sub-settlement. Much of the male youth and adolescent culture – based upon gangs, games, and petty gambling – that flourished on the streets of nineteenth- and early twentieth-century towns, and so perturbed the authorities, was built around minutely defined territorial loyalties. In early twentieth-century Salford, 'All the warring gangs were known by a street name and fought, usually, by appointment – Next Friday, 8 p.m.: Hope Street *v*. Adelphi!'[10] On a more organized level the inhabitants of the opposite sides of the street that ran from Queensberry Square to St Andrew Street, Dumfries, contested a curling match in 1831 for the Queensberry Street medal.[11] The rivalry between the industrial communities of Merthyr and its close neighbour Dowlais, fought out on the musical rather than the military field, reached epic proportions in the late Victorian era, and prompted charges of betrayal when the conductor Dan Davies migrated from Dowlais to Merthyr choir in 1892.[12]

The above cases illustrate the importance of what is termed 'relational identity': establishing the character of one place by relation to that of another.[13] In this 'shared system of differentiation',[14] historically some of the fiercest loyalties have been engendered by ecclesiastical and administrative divisions such as the parish and township, whose origins date back to the medieval period. Beating the bounds of these territorial units, a ritual that might literally involve the old knocking the heads of the young against marker stones to ensure the passage of knowledge from one generation to the next, was accompanied by liberal quantities of food and drink, and was part of the local festive calendar.[15] Inter-parochial competition was reflected in a wide range of sporting contests such as football, curling, and bell ringing, and could involve raids to steal symbolic items like a maypole.[16] Changes to the operation of poor relief, for which the parish was responsible, accentuated territorial tensions and consciousness. Richard Suggett suggests that the 1662 Act of Settlements placed parishes in Wales in 'a state of latent hostility', reflected in conflicts during festivals such as the *gwylmabsant* (wake) and *bedwen haf* (maypole).[17]

The town and city represented a further level of place identity. Though much of the ritual associated with medieval and early modern civic life focused upon the ruling elite, ceremonial was often carefully constructed to incorporate the populace, such as by elaborate public processions and the distribution of food and drink.[18] Urbanization meant that a growing proportion of the population were living in towns, at the same time as increasing the size of urban settlements to the point where it was potentially difficult for them to operate as viable local societies. None the less, considerable efforts were made in the nineteenth and twentieth centuries by urban authorities and wealthy benefactors to create and promote cultural institutions such as parks, libraries, museums, art galleries, bands, orchestras, and choirs that symbolized a common civic identity. Popular sports teams served a similar function, and the inter-urban rivalries generated during competition, especially in local 'derbies', reinforced urban loyalties.[19] By the late 1930s most First Division soccer sides in the north-west of England could enjoy average crowds equivalent to 15–20 per cent of their host town's population, and success would invoke mass celebrations. When Preston North End returned victorious from their FA Cup final in 1938, some 50,000 people lined the streets and 30,000 gathered in the Market Place.[20] Small towns have also proved adept at promoting distinctive local customs and events to assert a special identity, such as the Padstow Hobby-Horse and the Keaw Yed (Cow's Head) festival at Westhoughton in Lancashire.[21]

On the face of it, there would seem sense in the argument that place identities are strongest the smaller and more intimate the geographical entities involved. None the less, regional units have also been the focus of deeply felt loyalties. For the early modern gentry this was the case with the county, around which developed during the eighteenth century a rich package of fashionable recreations, focused upon the county town and events like the assizes and race week.[22] Participation in such events was a sign of regional loyalty and helped integrate the local ruling order. Inter-county rivalries could be expressed through cockfighting, and in 1710 it was claimed that 'cocks from the same neighbourhood or county do not willingly attack each other, so those from different parts are set to fight'.[23] The county provided the organizational template for the development of cricket, and given the large crowds that county cricket attracted from early on – it was claimed that a match in 1738 between Kent and London drew 10,000 spectators and by the end of the nineteenth century 15,000 to 20,000 were attending the most popular county contests – and the intense rivalry that emerged between areas like Lancashire and Yorkshire, it is clear that the county enjoyed a loyalty beyond that of the elite.[24]

Matches between Yorkshire and Middlesex generated an especial degree of hostility and this reflected a wider tension that existed between metropolis and provinces. In the south-east of England, tied umbilically to London, this led to the nurturing of intensely local customs such as the 'Hooden Horse' (recorded 1807–1908, and revived 1952), whose 'success', it is argued, 'has been due largely to the desire of many people in Kent to preserve a separate identity from London'.[25] Further away from the capital hostility could give rise to a more concrete sense of regional identity. The north–south divide in England is based upon long-term differences in economic, social, and political development that were accentuated by the Industrial Revolution in the eighteenth and nineteenth centuries and the decline of heavy manufacturing industry in the twentieth century. The impact on the evolution of leisure has been substantial, from major divisions such as the 'great schism' in rugby, to ongoing conflicts over the distribution of central government funding for the arts and sport. The effect has been that pastimes like football, cricket, and music have, in Dave Russell's words, provided 'a rich site for the creation of pan-class regional identities'.[26] Some of these admittedly cut across the north–south divide, such as the north-east, the north-west, East Anglia, and the south-west. Mike Huggins in his study of sport in the north-east has emphasized the importance of intra-regional loyalties, and suggested that from the mid-1870s the north-east defined itself against Lancashire and Yorkshire, which constituted its notion of 'the south'. However, he also argues that before this date, and after some point in the early twentieth century, the real anti-presence or 'relational other' was not some vague southern entity, but London.[27] This may be the case for most of the 'peripheral' regions. How far 'core' areas, closely tied to the metropolis – such as the Midlands, the south-east and the Home Counties – have been able to generate strong regional identities is questionable. Moreover, there remains the intriguing question of to what extent London and 'the south' possess a regional sense of identity, and whether regionalism is an asymmetrical concept, dependent upon metropolitan paramountcy, and available only to those outside the immediate influence of the capital.

NATION

When compared with that in many European countries, regionalism has been a weak force in the British Isles. In part this reflects a long-term trend, well under way by the early modern period, towards economic and political integration. However, the presence of several nations within the Atlantic Archipelago has also provided a powerful alternative focus to the region. The character of the four nations, and their relationship and interplay with each other and with the wider entity called Britain, have been in a constant state of flux since 1500, and there is little evidence of a closure to this process. That the nations exist cheek-by-jowl, with ill-defined borders, regular and substantial flows of migrants, and large diasporas embedded within each other, adds to the endemic instability. Despite, and perhaps because of, this fluidity and complexity, the nation in Britain has proved a potent site of place identity. It is at this level that the idea, suggested by Benedict Anderson, of an 'imagined' or 'symbolic' community takes on a particular force, since the 'nation' is so large that its members can have little face-to-face knowledge of each other.[28] Leisure has provided a crucial mechanism for transcending anonymity by providing a series of shared phenomena, often of a competitive nature, around which a people can conceive of themselves as a national community.

How long leisure specifically has been put to the purposes of creating national identities is debatable. The later eighteenth century is often taken to represent an important turning point in the construction of national consciousness. Among the elite in some European countries, especially those on the 'periphery', such as Scotland and Wales, there was a reaction against the universalist, centralizing, and French connotations of the Enlightenment, and this was reflected in a revival of interest in national 'folk' cultures.[29] The American and French Revolutions are seen as critical in the emergence of a popular patriotism, based on the notion of a 'mass' society of citizens, which laid the foundations for the recreational nationalism that emerged in the nineteenth century.[30] There is little evidence of substantial international sporting contests in Britain before the late nineteenth and early twentieth centuries, with the first matches within Britain between sides representing the four nations, and between those sides and representative teams from overseas. The first official 'England versus Scotland' rugby and soccer internationals were played in 1872 and 1873, the first fully representative Australian cricket side arrived in

1878, the first Rugby League tour from New Zealand arrived in 1907, from Australia in 1907–8, and the first English (Northern Union) tour to Australia took place in 1910.[31] It has been argued that 'at first English patriotism in sport was relatively weak', held back by the prevailing amateur code and cross-loyalties of class and region.[32] Though the new mood of nationalism abroad in the late Victorian and Edwardian years is clear enough, we should be cautious about dismissing leisure-based patriotism from an earlier period. In late medieval England St George was promoted as a symbol of national identity and a rival to the French St Denis, and in a number of communities the festivities mounted on the saint's day included a procession with a suitably ferocious dragon. Though remnants of the spectacle lingered on into the eighteenth century – the dragon was present during mayor-making at Norwich – the Reformation's attack on saints undermined the festival. However, from the late sixteenth century Protestantism brought with it, as David Cressy has shown, 'a new national, secular and dynastic calendar', focused on the monarchy, and including events such as Gunpowder Treason Day, that offered rich opportunities for patriotic recreation.[33]

A calendar which was Protestant and royal was never going to possess a universal appeal in the British Isles, and it therefore became one of a series of recreational markers around which a non-British national identity could be constructed. In Wales, merged with the English state and its religion from early in the sixteenth century, the Protestant calendar did not constitute a national differentiator. Guy Fawkes' Day was celebrated in Wales in the nineteenth century, if not before, though the occasion might be appropriated to local purposes, as when a doctor in Presteigne, who insisted on prompt payment of bills, was burned in effigy.[34] Wales developed other markers to distinguish itself, though with many of these it is difficult to determine how far participants perceived their activities in specifically national terms, and how far the nation as a whole shared in them. The Welsh bardic tradition, deprived of the patronage of a gentry class which had been seduced by the growing scope of fashionable metropolitan culture, collapsed in the late seventeenth century. However, a more popularly based Welsh-language poetry continued to flourish. In part this was supported in the early eighteenth century by the revival of the *eisteddfodau* – closed assemblies of poets and grammarians, plentifully supplied with wine and ale, held in taverns in small market towns. However, more critical for survival was the emergence of a Welsh-language press, producing ballads, interludes, almanacs, and religious works. It was this which facilitated the shift of Welsh from an oral to a mixed print and oral culture, and protected the long-term future of the language and its capacity to act as a marker and agent of national identity.[35] Parallel with these developments went a more self-conscious Welsh 'renaissance' – manifested, for example, in the mounting of the first large-scale regular *eisteddfodau* at Corwen and Bala in 1789, and the first provincial *eisteddfod* at Carmarthen in 1819 (when the *Gorsedd* of Bards was first introduced) – which involved ransacking and where necessary inventing the past 'to create a new Welshness which would instruct, entertain, amuse and educate the people'.[36] Paradoxically, this new cultural consciousness was forged in the flourishing associational life of London, with clubs such as the Society of Ancient Britons (1715), the Honourable Society of Cymmrodorion (1751), and Gwyneddigion (1770), formed from middling-order exiles, reacting with and against the metropolitan 'other', a potent reminder of the interrelated and interactive character of the various national cultures within the British Isles.[37]

During the nineteenth century, *eisteddfodau* developed into one focus of Welsh identity. An observer commented in 1880, 'these assemblies are unique, they are not to be found anywhere but in Wales. . . . We do not want anything like home rule but we like to keep up a love for "Hen Wlad fy Nhadau [Land of my Fathers]" '.[38] Choral music was central to these occasions, so that Wales became known, and identified itself, as 'the land of song',[39] and this accounts for the great significance attached to the Crystal Palace choral victories of 1872 and 1873. But it must not be forgotten that the choir that achieved these triumphs was drawn from South Wales, and that *eisteddfodau* were mechanisms for articulating competition *within* Wales, and as such were as likely to assert local as national identities. The same could be said of sport, which emerged in the late Victorian period as an even more all-embracing – without the linguistic exclusions of the *eisteddfodau*, though with ones of gender – symbol of Welshness. The intriguing question in the case of Wales is not why sport should acquire this role, but why rugby, particularly after the fabled victory over the New Zealand All Blacks in 1905, should, in Gareth Williams's words, become 'a badge of national identity'.[40] Cricket and especially soccer had the potential to fulfil this role, as they did in England. But therein lay the problem. Both sports were simply too associated with the country against which Wales defined itself, and whose superior playing resources would make any long-term prospect of success unlikely. Moreover, cricket and soccer in England had class-specific connotations, one aristocratic and bourgeois, the other proletarian, whereas what was needed, in the eyes of an upwardly-mobile Welsh middle class that participated in and sponsored club sport, and was keen to find a means of defusing political tensions, was a recreation that could cross class barriers and provide a pole around which a Welsh identity could be built.[41] Once the sport and Welshness were welded together, and the association had been boosted by heroic memory, then little could be done, despite any empirical evidence to the contrary, to break the link. As one devotee of rugby claimed, during a moment of national soccer success, 'The facts cannot be disputed: rugby has a mystical, spiritual and emotional grip over the Welsh population soccer cannot match. That is why rugby is the national sport of Wales.'[42]

Scottish sport followed a different course. Football 'held an extraordinary hold on the Scottish public'. In 1974 a quarter of the adult population paid to watch matches.[43] Why did soccer become the national sport? One reason was that rugby failed to provide an adequate basis for working-class support. Compared with the game in Wales it was relatively conservative, sticking rigidly to the amateur ethos, and among the urban-based teams which dominated the Scottish Rugby Union it remained socially exclusive.[44] In addition, the character of Scottish industrialization and urbanization – longer term, based more around factories and established towns than in Wales – encouraged soccer. The principal focus of hostilities was England, and unlike the case in Wales, Scottish football had substantial playing resources to draw on, and could mount a credible challenge to the old enemy. Some have argued that recreational nationalism has detracted from political nationalism. Jim Sillars complained in 1992, 'the great problem we have is . . . that we have too many ninety minute patriots in this country'.[45] Devolution has reduced the need to invest so much national sentiment in sporting competition with England – during the 2002 World Cup finals, which Scotland failed to reach, some Scottish politicians suggested that it would be a sign of political maturity to support England[46] – and the abandonment of the annual round of Home internationals has limited the scope for conflict. Moreover, it may be questioned to what extent football was ever able to provide a true focus of national identity, with the class-specificity of the sport, its domination by Glasgow-based clubs, and the bitter sectarian divisions that riddled the game.[47]

Other sports have also been used to express a Scottish consciousness. A poem of 1715 called curling 'a Manly Scotish Exercise', an account of 1774 described curling and golf as diversions 'peculiar to the Scots . . . the standing winter and summer diversions of Scotland', and the Duddington Curling Society's motto, inscribed on a medal of 1802, was *Sic Scoti: alii non aeque felices* (This is the way the Scots play; the rest of the world isn't half so lucky).[48] It was curling, golf, and bowls which the 'sporting patriot', the thirteenth Earl of Eglinton (1812–61), lent his considerable support to.[49] The problem from a Scottish perspective is that these would always remain minority and somewhat esoteric sports, incapable of rousing the passions of the mass of the population – other than momentarily, as during the women curling team's success at the

2002 winter Olympics, and then it was under a British flag.[50] The same was the case with Highland Games. That these were 'not so much an invention of tradition as a selection of tradition' mattered less than their narrow appeal.[51] Indeed, this was the case with the whole Highland myth, around which a sophisticated tourist industry was built in the nineteenth and twentieth centuries. Many of its features were geared specifically to servicing the recreational needs of well-off foreigners. Though it is true that there emerged a brand of popular 'Tartanry' that filled the new music halls of the late Victorian and Edwardian periods, it created a representation of the nation 'that trivialised, distorted and sentimentalised Scotland's self-image in a particularly grotesque manner',[52] and ultimately possessed only limited relevance to the highly urbanized proletarian population that filled the Lowlands. Of more importance to the development of a Scottish identity was the growth in the nineteenth century of a popular press – such as the *People's Journal*, whose weekly circulation rose from 58,000 in 1864, to about 250,000 by 1914 – which included pieces on Scottish customs and history, and fiction that was not exclusively rural but contained a good deal of urban reference. On occasions it also deployed Scots vernacular, and was characterized by 'its unique openness to its readers', though it must be said that by 1900 the 'cultural autonomy' of the Scottish press was declining, as more and more copy was taken from London and English syndicates.[53]

Elizabeth Malcolm has noted the extent to which the popular nationalist meetings and movements of early nineteenth-century Ireland afforded the opportunity for leisure, and speculated that from the 1830s and 1840s 'nationalism . . . was not merely a political ideology, but also a form of recreation'.[54] That protest movements could be vehicles for fun, and politics a form of pleasure, was not something peculiar to Ireland. Though the line between recreation and revolt is often a thin one, in most societies an invisible boundary is maintained between the two. In the case of Ireland the barrier to some degree collapsed. Quite how far is a matter of debate. Irish men and women have for centuries engaged in countless recreational acts which are quite unaffected by the politics of nationalism, and participated in many cultural forms found elsewhere in the British Isles. For example, though an Irish television service was inaugurated in 1961, eventually supervised by Radio Telefis Éireann, a significant proportion of east coast homes already had aerials enabling them to receive broadcasts of BBC and ITV programmes from Great Britain and Northern Ireland, and British stations, boosted by the introduction of cable TV, have continued to attract a wide Irish audience.[55] None the less, it is difficult to avoid the perception that for some participants street-based conflict and ritual in Northern Ireland has possessed a recreational element, and that in a numbers of areas of leisure the intangible membrane that separates politics and play has been breached by the sheer force of nationalist and sectarian sentiments.

Joseph Ryan has argued that 'nationalism . . . is the crucial determinant on the course of music in Ireland in the past two centuries'.[56] This is reflected in the development of a folk tradition in music that became a major signifier of Irishness. Dating back to the European-wide revival of interest in folk culture in the eighteenth century, it was a 'tradition' that in practice owed much to elite support and to invention and innovation.[57] The fiddle, for example, which is now central to the image and performance of Irish folk music, was not introduced into the country until the mid-seventeenth century at the earliest, where it caught on very rapidly because of its relative cheapness to produce.[58] It is argued that after the Act of Union nationalist sentiment in Ireland resisted new trends in classical music and focused upon the folk tradition, which was treated in an increasingly protected and insular manner and, in contrast to the cases of Kodaly and Bartok in Hungary, was not permitted to fructify with art music. The result, in Harry White's words, is that 'The condition of music in modern Irish history can briefly be characterized as a more or less polarized development of colonial and ethnic ideologies of culture.'[59]

Much the same could be said of sport. The explosion of organized recreation in late Victorian mainland Britain, and the rapid process of 'ludic diffusion' by which the new sports were spread through Europe and the Empire, left Ireland vulnerable to a massive injection of 'colonial' culture. The response within the nationalist community, unlike Wales and Scotland where the Union was more deeply embedded, was to create a uniquely Irish sphere of Gaelic sports, encompassing in particular Gaelic football and hurling. The sports were promoted by the Gaelic Athletics Association (GAA), founded in 1884. Members were banned from participating in or watching 'imported' games, including rugby, which was seen as socially exclusive, Protestant, and English. Gaelic sports enjoyed substantial popular support north and south of the border and their success has been closely tied to the strength of the nationalist political movement.[60] However, the GAA based itself upon the English county structure and borrowed from the ethos and organizational forms of Victorian sport. In general it has retained a certain distance from the more radical elements in nationalism, and has slowly adapted itself to the changing political climate. The ban on participating in 'foreign' sports was lifted in 1971, that on members of the Northern Ireland security forces joining the organization, in 2001, and on the use of its stadium for soccer and rugby internationals, in 2005.[61] None the less, the very insularity of Gaelic sports limits their role as a symbol of national identity. Mike Cronin has argued that 'they are ultimately a parochial sport in a globalized world . . . while Gaelic games seek to define Irish nationalism in an insular thirty-two county context, soccer defines Irish nationalism in the context of the global'.[62] For him this represents the contrast between old and new versions of Irish nationalism, one inward the other outward looking. However, following on from the débâcle when Roy Keane was sent home during the 2002 World Cup, Fintan O'Toole has maintained that Irish soccer is itself divided between 'the new Ireland . . . rich, upwardly mobile and driven by a ruthless work ethic' and the older, more relaxed, 'have a good time what ever the result' version of Irishness, willing to celebrate heroic failure.[63]

The case of Ireland reminds us that that there can be multiple notions of national identity within the same country. The linguistic divide in Wales, and its cultural ramifications, provides an obvious axis around which different definitions of Welshness revolve. In the case of Ireland, where the persistence of Catholicism has offset the need to sustain the indigenous language as a national marker, the division is not simply between a backward- or forward-looking version of Irishness, or even, in an all-Ireland context, between a Catholic and a Protestant one, but more critically between what constitutes the 'other' against which the country defines itself. For the progressive version, that other is globally defined; for the traditionalist version it is inevitably England and Britain. England has also to a considerable, though not exclusive extent – the supporters of Rangers football club can look to England or Ireland depending upon which identity they are assuming – formed the relational body against which Wales and Scotland have defined themselves. In England's case the big 'other' has in recent centuries tended to be located outside the British Isles. This was much less the case in the early modern period. In the seventeenth and eighteenth centuries the 'Celtic' peripheries were used in literary and visual works, and by the growing numbers who toured Britain, to define what it was to be Protestant, civilized, and English.[64] None the less, in the long term the 'other' for Englishmen has principally been located on the Continent, and with the expansion of the Empire, in the Orient and Africa. Visual depictions of the French as scrawny, impoverished, and servile (as in Hogarth's *Calais Gate, or the Roast Beef of Old England*, 1748, and *Beer Street*, 1751), of Russians as bloodthirsty and devious (as in the Great McDermott's jingoistic music hall turn 'We Don't Want to Fight', sung during the Eastern Crisis of 1876–8), and black Africans as murderous savages (as in the twentieth-century filmic representations of the Zulu Wars) all helped to construct a notion of Englishness.

Englishness, of course, was not only about not being something else. Various forms of leisure have been invested with positive patriotic meaning. The concept of a pantheon of national cultural heroes has a long history. Poet's Corner in Westminster Abbey began with the interment of Edmund Spenser and others near a monument to Geoffrey Chaucer erected in the 1550s. During the eighteenth century the idea of a national pantheon, and one with a markedly literary slant, solidified.[65] Representations could be found in a variety of places. The ceiling, for example, of the library in Berrington Hall (built c.1778), Herefordshire, contains painted medallions of Joseph Addison, Francis Bacon, Geoffrey Chaucer, John Milton, Isaac Newton, Matthew Prior, Alexander Pope, and William Shakespeare. The last of these in particular became, during the period, a national icon, his deification culminating in the three-day Jubilee, masterminded by the actor David Garrick, at Stratford-upon-Avon in 1769.[66] The presence of the 'other' was not entirely absent in the appreciation of the Bard, since his imaginative style of writing was favourably contrasted with the rigidities of French authors, and seen as symbolic of English liberties. It is difficult to know how far Stratford's involvement in the Jubilee was a deliberate strategy to develop the town's role as a tourist centre. By 1806 about a thousand people a year were visiting the poet's birthplace, but it was the purchase and restoration of the birthplace in 1847, the formation of a body of trustees (later to become the Birthplace Trust) to manage this and preserve and publicize the Shakespearean material heritage in the area, and the construction of a permanent Shakespeare theatre from 1827 (demolished in 1872 and replaced by the impressive Memorial Theatre in 1879), that really established Stratford's role as a place of literary and national pilgrimage. By the eve of the First World War about 50,000 people annually were visiting the birthplace (rising to almost 200,000 by 1950) and the town had become one of a growing series of urban and especially rural locations trading heavily on their associations with Englishness.[67]

Literature and landscape were to prove England's strong suit. The musical heritage was more problematic. The principal musical symbol of national identity in the late eighteenth century was Handel (1685–1759), his role in this respect boosted by the Handel Commemoration of 1784 in Westminster Abbey.[68] But he was a German by birth, though he lived in England for the great bulk of his creative life, and this is indicative of the fact that throughout the eighteenth and nineteenth centuries the principal influences on the English art musical scene emanated from the Continent. That the so-called 'English Renaissance', in which Edward Elgar emerged as the inspirational figure, should coincide with the surge in nationalist sentiment evident at home and abroad in the later nineteenth century, is hardly surprising. The movement was no doubt given a boost by the German author Oskar Schmitz's provocative description of Britain in the early months of the First World War as 'Das Land ohne Musik' (Land without music).[69] However, in practice this 'renaissance' drew heavily upon German models (Elgar was deeply affected by German music, in particular Wagner, and enjoyed extensive visits to Germany), incorporated strong Celtic and especially Irish elements (Philip Heseltine and Arnold Bax, for example, were heavily influenced by Celtic culture, and the latter was passionately committed to the Irish nationalist cause), and drew upon a range of non-Protestant elements (Elgar was a Catholic, Gerald Finzi Jewish, and Ralph Vaughan Williams's inspiration came in part from a recusant tradition of Tudor music).[70] Such eclectic influences were largely submerged beneath the self-induced conviction, what can be dubbed an 'invented tradition', that a music had emerged that was quintessentially English.

The nature of that essence is difficult to define. Imprecision and obfuscation are part and parcel of the creation of a national myth. However, in the early twentieth century a mixture of the past and the pastoral, embodied in a vision of the village green, gets as close as anything to what was felt to be English. It was a similar vision that underpinned the role cricket – in Rob Colls's words, 'the identity of England in flannels' – came to play in constructing and expressing a national identity. The game's perceived origins in a mythic rural past ensured that it became the English sport *par excellence* during the nineteenth and for much of the twentieth century.[71] In 1945 Neville Cardus likened the game to an English 'tribal rite', and in their inter-war history of cricket H. S. Altham and E. W. Swanton mused, 'victory is not everything: Test Matches and championships are but of modern growth when set against the background of the downs and woods of the Weald; and the cricket that really matters is the game that Englishmen play the world over because they cannot help it, because it answers some need deepest in their blood and hearts'.[72] Part of cricket's appeal, as with rugby for the Welsh, was that, unlike soccer, it seemed to span the classes. Undoubtedly cricket did enjoy widespread popular support. But, as Dave Russell has argued, during the inter-war years soccer increasingly took on the mantle of a 'national' sport, epitomized in the manner in which the Wembley FA Cup final, invested with a new meaning by the presence of the King and the cameras of the BBC, became part of the package of national rituals, to rank alongside the Boat Race and the King's Christmas Message.[73] As cricket's mass support diminished in the later twentieth century, as it increasingly become the sport of the independent school sector, and as decolonization removed the imperial rationale of the game, so cricket lost its iconic role to occer, and to a lesser extent rugby, as the national sport.[74]

Wales, Scotland, Ireland, and England constitute separate, if complex and changing place identities. Their histories have been inextricably intertwined, and to that extent they constitute a single economic, social, cultural, and political system in which the parts are to a substantial degree – though not exclusively, and with the growth of the European Union arguably less and less so[75] – shaped and defined in relation to each other. There remain the questions: To what extent do they collectively constitute not only a system but also a place identity? Is it possible, at least in the context of leisure, to talk of a British identity? The general failure in the modern era to create all-British sports sides – the Olympics team and the rugby Lions are notable exceptions, as was the Ryder Cup team until it incorporated European players – suggests an ambivalent response.[76] None the less, a number of factors have come into play to generate a collective consciousness. The long-term trend towards the common deployment of the English language, with the exception of pockets of Welsh and Gaelic speakers, marks off the British Isles from the Continent and has provided the basis for a rich interchange of literary and theatrical cultures. A broad acceptance of the Reformation and Protestantism, with the exception of Ireland, has also helped define a British identity against large swathes of Europe. The extraordinary growth of London since the early sixteenth century, and of the metropolitan network (including Dublin, Edinburgh, and the leading spas and seaside resorts) of which it was the hub, played a vital role in facilitating interchange between the cultural producers and elite consumers of the four countries.[77] Arguably the BBC is part of this network, an institution, despite its concessions to national and regional diversity, that has proved a powerful tool in conveying a British identity at a time when pressures towards political and cultural fragmentation were building.[78]

As early as 1923 John Reith, then general manager of the BBC, had suggested to George V that he deliver a Christmas or New Year message, but it was only in 1932 that the king conceded, and established another 'festive' moment in the modern British ritual calendar.[79] The monarchy has been one of the key institutions involved in creating a British identity. At various times its influence has been deeply divisive. This was the case for much of the seventeenth and eighteenth centuries, with the situation complicated by dynastic change. Yet, as Linda Colley has shown, a concerted effort was made in the latter part of George III's reign both to elevate the profile of the monarchy and to enhance its British credentials. The secular patriotic calendar, which had been in the process of construction since the seventeenth century, and in which the royal family's birthdays, coronation days, and jubilees were a central feature, was strengthened, and was intended to provide the basis for British-wide celebrations. The first royal jubilee was arranged in 1809, with events in Scotland, England, and Wales, and this proved the precedent for the even more spectacular jubilees (1887 and 1897) of the latter part of Queen Victoria's reign, another period which saw a surge forward in the monarchy's kudos after a phase of some unpopularity.[80] One of the Crown's functions was to incorporate the various parts of Britain into the whole. With their patronage of Walter Scott, their promotion of the Highland myth, and the process of 'Balmoralization', George IV, Victoria and Albert, and then the Windsors have drawn a largely willing Scotland into the British fold, and not so much erased as reconfigured the Jacobite and Highland heritage so that it united rather than divided England and Scotland.[81] On 29 November 1895 the prize-winning Treorchy male voice choir, having travelled from the valleys of South Wales to Windsor, performed privately before Victoria and her entourage. *Y Cerddor* reported that 'the "boys" have brought honour on themselves, their conductor and the land of their birth'. It was considered a great honour, not only because it elevated the status of the choir, which was subsequently able to use the royal prefix, but also because it was seen to incorporate Wales into the British family.[82]

After the Welsh victory over the New Zealand All Blacks in 1905 the *Western Mail* claimed that the Welsh team had 'come to the rescue of the Empire', and it is arguable that the success was seen as an imperial as much as a strictly national achievement.[83] This reflects the importance of the overseas Empire in structuring the British project. It provided a common enterprise, with potentially huge economic benefits, in which the four nations – though in Ireland this was more obviously the case in industrial Ulster – could share; it offered a space in which a purer version of Britishness, not coloured by the particular presence of any of the 'home' nations, could be cultivated; and it required a far more extensive and intensive contact with a non-European 'other' than ever experienced before, against which the essence of Britishness could be defined. Like monarchy, empire was a far from unproblematic category; it could divide as well as unite. But during the height of its influence in the late nineteenth and early twentieth centuries, when images of empire filled the music hall, panoramas, popular theatre, press, and literature,[84] it provided a sense of a common destiny and moral mission. The British could conceive of themselves as a chosen people, charged with spreading civilization to a backward and barbarian world.

Leisure played its part in this civilizing mission. Improvements in sea travel and the expansion of the rail network enabled the London theatre companies to tour the distant reaches of the Empire, such as North America, Australia, New Zealand, and India, 'a remarkable feature of Victorian cultural imperialism'.[85] But it was sport, more than any other pastime, which was seen to act as a conduit of civilization. The Victorian moralization of sport – the emphasis on rules, fair play, toughness, austerity, the corporate ethic (team before individual), service, gentlemanly behaviour, self-control, and muscular Christianity – made it an ideal vehicle for the dissemination of 'civilized' values.[86] In reality the new sports, and the ethic which they embodied, were intended primarily for two groups; on the one hand, the colonial cadre of officers, administrators, and settlers and, on the other hand, indigenous elites willing to be included within the structures of power that came with colonialism.[87] This ensured that civility remained the cultural property and signifier of the ruling order, while at the same time conveying the impression that Britain was engaged in a universal mission to civilize. The relative failure to promote soccer as a sport for imperial export[88] – in comparison with, say, horse racing, polo, tennis, hunting, rugby, golf, and cricket – owes much to its populist following back home, and the inherently uncivil elements contained within it. Moreover, in the long run it was precisely the lack of imperial baggage that was responsible for the fact that soccer became the most successful of all Britain's sporting exports.[89]

Empire helped to bond Britain together. Only in the case of southern Ireland, which felt more like a colony than part of the imperial core, did it have the opposite effect, and force a redefinition of what constituted Britain with the formation of an independent Irish state in 1922. In fact, there was no necessary contradiction between imperial and national identities and aspirations. As Tom Devine has argued, 'The British Empire did not dilute the sense of Scottish identity but strengthened it by powerfully reinforcing the sense of national esteem and demonstrating that the Scots were equal partners with the English in the great imperial mission.'[90] However, the decline of empire has started to dissolve the glue that held together the British project. Scottish and Welsh devolution reflects one outcome, but this in its turn has problematized the nature of Englishness, and exposed the once unconscious and easy assumption among the English that Britain and England were coterminous identities. It is an assumption reflected in the fact that there is no 'English National Museum' or 'English National Library'. It may be that the mixture of euphoria, paranoia, and self-laceration that accompanies the performance of English sports teams emanates from an identity crisis, though in truth such responses are hardly atypical of the media of most nations, not least Scotland and Wales. More plausible is the notion that such a crisis, to the extent that it exists, derives from the English failure to come to terms historically with the notion of dual or multiple identities, unlike the Welsh and Scots; and this may explain, as Keith Robbins has argued, 'why, of all the nations of the United Kingdom, the English appear to find it most difficult to be "European" '.[91]

7

SPACE

TOURISM AND THE 'OTHER'

In the previous chapter the 'other' was deployed largely in a negative sense. It was a space against which a familiar place could be defined. However, there is also a positive sense of the 'other', the celebration of a phenomenon precisely because it is different and 'exotic'. What motivates this? The structures and identities – state, class, gender, family, community, and place – within which we normally live, though they are fundamental to our being and satisfaction, depend for their effective operation upon powerful rules and norms. These generate huge pressures to conform, which by restricting unorthodox responses are potentially debilitating. The very rigidity of the structures can create frustration by suppressing multiple and contradictory identities that fail to fit the conventional categories. It is not always easy for an English person to be European and patriotic, for a woman to be competitive and feminine, and for a man to be caring and masculine. In this context the 'other' might be characterized as an escape route. But this both oversimplifies the distinction between the orthodox and the 'other' and seriously underestimates the potential for creativity and pleasure provided by the latter.

The most obvious recreational medium through which 'other' spaces are explored is tourism. We will come to this. It is important to recognize, however, that there is a multiplicity of forms which do not involve travel, through which unfamiliar spaces can be investigated. The global images used today in marketing food-stuffs, beverages, restaurants, and fast food outlets make it clear that they are frequently being sold for their associations with exotic locations. Similar processes were at work in the past. Chocolate, coffee, and tea were introduced into Britain in the mid-seventeenth century, and their drinking soon became both fashionable and recreational. Though some of this was due to their taste and mild narcotic qualities, their association with strange and glamorous territories, highlighted by the importation, and increasingly the home production, of tableware decorated with images of the Orient, suggests that much of their early appeal derived from the contact provided with exotic spaces. The craze for chinoiserie, particularly evident during the rococo phase in the mid-eighteenth century, can also be seen in the interior decoration and furnishing of well-off houses and in garden design and architecture, of which the pagoda at Kew is a memorable example.[1]

Gardening has proved one of the most enduring pastimes for accessing non-native cultures. Italian and French influences were evident throughout the early modern period, and from at least the second half of the seventeenth century there was a growing trade in so-called 'exoticks': plants, shrubs, and trees imported from the territories opened up by European commercial and political expansion. The opportunity for exploring further and further afield was enhanced by the growth of the British Empire, and the means for cultivating delicate imports by technological improvements during the nineteenth century, which made it possible to create large-scale artificial environments.[2] The appeal of the great Victorian conservatories, as of their successors – such as the domes in the present-day Eden Project in Cornwall and the National Botanic Gardens at Middleton in Carmarthenshire – was that they re-created a pocket of exotic space on British soil. Exhibitions of non-native wild life had a similar effect. Since at least the reign of Henry I, medieval and early modern monarchs had maintained collections of lions, leopards, and other wild creatures; since at least the Tudor period there were commercial shows displaying curious animals from overseas; and many eighteenth-century aristocrats kept collections of rare beasts and birds. Sometimes open to the public for a small fee, the private menageries were the forerunners of the public zoos, of which London was opened in 1828, and Dublin three years later.[3]

Dance and music have regularly acted as vehicles for foreign influences. French and Italian models were highly fashionable after the Restoration in 1660, and during the eighteenth century England swarmed with dancing-masters and musicians from the Continent.[4] In the twentieth century, American and Afro-Caribbean forms have had a huge impact on popular music and dance in Britain, as also has the US television and film industry on the visual media. To what extent these cultural imports are perceived as foreign and experienced for all time as such is a moot point. At some stage many are absorbed into the native tradition, so that, for example, few people today would look at a camellia and think of China, listen to Handel and imagine Germany, and hear the Beatles and think of Africa or the USA.

Dancing a French-inspired cotillion, watching a Hollywood film, and eating at an Indian curry house are all forms of virtual tourism. Visiting 'other' spaces should constitute a more intensive experience. The history of tourism can be traced back to the medieval pilgrimage. The most prestigious involved visits to key Christian sites in Europe and the Holy Land, but very large numbers of Britons also travelled to shrines in their homeland, which possessed a pecking order in much the same fashion as modern holiday resorts.[5] The Reformation officially destroyed saints' shrines and therefore the rationale of pilgrimage, hitting those towns whose livelihood had depended upon the trade. But early modern Britons travelled a great deal more than has been imagined. Sailors, boatmen, packhorse men, carters, soldiers, and shoals of migratory workers would be accustomed to moving around, and their numbers increased as the economy expanded and integrated in the period. Though most of this travel was for work rather than pleasure, it did not prevent those involved experiencing novel spatial sensations. A sailor who visited the Caribbean, or a servant girl who obtained seasonal employment in Bath, would grasp something of the special character of the place. Eric Hobsbawm has declared 'the story of nineteenth-century labour . . . one of movement and migration', and the desire to experience other places may have played at least a small part in this. The travelling harvesters who in the nineteenth century made the journey to London and back, some from as far away as Derbyshire, working in companies of young men, moving from job to job, and village to village, carrying their songs and dances with them, were tourists of a kind. The same might even be claimed of the Scottish fisher girls who decamped temporarily to Yarmouth to service the great annual herring fair in autumn.[6] However, limitations of time and wealth seriously restricted most working people's capacity before the late Victorian years to engage recreationally with 'other' space. Tourism as we now understand it requires full immersion in such space. This was pioneered by the well-off in the form of the Grand Tour and the spa and seaside 'vacation'. Over the long term, not only did the notion of the 'total holiday' away from home become available to a majority of the British population, but the volume and range of geographical destinations expanded enormously. Tourism became embedded in British leisure culture.[7]

In the tourist experience it is possible to identify four distinctive phases: planning and anticipation, travel, the holiday, and reintegration and recall. Presented in this way it constitutes a type of rite of passage.[8] This is reinforced by the linking of special holidays to key moments in the life-cycle: late adolescence – a favourite time for the Grand Tour and the modern transcontinental backpacking holiday; marriage and honeymoon; retirement; and wedding anniversaries. Of greater general importance has been the building of holidays into an annual seasonal cycle, during which everyday space is temporarily vacated. In practice this is overlaid by shorter-term breaks, though often taken to coincide with moments in the recreational calendar such as Christmas and Easter, but the principle of the regular need to visit other space remains the same. Planning can consume a considerable amount of time, adding to the anticipation. Critical is place programming, by which travel literature and imagery, including fictional accounts, are absorbed, so that the tourist *knows* the place of destination before arrival.

The journey can be as important as the holiday itself. In some cases travel is the *raison d'être* of the exercise. In the 1930s it is estimated that well over 150,000 Britons were enjoying the delights of the then newly fashionable pleasure cruise, a form of pastime in which travel and holidaying were inseparable.[9] The same is the case for the motor and coach tour, the cycling holiday, and even what is known as 'excursive walking', something that owes its origins to the Romantic poets.[10] Admittedly, practical considerations have often invested the journey with significance. Simply getting from London to Bath before 1680 took over 60 hours, and still consumed 36 hours in 1750, requiring overnight stops.[11] The Grand Tour was in another league. In order to make Rome by Christmas 1699, and traverse the 1,237 miles involved, the fifth Earl of Exeter and his entourage had to leave London three months earlier (25 September). Though time was taken out for sightseeing, the vast majority of the days involved a significant element of travelling.[12] Transcontinental tourism in the nineteenth and twentieth centuries added further distances, so that any visit was prefaced by a lengthy boat journey. Developments in transport have compressed time and space, but this should not lead us to imagine that the journey has become less important in the tourist experience. Its symbolic and psychological role has always been as critical as its real and practical one. Not only is it a rite of passage within a rite of passage, it also celebrates the *idea* of movement, and of unhindered mobility, that has become fundamental to the success of western economies and cultures. The air flight, as with the rail journey in the nineteenth century, might constitute only a small portion, in time, of the total holiday, but the rituals surrounding it, and the obvious tensions generated when technical problems occur, highlight its deeper meaning. The hijacking of two aircraft and their transformation into weapons of destruction for the attacks of 11 September was a way of turning one of the instruments and icons of western culture upon itself. The restrictions on recreational travel imposed by the tragedy threatened the 'apparently seamless harmony between liberal notions of freedom (of movement), cultural exchange, peace and prosperity' which the holiday journey and international tourism represent.[13]

The holiday itself, the third element in the tourist experience, is now defined by the notion of 'other' space. Today a vacation at home seems a contradiction in terms, though in pre-modern times home was where the majority of people, perforce, took their 'holidays'. However, it is arguable that the idea of the holiday as 'other' space can be exaggerated and is becoming increasingly anachronistic. Holidaymakers carry much of the baggage of their normal lives with them. This includes not only families and friends but in the case of late Victorian textile towns whole communities, which would shift *en bloc* to the same resort.[14] In reality, if not in the imagination, for most tourists adventure comes relatively low on the list of priorities when compared with comfort and familiarity. Seaside landladies, many themselves drawn originally from the towns of their clients, placed a premium on reproducing home comforts, and, far from seeking something different, visitors would often return to the same boarding house, year in, year out.[15] Today the plethora of pubs, fish-and-chip shops, and burger bars that fill the more popular Spanish resorts is testimony to the British holidaymaker's distaste for the unfamiliar. Moreover, it could be claimed that the notion of 'other' space is becoming less and less plausible. The separation of places of work and pleasure that fitted the needs of the developing industrial economy and labour force in the nineteenth century is less relevant in a post-industrial age. The 'de-differentiation of spaces and functions' is seen as a feature of postmodern tourism, in which, for example, people undertake work-based holidays, such as an archaeological dig or crewing a ship, and visit places of work, like a redundant industrial site or port, as part of heritage tourism.[16] Moreover, globalization, though it has opened up access to a huge variety of spaces, has by virtue of this eroded the differences between locations. Not only do multinational organizations import their branded products – one commentator has referred to 'the McDonaldisation of the world' – but it is now simply too easy for tourists, adopting real or virtual forms of travel, to flit from one part of the world to another. 'Time–space compression' has suppressed 'all sorts of differences between places', creating a planet of placelessness.[17]

Globalization offers a highly plausible framework in which to accommodate a wide range of recent trends. But it is a technology-driven concept, which assumes that developments in communications necessarily lead to a shrinking world and a flattening of space. In practice, differential access to technologies means that their impact will vary according to geographical location and categories like age, class, and ethnicity. Major cities and premier tourist sites become more connected while other spaces become relatively more isolated. The internet provides access to recreational hot spots across the globe, but this depends upon these locations having a website and the resources and inclination to invest in place promotion. Moreover, connectivity is not something new. Simple technologies such as the printing press, introduced in the fifteenth century, and postage – the first British public services date from the seventeenth century – allowed for considerable flows of spatial knowledge. Many among the early modern elite and middling orders were voracious letter writers. Visitors to eighteenth-century spas would send lengthy and regular missives compared with which the twentieth-century post-card pales into insignificance.[18] One consequence of this circulation of recreational knowledge was that long before globalization, spas, and then seaside resorts, pursued a policy of standardization, copying architectural forms, facilities, routines, and lifestyles.[19]

There is a risk of jumping from quantitative to qualitative judgements. There can, for example, be no crude correlation between a reduction in journey times and a diminution in the perception of spatial difference. If the tourist is prepared to conceive of space as different, whether it takes two hours or two weeks to reach a destination will not necessarily affect the experience. Nor *per se* will elements of familiarity. Tourism often involves mixing notions of home and away, the known providing a basis of security from which to engage with that which is different. The definition of difference has varied. For rural dwellers it might be the town. The prospect of visiting Stuart London, Georgian Dublin, and Regency Brighton would generate considerable excitement among those, especially women, immured for much of the year on a country estate.[20] For a later and more urbanized elite it was the prospect of abandoning London for the salmon rivers, deer parks, and grouse moors of the Scottish Highlands that would set the pulse racing.[21] For the urban working class it was exchanging the smoke, dirt, and noise of the industrial town and city for the clean air and water of the coastal resort that appealed.[22] In the twentieth century a release from the vagaries of northern European weather, the pull of the sun, and the exchange of white for brown bodies, proved a powerful allurement.

It would be wrong to conceive of otherness simply in environmental terms. Tourism and holidays provided the opportunity to engage in modes of behaviour not normally found in everyday life. Spas, seaside resorts, holiday camps, cruises, coach tours, and package holidays provided the context for intensely collective forms of social interaction, while in other types of tourism – though those involved would have probably called themselves 'travellers' rather than tourists[23] – like walking, backpacking, and motor touring, individuals or very small groups cut themselves free from society to pursue what they perceived as self-constructed, loner agendas. Some holidays were conceived as purposeful and educational, in others the focus was upon pleasure and hedonism. In the latter category conventions would be relaxed and even inverted to allow heightened levels of sexual anticipation and interaction. The Grand Tour and the London and Edinburgh seasons provided an opportunity for prostitution and sexual experimentation.[24] At the seaside 'the grotesque prurience of the comic postcard, the nudging innuendo of the down-market music hall and some kinds of end-of-pier show, the humorous sketches about landladies and lodgers, the stories of foreshore foreplay and sexual promiscuity current in pubs and workplaces' created a carnivalesque ambience.[25] On the beach and in the sea this was heightened by the loosening of many of the prevailing norms governing bodily exposure, posture, and clothing, though this did not go uncontested in the nineteenth and early twentieth centuries.[26] Sexual tourism, though it today conjures up lurid 'images of pot-bellied male European tourists to the Philippines and Thailand',[27] and drunken twenty-somethings engaged in rituals of corporate hedonism, builds on a broader and long-standing relationship between sexual libertinism and the otherness of the holiday.

The final phase of the tourist experience involves reintegration and recall. A return journey, invariably flat in comparison with the outward one, unpacking, and re-acquaintance with home and community are all part of the process of re-engaging with the familiar world. But the holiday does not end there. Most tourists will attempt to recall and review their holidays, reordering and re-evaluating their memories to filter out the mundane or unpleasant ones. This creates a resource that can be recalled throughout the year to counter low periods and provide an incentive to keep working until the next holiday. From the late nineteenth century the widespread availability of portable cameras and celluloid-based roll film provided the potential to create a personalized library of *aide-mémoires*,[28] and reviewing the holiday snapshots/ film/video has become a common post-holiday ritual. When this is done in conjunction with images obtained in previous years it becomes tantamount to an annual audit of how personal and family life has progressed. Tourists would also collect memorabilia to recall their travels. Drawings could be made, and for those with limited skills in this area equipment existed to trace something approximating to an accurate image. Indeed, it was Henry Fox Talbot's dissatisfaction with the results from using a *camera lucida* on the shores of Lake Como in 1833 that led him to engage in experiments which led to the British strand in the discovery of photography.[29] Those unable to draw could call upon the services of professional artists, and the printing press ensured that relatively cheap reproductions were engraved and printed. In the case of Bath, almost 500 views with some topographical content have been tracked down by David Ford for the period before 1830.[30] Some tourists gathered together prints collected on the Grand Tour and incorporated them into wall surface decoration to create a 'print room'.[31] Another recall mechanism was the physical souvenir. Already by the late seventeenth century the spa of Tunbridge Wells (Kent) was producing a special type of treen known as 'Tunbridge Ware', some of which contained marquetry inlays depicting local scenes. Sold from souvenir shops on the public walks this was the basis of a prolific local industry.[32] On a small scale the souvenir trade mimicked the acquisitive practices of those on the Grand Tour, for some of whom the exercise was first and foremost a shopping trip. Paintings, antique sculptures, intaglios, plaques, coloured marbles, and reproductions of antiquities would be assiduously assembled, often at huge expense, and shipped back home to fill the rooms and occasionally specially constructed galleries – as at Newby Hall, Yorkshire (1767–72), and Towneley Hall (*c*.1789) and Ince Blundell Hall (1802–10) in Lancashire – of town and country houses.[33] Homes in effect became memory banks, allowing collectors to luxuriate in the recollections of their travels. Even more importantly, the objects collected provided a spectacular means to show off, engaging in what became a widespread pastime, competitive tourism.

COUNTRY AND TOWN

The pursuit of 'other' recreational spaces is motivated largely by the search for environments different from that which a person occupies in normal life; substituting sun for rain, sea for land, and 'natural' for man-made landscapes. These are not simply or even primarily physical categories. All involve some element of cultural construction. This applies particularly to one of the key environmental dialectics of the past half-millennium, country and town.

Early modern Britain was a predominantly rural society, though as we shall see this was a far from static situation. Work and the festive/religious calendar were central features in determining the character of recreational life. Harvest, for example, was critical because it demanded the maximum labour input, which drew men, women, and children into the fields and focused the community's efforts on a single activity. This reduced the time available for formal leisure. However, engagement in a common enterprise, the high levels of earnings enjoyed, and the array of rituals associated with completion, prompted an explosion of post-harvest communal leisure.[34] The August grain harvest was a widespread but not universal phenomenon, particularly associated with the mixed economies of the lowlands. Other environments would support different crops with different periods of harvest, bark (March–April) and bracken (autumn) in the woodlands, peat (after May Day), lichen (summer) and rushes (late summer) in the moorlands, and sheep across upland areas.[35] Shearing day was the harvest equivalent for sheep, and according to Henry Bourne in 1725, 'is generally a time of mirth and joy, and more than ordinary hospitality . . . on the day they begin to sheer their sheep, they provide a plentiful dinner for the shearers, and for their friends who come to visit them on that occasion'. Llandysul in Cardiganshire also mounted a shepherds' feast (*ffest y bugeiliaid*) on 12 August when shepherds in the area gathered together on a hill top, paralleling practices in early August in the Brecon Beacons and the upper Swansea valley, and more commonly in Ireland, though there, associated with the opening of the cereal or potato harvest.[36] Shepherds led a very different life from that of cereal farmers and generated a different sort of recreational culture, more individual and less collective, depending more upon their own devices, such as playing solo musical instruments, but also needing to develop shared festivities 'in compensation for their lonely working life'.[37]

Agricultural regimes varied considerably across the British Isles. It must also be remembered that the countryside included craftsmen and industrial workers, and that the home itself constituted a site of work whose rhythms were not necessarily the same as those of the non-domestic economy. In these circumstances it is impossible to talk of a single rural pattern of leisure. What further complicates the position is the relational 'other' against which the countryside is defined: the town. The vast majority of pre-modern urban settlements were tiny. In the late seventeenth century over nine-tenths of the 1,000 towns in mainland Britain had populations of under 2,500 people, and two-thirds of under 1,000.[38] Though most of their inhabitants were engaged in non-agricultural occupations, there was a significant agrarian sector to their economies, and there was a constant flow of country people into and through the town. It was commonplace for country girls to obtain positions as servants in urban households and businesses, and virtually all villagers would make regular trips to towns for markets and commercial and hiring fairs. Many of the fairs were semi-recreational events, which was increasingly the case as trade was transacted through more permanent facilities like shops, and one of the functions of towns was to provide country people with entertainments.[39] For their part towns were only too willing to incorporate the rural world into their customs. Greenery was frequently introduced at points in the festive calendar, many features of which were common to town and country. Patrick Collinson has suggested that in sixteenth-century London 'the seasonal exits to the woods and fields to return with greenery and maypoles perhaps symbolized . . . the need to reconcile the teeming, crowded city

with the countryside'.[40] May Day, despite its controversial character for many puritans, was a celebration of the relationship
between the rural and urban spheres. In London from the mid-
seventeenth century there were special ceremonies mounted by
the milkmaids and later the chimney sweeps, shot through with
bucolic imagery. According to Joseph Strutt, the milkmaids
included a cow 'nearly covered with ribbons of various colours,
formed into bows and roses, and interspersed with green oaken
leaves and bunches of flowers', and the chimney sweeps had the
so-called Jack-in-the-Green, 'a hollow frame of wood, or wicker-
work . . . covered with green leaves and bunches of flowers inter-
woven with each other, so that the man within may be completely
concealed, who dances with his companions'.[41]

Charles Phythian-Adams has argued of the milkmaids' and
chimney sweeps' performances that 'what had originated in a
largely rural society ended up in London as a strictly limited ritual
dialogue between two separate urban "nations" '.[42] In Georgian
London a dialogue *between* town and country was being replaced
by one *within* the town. There had long existed a distinctive civic
culture, with a strong recreational input, directed in part towards
townspeople telling stories to townspeople.[43] None the less, there
was also a recognition that the events mounted would draw in
country people as observers, and that the town had a wider function to service the leisure needs of the majority rural population.
Over time, and in the bigger towns, this function began to alter.
Urban leisure became a more self-driven and autonomous phenomenon, but paradoxically one that also increasingly turned to
an idealized view of the countryside as a source of inspiration. This
reflected a profound process of economic and demographic
change under way throughout the early modern and modern
periods, which resulted in the reversal of the urban and rural
balance of society.

Urbanization has characterized the British Isles for most of the
half-millennium since 1500, and had dramatic long-term effects.
Measuring it, however, is fraught with difficulties. Table 1 shows

Table 1   Proportion of the population in settlements of over 10,000 people

	1500	1600	1700	1750	1800	1850	1890	1951
England and Wales	3.1	5.8	13.3	16.7	20.3	40.8	61.9	77.3
Scotland	1.6	3.0	5.3	9.2	17.3	32.0	50.3	60.2
Ireland	0	0	3.4	5.0	7.0	10.2	17.6	36.9
Brit.Isles	2.0	4.2	9.4	12.3	15.6	32.5	55.0	72.4
Europe	5.6	7.6	9.2	9.5	10.0	16.7	29.0	

calculations for the proportion of the population of the various parts of the British Isles living in settlements of over 10,000 people between *c*.1500 and 1951.[44]

The statistics demonstrate the long-term trend that transformed the British Isles from a predominantly rural to a predominantly urban society, and the variations in change between the different parts of the British Isles, notably Ireland and mainland Britain. Widening the perspective, it is important to emphasize Britain's position as the most dynamic urban society for the eighteenth and much of the nineteenth century in Europe (and possibly the world). These figures are crude and, in some respects, misleading; 10,000 is far too large a figure to provide a demographic delineator of a premodern town. Using definitions more related to the standards of the time, perhaps as many as a fifth of the population of England lived in towns in the late medieval period, and a third or more by 1700.[45] However 10,000 is too small to detect the tendency of people to congregate in large-scale urban settlements and conurbations, noticeable (see Table 2[46]) from the second half of the nineteenth century. It was a trend that 'was not only a matter of scale', but also introduced 'qualitative changes which, *in toto*, were transforming city life'.[47]

Demographic urbanization was accompanied by a series of other processes. The balance of economic output, to the extent that it is possible to apportion it between rural and urban sectors, switched from country to town. Industrialization, from the later eighteenth

Table 2 Proportion of the population in cities of over 100,000 and 500,000 people*

	1800	1851	1871	1891	1911	1951
England	10.7	24.9	32.6	39.5	43.8	52.7
and Wales	(10.7)	(13.9)	(19.3)	(19.5)	(19.6)	(39.6)
Scotland	0	19.9	27.3	34.4	37.4	37.6
	(0)	(0)	(16.7)	(19)	(21.7)	(21.4)
Ireland	3.6	3.8	7.8	10.6	15.8	26.1
	(0)	(0)	(0)	(0)	(0)	(13.3)

* Numbers in parentheses are for cities over 500,000 people

century focused increasingly on the town, was a crucial factor in this process, alongside the marginalization of agriculture from the later Victorian period as foreign imports of cheap food began to flood in. The effect on the countryside was to prove dramatic. From being by far the dominant zone of production in the early modern period, by the twentieth century – in mainland Britain if not in Ireland – it was being driven increasingly to the fringes of the 'productive' economy. Urbanization also shifted the balance of power between town and country. Though the rural elite, who had been the pre-eminent if not exclusive political force in pre-modern Britain, were remarkably successful at retaining the levers of power in the eighteenth and nineteenth centuries, control of the local and national state shifted remorselessly towards largely urban-based elites.[48] It was here, in the long term, that decisions about leisure and the recreational use of space were to rest.

The impact of urbanization and the broad processes that accompanied it, on leisure and space are complex. For the seventeenth and much of the eighteenth century there is evidence of fashionable urban and especially metropolitan culture rising in kudos. To link this directly to urban growth would be too simplistic. However, it cannot be disconnected from the remarkable expansion of London, from an important but not top-tier European city in 1450 of about 40,000 inhabitants, to the leading city in western Europe by 1700 with 500,000 people, and one of the three leading cities in the world by 1800 with almost a million souls.[49] The metropolitan centres of Britain became engines of cultural innovation and power in fields such as architecture, music, theatre, publishing, and gardening.[50] They were aided by a Europe-wide development, evident during both the Renaissance and the Enlightenment, which emphasized the Classical past and the virtues of civility and politeness, all of which were seen to be rooted in city life. This was accompanied by an element of anti-rural satire, such as was conveyed in the influential issues of the London-based journals the *Tatler* and *Spectator* (1709–12), which portrayed country culture as boorish and backward.[51] Urbanism became chic among the ruling order, many of whom set up lavish establishments in the metropolitan centres, often living in the newly created urban units of classical terraces, squares, and crescents.[52] However, the elite retained deep roots in the countryside. Landed property remained the most important source and symbol of wealth, status, and power, and this was reflected in the heavy investment in country houses and estates, and the lifestyle that emanated from them.

The social elite were therefore a culturally amphibious group. Though town living became more fashionable and comfortable, this did not necessarily lead to a diminution in the status of country living. Moreover, beneath the surface of change a dialectical process was under way. As urbanization bit deeper and deeper, and as, in the long term, the economic and political importance of the countryside declined, so paradoxically rural living and culture became more and more valued.[53] This reflected the pursuit of the 'other' evident in tourism, in this case energized by a powerful sense of nostalgia for a world that seemed to be vanishing and appeared to embody the virtues of a traditional society. This demand came primarily from within urban society itself, or those who made heavy use of towns. The outcome was the construction of a leisure culture that looked towards nature and the countryside for its inspiration, but since it derived from the town, was fundamentally urban in character.[54]

It is arguable that the pre-modern custom of bringing greenery into the town was in part motivated by a sense of rural loss, particularly in the capital. However, the 'greening of the town' also took on a more formalized character, with the emergence from the early seventeenth century in the case of London, and rather later in the provinces, of formal public walks and gardens. By the mid-eighteenth century most towns of any pretensions sported some form of public promenade. Invariably lined with trees, often located on the edge of the town, close to a river, and possessing a fine prospect of the surrounding countryside, walks drew nature into the town.[55] This effect was reinforced by the growing number of commercial pleasure gardens in the larger towns – the great London ones, such as Vauxhall and Ranelagh, were effectively theme parks – and a rising interest at the time in domestic gardening, underpinned by a commercial sector of nurserymen and professional gardeners and a proliferating body of floral societies and competitions.[56] The public parks movement of the nineteenth century built on these developments. It was financed by a mixture of private philanthropy and public monies, and was driven by an anxiety about the impact of rapid urban expansion on the working class and the perceived need to create symbols of civic progress. 'In many ways the most substantial achievement of the rational recreationists', the provision of parks intruded nature into the city to compensate for the damaging environmental and social effects of urbanization.[57] Domestic gardening has proved to be one of the pivotal pastimes of the modern town dweller. In the mid-1960s it was the second most popular recreation, after television, among males (the fifth among women and the highest of any outdoor pastimes), with 80 per cent of homes in Britain possessing gardens.[58]

One way that the town embraced the countryside was to appropriate some of its activities. Football appears since medieval times to have had strong urban associations,[59] but cricket emerged in the early eighteenth century as an essentially country pastime. However, the late eighteenth and early nineteenth century saw, with the formation of the Marylebone Cricket Club in 1787, 'the transfer of the game's centre of gravity from rural England to London'.[60] It was not just a question of the capital's influence, since at the time, towns such as Birmingham, Leeds, Nottingham, and Sheffield, in the industrial areas, were also beginning to establish teams, a sign of developments that in the nineteenth century were to reinforce cricket's urban base and lead, for example, to the emergence of competitive league cricket in the English North and Midlands, based upon industrial towns and villages.[61] Cricket in South Wales may have begun in the 1780s in the bucolic surroundings of Court Henry Down in the lower Towy Valley but teams from fashionable towns in the south-east were prominent in the early years of the game, and from the late 1840s the growth points for the sport were the coastal towns – Cardiff, Newport, Neath, Swansea, and Llanelli – while during the 1850s and 1860s new clubs were being established in the 'booming industrial valleys of Glamorgan and Monmouthshire'.[62]

Despite the urban input the *image* of cricket has remained rural, and when musing on the game it is the village green rather than the town recreation ground that springs to mind. This reflects the townsman's desire to retain the country profile of the sport. The same may be argued of horse racing, which possesses a strong rural image, but since its origins in the early sixteenth century has been based around towns. Almost all the Scottish meetings were held in royal burghs, and about three-quarters of recorded courses in England in the early modern period were located in market towns. The latter proportion strengthened during the development of the sport in the eighteenth century, as a mixture of growth and rationalization urbanized and modernized racing's infrastructure.[63] It is likely that the rationalization of racing in the later nineteenth century, after the introduction of enclosed courses in 1875, had a similar effect. Roger Munting has argued of steeplechasing in the half-century before the First World War, that it 'certainly retained links with the hunting world and "rural England" but that rural setting was increasingly penetrated by urban society.

The major racecourses for National Hunt racing were suburban rather than cross country courses.'[64]

A proto-suburbia had begun to emerge in London from at least the late seventeenth century, with villas that were designed to be a pocket-sized version of the elite country house. According to Carl Estabrook, such developments did not impinge on the provincial town until the mid-eighteenth century; moreover, he emphasizes that when the number of suburbanites began to grow, their objective 'was not to insulate themselves within rural surroundings; their aim was to make the rural retreats an extension of their urban world', promoting 'the merger of urban and rural social spheres in an entirely new context'.[65] Suburbia became the quintessential locale of the middle class in the nineteenth and twentieth centuries, as its members fled the centre of the town, their traditional home in the pre-modern period, for the urban periphery. The marginal space between town and country was systematically reconceptualized and reconstructed.[66] In the early modern period it was the poor who tended to occupy the extra-mural suburbs, together with insalubrious industrial processes, and the urban edge would be the location of substantial tracts of common land, much of it heath, moor, and woodland, often interspersed with 'rough' hamlets and settlements beyond the immediate control of the urban authorities.[67] The remodelling of this marginal zone could lead to short-term conflicts – often over access to economic, and sometimes recreational resources – between the indigenous population and town leaders, as in the 'battle' for Mousehold Heath in mid-Victorian Norwich, but the long-term incorporation of the space involved into the urban sphere was unstoppable.[68] However, though suburbia was *urban* space it was fundamental to its meaning that it conveyed the impression of being *rural*. Greenery became bound inextricably into the notion of the suburb, with the extensive planting of trees and shrubs, and domestic gardens *de rigueur*. So pervasive was this horticultural influence that 'the contribution of the British' to the town-planning movement that emerged in the late nineteenth century was the idea, pioneered by

Ebenezer Howard, of the 'garden city'.[69] In addition to gardening, from the late Victorian era inhabitants of suburban estates developed and institutionalized a range of recreations – such as lawn tennis, croquet, golf, bowls, and rowing – which exploited the semi-rural environment and possessed a strong green profile.[70] Today a recreational event and lush suburban location like Wimbledon – all summer, strawberries, and lawns – embodies the pastoral paradox, by which an urban civilization defines itself in terms of its antithesis.

Where the suburb ends and the countryside begins is a moot point. It is an issue which exercised the minds of rural campaigners and town planners in the twentieth century, haunted by the prospect of urban sprawl, and led to the introduction of the concept of the 'green belt'. First legislated for in the case of London in 1938, it aimed at arresting ribbon development and protecting the rural environment.[71] However, the policy was not designed to prevent the *recreational* penetration of the countryside by townspeople. Long-term economic changes in agriculture encouraged the conversion of the rural world from a productive to a recreational resource.[72] The open air movement, which flourished in the inter-war years (the Youth Hostel Association was founded in 1930, the Ramblers' Association in 1935), was based on walking,[73] but developments in transport technology made the countryside far more accessible. It was the 'railway revolution' which linked the cities to the major hunting meets and greatly increased the size of fields.[74] Rambling clubs, antiquarian societies, and field clubs made regular use of the rail system for their rural excursions, branch lines extending deep into the countryside by the time the system reached its zenith, with over 20,000 miles of track in the years before the First World War.[75] In June 1889, for example, 50 or so members of the Woolhope Club occupied a special carriage for the journey from Hereford to their destination, Newland in the Forest of Dean, and the Great Western Railway ran a special train from Monmouth to enable members to catch evening trains home from Hereford.[76]

Cycling became a major pastime in the late nineteenth century, with the formation of the National Cyclists' Union and the Cyclists' Touring Club (CTC) in 1878. It provided its devotees with a highly flexible mode of transport with which to explore the nooks and crannies of the rural districts surrounding their towns. The introduction of motorized transport took this flexibility one step further for those able to afford it, and may be one factor accounting for the temporary decline in the fad for cycling (membership of the CTC dropped from a heady 60,000 to around 15,000 by 1914).[77] Not only did the automobile mitigate the problems of physical incapacity and the weather, and provide ample space to carry refreshments, it also offered a high degree of control over the time, duration, location, and range of trips undertaken. The car was the perfect instrument with which to explore the hidden secrets of rural Britain. All this was reinforced by a growing torrent of maps and guide literature, which reached a first peak in the 1930s. David Matless has claimed that 'if one book can be credited as establishing a motoring pastoral genre it is H. V. Morton's 1927 *In Search of England*, which by 1939 had reached 26 editions, and early on observes that 'The village that symbolizes England sleeps in the sub-consciousness of many a townsman.'[78] Literature of this type enabled the urban visitor to the countryside to conceptualize and navigate the new, old world they journeyed into.

Many of the 'imagined' countrysides were effectively created in the late nineteenth century as urbanization deepened and became more concentrated,[79] and most were in striking distance of large urban concentrations. Those living in London, for example, had Epping Forest, Box Hill, and the Sussex Weald, those in Birmingham the Forest of Arden and Shakespeareland, and both could enjoy the Cotswolds. But the British Isles possessed its remoter countrysides. The creation of Britain had involved the incorporation into the English core of huge swathes of 'wild' areas; the Scottish Highlands, much of Wales and Ireland, not to mention also great tracts of the north of England. During the early modern period these were perceived as uncivilized territories stocked by a simple and uncouth peoples. In 1799 James Plumptre, a young clergyman from Essex, complained of the Scots, 'their language at times unintelligible to me . . . the accommodations were at the best indifferent, and often dirty. . . . I was exposed to continual extortions', and described the inhabitants of Glen Falloch as 'savages'.[80] Plumptre was engaged in a walking tour, and his very decision to explore the mountains and lochs of the Highlands, whatever prejudices he may have brought with him, reflects the fact that from the later eighteenth century, under the influence of the picturesque and romantic movements, the 'peripheral' areas of the British Isles began to be re-conceived. Mountains and moorlands, valued increasingly as the repositories of a natural world whose kudos was rising, were no longer simply a nuisance and danger, something inhibiting movement between towns and centres of civilized living. They became the focus rather than marginalia of guide literature. Romanticism was a European movement, but it is hard not to see it in Britain's case as a reaction to the gathering forces of urbanization and industrialization. Much industry was located in the upland zone, and there was a tendency among early travellers to see furnaces, forges, mines, and mountains equally as manifestations of the sublime. However, as industry migrated into towns and its damaging environmental effects became more discernible, so it lost its romantic appeal.[81]

Already by the late eighteenth century there is evidence of an anti-urbanism emerging among the aristocracy and gentry, building on a persistent if not dominant early modern tradition that stressed the corrupting influences of the town, and especially London. The landed elite began to withdraw from contact with towns, though interaction with the metropolitan centres remained essential.[82] One aspect of this rural tendency was for landowners to re-landscape their country estates to appear more 'natural', a movement already evident from the mid-eighteenth century in the work of Capability Brown, operating from his extraordinarily successful London-based gardening practice, and intensifying with the rise of the picturesque movement at the end of the century.[83] A key theorists of the latter was Richard Payne Knight, and a close neighbour of his in Herefordshire, Thomas Johnes, took the process of withdrawal one step further by transforming an estate (Hafod) he had inherited in the remote uplands of Cardiganshire, into a picturesque paradise, planting perhaps three or four million trees between his arrival in the 1780s and his death in 1816. Johnes also consciously encouraged tourism, improving the road system and establishing a hotel at the suitably dramatic site of nearby Devil's Bridge, while a guide book was also published for the gardens.[84] This became one of the multiplying areas of the British periphery being modelled – through works of fiction, guidebooks, paintings, prints, and investment in tourist infrastructure – into areas of romantic tourism, including Snowdonia in Wales, the Wye Valley on the border of Wales and England, the Lake District and the Peak District in England, the Scottish Borders and Highlands, and the Lakes of Killarney in Ireland. New pastimes, like rambling and mountaineering, and old ones, like hunting, shooting, and fishing, geared to the recreational potential of these 'wildernesses', were developed.[85]

In the early nineteenth century Wordsworth deemed the Lake District 'a sort of national property, in which every man has a right and interest who has an eye to perceive and a heart to enjoy'.[86] The notion that certain areas were super-charged with untainted nature, that these areas constituted a national resource which had to be preserved, and that there was a close relationship between nature and national identity, was re-drawing the mental map of Britain. Symbiotic but separate zones of nature and mechanism, recreation and production, preservation and progress, stasis and change, beauty and ugliness, were being created. Geographical space was being cut and parcelled up in a quite new way, linked, directly or indirectly, to urbanization and industrialization. The establishment of organizations like the National Trust (1895) and the Council for the Preservation of Rural England (1926) reinforced this process and culminated in the legislation of 1949 that led to the establishment of a National Parks Commission, and the formation of ten national parks by the mid-1950s, covering 9 per cent of the area of England and Wales (Scotland was excluded from the Commission, presumably because so much of the country was considered 'wild' that there was felt to be less need to protect it). Located exclusively in the upland zone of Britain, they demonstrated the extent to which mountain and moorland had become the symbols *par excellence* of wild nature, the ultimate retreat from the town.[87]

There is one final dimension to the process of urban escape, the rise of the watering-place.[88] Though there was a long popular tradition of visiting magical and sacred wells and springs, the Reformation had undermined this in Protestant Britain and opened the way, from the late sixteenth century, for the secular development of springs, on an up-market commercial basis. Health was and remained a very important function of these places, until at least the early twentieth century, but pleasure was also a part of the package, a point that became obvious as spas proliferated in the later Stuart period. By the mid-eighteenth century they were joined by the seaside resort. Most spas and resorts had an underlying urbane character to their culture; but many, especially in the early stages of their development, were very tiny, often little more than villages or hamlets. Almost all exploited their rural location – even the metropolitan spas such as Islington and Hampstead were originally situated in the rural penumbra of the capital – and cultivated a pastoral strand in their make-up, with walks, pleasure gardens, parks, and forms of residential architecture which embraced the natural environs. In the seaside resort the fashionable crescent and terrace would usually be perched on a cliff-top location, contrasting with the cottages of the fishermen, which turned their backs to the shore, seeking protection from the elements. This reconfiguration of marine architecture and landscape reflected a transformation in how the sea was perceived. From being something destructive and demonic, to be feared and avoided, it became, under the influence of the picturesque and romantic movements, creative and sacred, an object to contemplate, immerse oneself in, and celebrate.[89]

Thus it was that when British townspeople turned to nature, as an antidote to urban living, they sought out not only the countryside, mountains, and moorland, but also the sea, of which, given the island geography of the British Isles, there was a bountiful and easily accessible supply. The twin foci of land and sea, both equally redolent of nature – and since the late eighteenth century giving rise to equally powerful traditions of landscape painting that moulded perceptions of these forms[90] – gave urban Britons a choice of where to locate their natural worlds and pursue their recreations. Selecting one environment has not necessarily involved rejecting the other. Most resorts back on to areas of rural beauty and some to mountainous zones, and touring holidays were easily capable of merging coastal and inland sites. None the less, Britons since early times have had a real choice where to head for when escaping the city and this has complicated and enriched both the practice and meaning of leisure. By and large a visit to the mountains and moorlands is likely to be a more individualist experience, one to the seaside a more collective one; and the land, challenged by the appeal of the sea, has never been allowed to acquire that centrality in recreational culture and national consciousness that it has in parts of land-locked central and eastern Europe.

8

TIME

Just as leisure is both defined by and defines space, so it is also determined by and determines the nature of time. For humans to function effectively there is every reason to treat time as a given; an objective and inflexible phenomenon. How would it be possible to play a football match if there was no absolute measure of when the game started and finished? However, though powerful boundaries are set by natural phenomena – night and day, the phases of the moon, the seasonal cycle – time is a fluid category. Maureen Perkins has argued that 'The nature of time is not simply "there", waiting to be discovered. It is a component of cultural communication. . . . Each society formulates its own understandings of different kinds of temporality,' and John Urry has emphasized that 'the category of time is not natural but social'.[1] This chapter will argue not only that time is defined in different ways within different societies at different periods, but also that within any given society different conceptions of time co-exist and compete. The second section will tackle this issue by discussing typologies of time. The third section deals with time not as something which passes, but as something which has passed; time as memory and recreative past. The chapter will begin with the more prosaic aspect of simply having time for leisure.

TIME, WORK, AND LEISURE

As we saw in the Introduction, leisure is frequently defined as activities undertaken in 'free' or 'unobligated' time. When these terms are unpicked, what is meant by 'free' is usually 'time free from work'. This seems commonsense. Work is our principal occupation and obligation since it is the means by which we live. The opportunity for leisure, therefore, is directly related to the volume of work that we have to do and the time that this takes. Leisure takes place in the time that is left over. The key factor in understanding the relationship between time and leisure is, therefore, work. Broadly speaking the view has been taken, though the statistics are difficult to establish, that industrialization initially increased working hours and squeezed the time available for leisure. Thereafter the story is one of a slow but steady reduction in work time, with a diminished total number of hours worked and growing opportunities for time off, due to improved weekend breaks – the introduction of the Saturday half-holiday, and a reduction in Sabbatarian influences – and increased public holidays and extended periods of vacation, eventually supported by pay. Hugh Cunningham has suggested that by the mid-eighteenth century a working day of 6 a.m. to 6 p.m., with two hours for lunch, was the norm in most industries, a reduction compared with the position in the seventeenth century; by the early nineteenth century the situation had deteriorated, with the norm in textile factories being 6 a.m. to 7 p.m. or 8 p.m., with an hour for meals; from the 1840s/1850s the trend is again towards a reduction in hours, with gains concentrated in three periods, the early 1870s, 1919–20, and 1946–9.[2] In their study of leisure (1951) Rowntree and Lavers concluded that 'the general situation in this century has been that a larger and larger number of people have enjoyed a steadily rising standard of living, while, at the same time, their normal period of leisure has increased by ten or more hours a week'.[3] Though this may be a little optimistic, across a sample of towns and industries there appears to have been a reduction in mean 'normal' weekly hours from 57 in 1870/1 to 45 in 1950.[4] Twenty years later the figure for manual workers had dropped to 40, though this reflects 'normal' rather than actual hours (46) worked.[5] The long-term decline may have been reversed thereafter, with claims that by the end of the millennium over a quarter of male employees were working more than 48 hours a week, that 44 per cent of British workers came home exhausted, that 'Right across society there is a sense of time being squeezed', and that the period saw the emergence of a 'harried leisure class'.[6]

It is difficult to evaluate this sort of data. The problems in establishing the statistics, and above all in calculating some sort of 'norm' that smoothes over variations in occupation, region, class, and gender, become even severer the further back we explore. We are told that 'working hours were generally long' in early modern England, and cases are cited of artisans undertaking 13- to 18-hour days, but so many variables and complexities come into play that an overall assessment of the length of the working day/week/year is deeply problematic.[7] Underemployment was widespread. The majority of eighteenth-century male farm labourers, for example, were engaged on contracts that fell well short of the entire year, and were hired sometimes simply on a seasonal basis.[8] In theory, underemployment and unemployment provided more time for leisure, but, given the limited resources of the individuals involved, the reality was likely to have been very different, as it was in the 1920 and 1930s. However, it may be that the time–work–leisure equation, critical as aspects of it are, is misconceived. It cannot be assumed that work constitutes the primary human activity, and that leisure simply picks up the crumbs of time left over. Recreation is also a necessary form of behaviour, capable of demanding and receiving a portion of a person's time. Michael Thompson has written of one of the worrying paradoxes that face historians of the early nineteenth century:

> Yet the time when the life of the labouring classes was being portrayed as one of unremitting toil was also the time when there

were loud denunciations of the undesirable and vicious habits of the poor at play, and strenuous efforts to steer workers' recreations into approved and rational courses. . . . The explanation of this is that hours of work were never so long, so continuous, or so regular as the employers might have wished or the opponents of the exploitation of labour might make out by portraying peak-period workloads as the workaday norm.'[9]

Workers, willy-nilly, would carve out leisure time, however restrictive the structure of work that surrounded them – and in all probability this did tighten up during the course of the Industrial Revolution – because recreation was fundamental to the way they conceived of and ran their lives.

It should also be remembered that there were other calls on time than simply work and leisure, of which sleep and eating are the most obvious, which provided scope for varying the volume of leisure time. Moreover, the distinction between work and leisure – even if it has become sharper in the last two centuries – remains a blurred one. Middle-class managers and professionals may work long hours, but within these are often embedded semi-recreational phases, for example, dining with colleagues or entertaining a client.[10] Housewives and domestic servants would frequently clock up a daunting working day, 'on call' for the majority of their waking hours, but they would engineer their timetable to include periods of semi-relaxation – for example, sewing, embroidery, and playing with the children – or snatch a moment of conversation with fellow workers, friends, and neighbours.[11] Often such strategies involved engaging in work and leisure simultaneously. In the 1660s Thomas Baskerville observed how Suffolk women 'go spinning up and down the way . . . with a rock and a distaff in their hands, so that if a comparison were to be made between the ploughman and good wives of these parts, their lives were the more pleasant, for they can go with their work to good company, and the poor ploughman must do his work alone', and saw in Gloucestershire, 'many women of the older sort smoking their pipes of tobacco and yet lost no time, for their fingers were all the while busy at knitting'.[12] Today women are likely to combine watching television or listening to the radio with domestic tasks.

TYPOLOGIES OF TIME

A more fruitful avenue of investigation than viewing leisure time simply as the obverse of work time is to think in terms of typologies of time. In a classic study of changing patterns of work during the Industrial Revolution, Edward Thompson drew a distinction between task-oriented and clock time.[13] In the former, time was determined by the task or job in hand. Since the pace of much pre-industrial (especially agricultural) work was highly irregular in character, varying according to the vagaries of the weather and seasons, so the perception of time was uneven. In contrast to this, clocks represented a form of time in which every moment was of equal duration. Delivered by a machine, clock time was the medium of mechanization. Fostered by the widespread adoption of clocks and watches, it became a key tool in the training and disciplining of the expanding factory workforce. However, it is an open question how far the adoption of clock time can be linked to industrialization, and to what extent it is possible to talk of a transformation in attitudes to time at this period. As Thompson was well aware, clocks (not to mention bells that tolled the hours) had been placed in churches and town halls in England and Scotland since the late medieval period,[14] and must to some degree have regulated working and commercial behaviour. In the sixteenth century Bishop James Pilkington, while criticizing the work habits of the labourer, suggested that notions of clock time were already rooted in popular consciousness, and being turned to the worker's advantage: 'At noon he must have his sleeping time, then his bever in the afternoon, which spendeth a great part of the day; and when his hour cometh at night, at the first stroke of the clock he casteth down his tools, leaveth his work, in what need or care soever the work standeth.'[15] Rather than conceiving of a dramatic switch from task to clock time it is more plausible to think of the two operating in tandem over a long period. Indeed, even today both types of time co-exist in the workplace, and task time can predominate in the case of certain types of occupation. Students, for example, engage in intensive bursts of work close to essay deadlines and exams, followed by phases of relaxation, pursuing a pattern of work and displaying an attitude to time very similar to that of Thompson's handloom weaver and artisan.[16]

None the less, it is still arguable that the *relative* influence of task time declined, and, with a growth in time-pieces, that of clock time increased, especially in the towns, during the eighteenth and nineteenth centuries.[17] Other historians have argued for a shift of a similar sort in the significance of one type of time over another. Robert Poole sees an older 'natural time' and a new 'Newtonian' or mathematical time in competition during the eighteenth century, with the latter dominant among the educated classes in England by the middle of the century. Maureen Perkins contends that there was a 'reform of time' in the nineteenth century, with the displacement of a pessimistic and fatalistic notion of time, based on magic and superstition, by one that was optimistic and progressive. John Sommerville sees a similar process of change as early as the Reformation, with a movement away from a religious, ritualistic, and repetitive idea of time to a secular one in which moments were more even and moved in an 'irreversible direction'.[18] There is certainly some evidence that clock time exerted considerable influence on the timing and organization of elite leisure in the Georgian period. *The New Bath Guide* of 1809 included among the regulations for the Upper Assembly Rooms one requiring 'That the Dress and Fancy balls shall begin as soon as possible after seven o'clock, and conclude precisely at eleven, even in the middle of a dance.' In the 1740s John Wood's guide to the spa included an extensive daily itinerary, in which it is clear that at particular moments in the day the company moved *en bloc* from one event to another. Though generally Wood fails to give a precise time as to when these changeovers occur, he does record that 'the Balls begin at six o'Clock, and end at Eleven;

nor will the King of Bath [Beau Nash, the Master of Ceremonies] suffer them to continue a Moment longer'.[19] The explosion in printed information during the eighteenth century advertising public entertainments – guidebooks, bills, and especially newspapers – provided a potentially powerful medium for inculcating clock time. The need for an extrinsic temporal framework was in part driven by the fact that as pastimes became more public and commercial, so the circle of those who might attend would expand, and there would be less 'in-built' knowledge about social chronology. This would be particularly so on the case of the larger spas, which would be drawing visitors from a wide geographical area.

Precise times were not always included in Georgian advertisements. The crucial point is the extent of information needed by those expected to participate. This raises a more fundamental issue. Was clock time being more widely publicized for pragmatic reasons, so as to organize an expanding and increasingly anonymous market; or because there were qualities inherent to clock time that represented a shift in cultural attitudes? The evidence is difficult to interpret. Failure of a source to specify a starting or finishing time does not necessarily mean that there was no temporal framework. It is implausible to imagine that there was not some understanding about when, for example, a bull baiting or a football match started, even if the records fail to mention this. Broad 'natural' markers such as dawn, early morning, noon, and afternoon might be used, along with human-based referents such as 'after Sunday afternoon prayers' (1672), and 'after the conclusion of the service' (1822).[20] But these were inexact. Given the availability of clock time throughout the early modern period it is likely that there was a growing resort to it where this proved advantageous. Precise times existed by the Georgian period for the start of the famous Derby football match (2 p.m.) and the Stamford Bull Running (11 a.m.).[21] Once an event was under way it was not always or even generally necessary to have a pre-set finishing time; horse races would be determined by the length of the race, cockfights by the death of a bird. Carew's account of hurling in Tudor Cornwall shows that the match was completed when a 'goal' was scored, and this also appears to be so in the Derby football match.[22] In such cases task time ruled. This is different from a modern sporting contest, where strict temporal limits operate. Anybody watching a contemporary football match will be acutely aware of the passage of minutes and even seconds. Players will be substituted according to the time left to play, or to waste an extra few minutes, and serious disputes can arise over the precise moment at which a match finishes. In these circumstances it can be argued that clock time doesn't just provide the frame within which an event takes place, but is part of the very event itself, determining the strategies employed by those involved.

The shift from task to clock, natural to Newtonian, cyclical to progressive time in leisure can be seen as part of a wider process of modernization by which new attitudes to time, critical to the efficient operation of a commercializing, industrializing, and urbanizing society, were inculcated in the population. The draconian rule books which early factory employers like Josiah Wedgwood and Ambrose Crowley felt it necessary to deploy to counter the prevalence of traditional attitudes to time became less of a requirement as workers internalized the new approaches.[23] But we should be cautious about taking the thesis of modernization too far. As has already been noted, clock time was available throughout the early modern period, and task time continued to be a significant feature of leisure in the modern era. Sports like tennis, golf, and snooker have few time restrictions as such, but are allowed to unfold according to the task in hand. Clock time is an important part of modern cricket, but (restricted matches apart) the game is permitted to follow a remarkably protracted timetable that bears little relation to the demands of the workplace. Natural events such as the weather and the state of the light play a critical part in the game, as they do in golf, horse racing, and fishing. Looking at modern sport one might be inclined to belief it was designed to reflect the 'natural' order, and create an 'other' time zone than that in which industry and business operate.

Soccer and rugby, however, appear to make the opposite case. In their modern version, compressed from the rambling spaces and chronologies they occupied in pre-industrial times into the tight confines of the city stadium and the $2 \times 40/45$ minutes timetable, they seem shaped to service the needs of an urban industrial civilization. However, the way that time is *experienced* by players and spectators is anything but Newtonian. Each moment of time varies hugely, not least according to the affiliations of those involved. During the climactic final phase of a game, assuming that the outcome still hangs in the balance, then for the team in a winning position minutes will seem to drag interminably, while for those losing, the moments will fly by. Time in this sense is highly variable. In truth, the game is being played in a double time frame, in which neither clock nor task time are predominant, but both complement each other. It is the existence of an 'objective' regulatory framework, including rules of time, which ensures that those engaged in the event have a common understanding of what is happening. However, this framework also creates the context in which varying individual and collective perceptions of time, a result of the differing tasks in hand, can flourish.

One distinction which is often made between traditional and modern notions of time is that between cyclical and linear time. The former is associated with the pre-modern world, and put crudely, the argument is that our ancestors advanced only slowly because they were locked into ideas of time, particularly associated with the 'stations of the sun', in which life simply repeated itself. Modern concepts of time, however, look continuously to the future; there is no notion of return, only of an endless sequence of forward movements. This is taken to be the engine that drives economic and social progress. In the pre-modern world the principal temporal vehicle for carrying recreations was the festive or customary calendar, with cyclical occasions such as Christmas (*y Gwiliau* in Wales), New Year, Shrovetide (Fastern's E'en in Scotland), Easter, May Day (Beltane in Scotland, Bealtaine in Ireland, *Calan Haf* in Wales), Whitsuntide, Midsummer (Johnsmas in Scotland),

Harvest, and Hallowe'en (31 October) or Samhain (1 November, the first day of the Celtic year in Ireland and Scotland, *Calan Gaef* in Wales).[24] Embedded in this were events specific to a particular community, such as fairs and wakes (parish feasts, *gwylmabsant* in Wales). Cyclical in character, the calendar combined seasonal, secular, and religious elements.[25] Charles Phythian-Adams has suggested that there were sacred and secular halves to the year, divided at Christmas and Midsummer, and argued that the Reformation in mainland Britain instituted 'the modernization of . . . [the] late medieval framework . . . characterized by the triumph of the secular half over its ritualistic counterpart, as, one after another, the principal ceremonies vanished'.[26] Though the Reformation did not strip the calendar entirely of its religious associations, its impact reminds us that the annual cycle of festivities was not a static phenomenon, but one constantly being re-fashioned under the impact of changing economic and political circumstances. Nor was it a universal one, with different places and regions establishing their own version of it, not least because the Reformation affected Britain in different ways.

The traditional festive calendar no longer plays the primary role that it did in the organization of leisure in early modern society. The agricultural economy which underpinned it has lost its dominant influence. None the less, the festive calendar and the cyclical notion of time that it embodies did not vanish with the coming of the modern age, but demonstrated remarkable staying power, not least in urban industrial communities[27] (though it must be remembered that there is always the problem as to whether the practice under consideration is a continuous custom or a revival). 'Whitsuntide celebrations were observed in almost every town and settlement in south Wales throughout the second half of the nineteenth century,' with the mounting of special fêtes, fairs, excursions, and parades. Walks were an important feature of Whitsuntide events in early twentieth-century Manchester and Salford, where May Day was also celebrated with parades and maypoles, and in Bolton children went pace-egging on Good Friday.[28] Wakes in

Lancashire showed a remarkable persistence, sustained rather than undermined by rapid economic change, benefiting from extra participants, rising incomes, and the opportunities developments in transport provided to draw in revellers from outside. In August 1860 one correspondent reported, 'It being Oldham Wakes there will be no working on Monday. . . . There is an omnibus leaves Manchester at 10 a.m., but it will be crowded with people going to Oldham Wakes, so that I should prefer the railway.' Richard Hoggart remembers a lively customary calendar in pre-Second World War Leeds, 'Pancake Tuesday, Voting Day, which is always a holiday, Hot-cross buns on Good Friday, the Autumn "Feast", Mischief Night, and all the weeks of cadging and collecting for Bonfire Night'. Ronald Hutton, at the end of his monumental survey of *The Stations of the Sun* (1996), concludes, 'When all is said, a vigorous seasonal festive culture survives and continues to develop among the British.' But, he argues, it is a culture that has changed from the one operating in the early modern world: 'The ritual calendar . . . is becoming a celebration of . . . the individual lifecycle. Humanity has come to replace the natural world at the centre of the wheel of the year.'[29]

The festive calendar has never been a static phenomenon. After the Reformation a sea-change occurred in its character. Protestants, particularly among its more committed devotees, were hostile to its late medieval form, seeing it as a repository for Catholic superstitions.[30] Pressure was exerted to suppress elements of it, not only openly Catholic festivals like Corpus Christi and saints' days, but also occasions such as May Day and Christmas. In Scotland, Yule or Christmas felt the full force of the Kirk and was eventually sidelined, except in parts of the Highlands and Islands, and effectively replaced by New Year celebrations. In England, during the Puritan 'cultural revolution' of the later 1640s and 1650s, when royal government was displaced, Christmas, along with Easter, Whitsun, and all 'holy-days' were abolished, and replaced with a Puritan calendar, which included both secular and religious holidays based on days of fasting, humiliation, and thanksgiving.[31] Though such radical changes generated considerable resentment and opposition, and were rescinded at the Restoration, they do highlight the emergence in the early modern period of a new type of Protestant calendar, which throughout much of Britain came to replace the older Catholic one. Traditional festivals were not necessarily abandoned. In the long run, Christmas (outside Scotland) and Easter survived remarkably well. John Golby and William Purdue have argued that between the Restoration and the early nineteenth century 'there was a waning of Christmas', but then it underwent a dramatic 'reinvention' under the Victorians, a revival felt equally in nonconformist Wales and Anglican England, to achieve the pivotal, if largely secular role that it now plays.[32] However, the new calendar was not simply a reshaping of the old one. The emphasis shifted from the Catholic to the Protestant, the sacred to the secular, the 'magical' to the 'rational', and the naturally determined to the man-made event. Patrick Collinson has observed that in the late sixteenth and early seventeenth century, 'out of the detritus of remnants of the old pastimes, there emerged in the towns a new slimmed-down, secular and increasingly civic-cum-martial festive culture', and this emphasizes the importance of celebrations and commemorations associated with the local and national state – such as mayor-making, the Fifth of November, military victories, and royal birthdays – in determining the 'festive' points in the new Protestant calendar.[33] In Ireland a rather different version of the Protestant calendar emerged during the eighteenth century, with celebrations of William III's birthday (4 November), the battles of the Boyne (1 July 1690) and Aughrim (12 July 1691), and from the 1820s the Apprentice Boys' celebrations (12 August, 18 December). For the Catholic community such a calendar understandably had limited appeal, and was countered by one that included St Patrick's Day (17 March), the Easter Rising (24 April 1916), and the Catholic festival of the Assumption of the Virgin Mary (15 August).[34]

The Protestant calendar may be very different from its Catholic predecessor, but it was still a calendar. It still measured time in a cyclical way. There may be linear and progressive elements. New dates were regularly being added as political circumstances changed, and there was a sense of an unfolding Protestant destiny. But older features were retained and the annual cycle remained the organizing principle. The same can be said of the new calendar that emerged to govern the recreational life of the elite. During the late Stuart and Georgian periods there was constructed a polite calendar which accommodated and organized the expanding range of fashionable entertainments available to the ruling order. It was based on a twelve-month cycle, and within this the fundamental division was the 'season'; a winter phase residing in or visiting a fashionable town, and a summer phase spent in the countryside or visiting a watering-place. The bifurcation of the year can be seen in the way over four-fifths of the assemblies in early Georgian York, the social capital of the North, were packed into the months October to April, whereas race meetings largely took place between April and October, and cricket matches from May to September.[35] Building a recreational calendar around the idea of the seasons reflected the continuing importance of natural elements to elite leisured life; not only in a pragmatic sense – being based in town eased the problems of travelling to events in the winter – but also because retaining a connection with 'nature' became important to the ruling order's perception of itself. The polite calendar evolved in the nineteenth century into something on a larger, more formalized and integrated scale, leading Leonore Davidoff to argue that by the 1870s, 'the calendar of events for a national Society with its blend of rural and urban pursuits was almost complete'.[36]

Various elements of the Victorian and Edwardian 'season' continued to exert an influence in the twentieth century – The Boat Race (established 1829, in April), the Lord's Cricket Test, Royal Ascot (in June), Wimbledon (inaugurated 1877, in June), Henley Royal Regatta (inaugurated 1839, first week in July), Cowes Week (early August), the Glorious Twelfth (August, start of the grouse shooting season) – and were integrated into a British 'national' recreational calendar that embraced more popular events like the Grand National (April) and the Cup Final (May). Sport dominated, providing the majority of iconic events, but occasions like the Last Night of the Proms, Glastonbury, the Eurovision Song Contest, and Children in Need could be added, as new festivals were invented and others were quietly dropped. The notion of a single 'national' calendar is problematic, both historically and contemporaneously, with the different parts of the British Isles possessing their own takes on the turning year. Indeed, in a general sense it might be better to think in terms of recreational calendars in the plural, with different forms of leisure and different ethnic, gender, religious, and regional constituencies developing their own versions. The signs of this were already present in post-Reformation Britain, with the decline in religious uniformity, but the pluralist character of modern society has accentuated it. None the less, most recreational calendars possess a strong ritualistic, cyclical, and seasonal character.[37] Even the most commercialized of modern sports, soccer, still operates to an annual cycle that is at least nominally seasonal.

Until relatively recently, and with the rearrangement of matches to dovetail with television schedules, soccer was indelibly associated with Saturday afternoon. For those hooked on the sport this was the high-point of the weekly recreational cycle, a moment of explosive psychic tension and release, but also of comforting familiarity as a whole range of petty rituals were repeated, such as the pre-match purchase of fish and chips. In Barrow-in-Furness, midday on Saturday was one of the peak moments of demand in the local chip shops, as men called in on the way to the afternoon's football or rugby league match.[38] The Saturday afternoon half-holiday emerged in the industrial towns, though at variable rates, from the 1840s. Cast publicly as a philanthropic gesture on the part of employers, one of its principal functions was to undermine the credibility of St Monday. This was a widespread weekly 'holiday' that many artisans, particularly those who were better paid, took of their own volition, and was an assertion both of the workers' leisure preference and their independence. For some, depending upon how much alcohol was consumed, it also crept over into St Tuesday. The Saturday half-holiday was used as bait to woo workers away from this unofficial, and from the employer's point of view disruptive and wasteful, break.[39] Saturday had been one of the days least likely to accommodate sport; now it became the most popular.[40] Moreover, the effect spread beyond physical recreation. Saturday evening became a peak time for attending the music hall, cinema, and the Palais de Dance, and crowds of 15,000 to 20,000 were said to have congregated at the Saturday evening Shude Hill Market in Manchester, established in 1870.[41]

It took some time to eradicate St Monday – fishing competitions were still being arranged in Sheffield on a Monday up until the First World War [42] – but the eventual success of the policy had the effect of creating one of the central planks of the modern recreational calendar, the weekend break. Sunday was an important part of this package given its traditional role as a day of rest. The Puritan drive to elevate the significance of the Sabbath, and to keep it free of all human activity other than spiritual exercises, dated back to the Reformation era, and seriously constrained its recreational use. However, that pressure also protected Sunday from work and therefore enhanced its potential for leisure.[43] The impact of Sabbatarianism varied across our period. Bills promoting its aims were regularly introduced into Parliament in the seventeenth century, though most failed to reach the statute book or were heavily amended.[44] The growth of evangelicalism hardened attitudes.[45] The Sunday Observance Act of 1780 imposed serious restrictions by preventing entertainment venues from charging, and the Lord's Day Observance Society (founded 1831) sought to influence legislation and bring individual prosecutions. But the Society's support was always limited – four bills it inspired in the 1830s failed to make the statute books – and during the late Victorian period Sabbatarianism was a fading force. Inexorably if slowly – as late as 1901 the London County Council banned Sunday football, and the Football Association's ban on professional football was only lifted in 1981 – Saturday and Sunday merged to create the recreational weekend.[46]

The weekend's existence was always something of a chimera. To service the leisure of some people others had to work. The arrival of Friday night did not signal a hiatus in domestic duties, the majority of which were carried out by women, or for caring for animals, the burden of which fell on farmers, and for many people, such as pensioners, the weekend break was rendered relatively meaningless by the fact that they worked part time or not at all. None the less, the Saturday to Sunday package – iconicized in Karl Reisz's film *Saturday Night and Sunday Morning* (1960) – became embedded in the national culture, and represented a major re-orientation of the recreational calendar. In effect it was the trade off for dropping most of the irregular and fluid holidays that filled the traditional festive calendar. It was a bargain between employers and employees, in which the former obtained consistency and concentration of work and the latter a guarantee of leisure. However, important as this change was, it did not represent a move from task to clock, repetitive to linear, or ritual to rational time. The week is a form of cyclical time, and the recreational weekend is layered with a myriad of rituals, such as the weekly worship at the temples of sport, and binge shopping and drinking, that are fundamental to its meaning. Clothes shops pipe in different music to signal the arrival of Saturday, 'brighter, funkier' sound, 'more up-tempo music when . . . people [young women] are shopping for outfits for that evening'. In fact, as Tia DeNora has shown, 'some of the stores also use music to mark seasonal changes and events', such as St Valentine's Day and Christmas, an affirmation of the persistence of the festive calendar and cyclical time at the heart of a commercial society.[47]

MEMORY AND THE RECREATIVE PAST

Cycles are about historical time. They are about remembering what has happened in the past and regularly repeating it. Memory, individual and collective, is fundamental to this process and to leisure. This is not to argue that change is not also a central feature, but to give that change meaning, to give it a framework against which to operate, elements of continuity are also critical. Peter Burke argues that 'folksong and folktales, popular plays and popular prints all need to be seen as combinations of elementary forms, permutations of elements which are more or less ready-made'.[48] Opportunities for contemporary variations are endless, but the repetitive character of folk genres is fundamental.[49] The appreciation of music depends upon complex processes of memory, recalling themes, motifs, and forms internal and external to a piece. Audiences do not enter a gig or concert with an 'innocent ear', but are expected to bring with them an extensive library of musical experiences. Once a piece is under way it builds up its own internal memories through repetition and variation of forms and themes. The same applies to a sporting contest. Much of the meaning of the event derives from what has happened in the past. Some of this is drawn from relatively recent events: how a player, team, or animal performed in their last match. Gambling on the football pools and animal contests depends upon close knowledge of recent performance. In the case of horse racing, information on breeding history and lineage is also important. Knowledge of the careers and personal lives of sports, music, film, and TV stars is critical to building their heroic persona. Longer-term memories are also vital. They have, for example, underpinned the performances of every Manchester United side since the Munich air crash of 1958, which killed many of the side – a clock, showing the date and precise time of the tragedy, stands as a memorial outside the ground – and has been seen by some as creating a mythology that contributed to the club's super-team status. In Welsh rugby, recollections of the 1905 victory over the New Zealand All Blacks will always colour contests between the two sides, as will the 1966 soccer World Cup final England's matches with Germany.[50] Even after an event has started, memory plays its part. Tony Mason has emphasized that 'Football matches are like a story. They have a beginning, a middle and an end.'[51] Each sporting occasion has an internal history – a breathtaking try, a snooker ball missed, a dubious LBW decision, a foul committed – which is re-played and constantly re-fashioned in the mind of player, spectator, and commentator alike, determining the action and perception of the game even as it unfolds. And once all is over there are the endless post-match analyses, creating a mental record of the occasion, and integrating this into the long-term history of the sport. As a poem of 1773 observed, after a curling match:

> The *bonspiel* o'er, hungry and cold, they hie
> To the next ale-house, when the game is play'd
> Again, and yet again, over the jug;
> Until some hoary hero, haply he
> Whose sage direction won the doubtful day,
> To his attentive juniors tedious talks
> Of former times; – of many a *bonspiel* gain'd,
> Against opposing parishes; and *shots*,
> To human likelihood secure, yet storm'd:
> With liquor on the table, he pourtrays
> The situation of each stone. Convinc'd
> Of the superior skill, all join, and hail
> Their grandsires steadier, and of surer hand.[52]

For the veteran curler, remembering past achievements was a patently enjoyable experience. Perusing the past has proved to be one of the most pleasurable and popular pastimes of all. Today, the commodification and consumption of time has become an industry and entertainment in itself. However, an interest in the past is not a new phenomenon. From the very start of the early modern period in England there was an elite interest in antiquarianism that was closely tied to landscape and material culture. The Reformation and its wholesale destruction or remodelling of the Catholic medieval church raised awareness of the native religious fabric, and the potential for and actuality of loss. John Leland, appointed 'King's Antiquary' in 1533, and often called 'the first English topographer', injected a touristic element into antiquarian studies with his travels around the country to search the records in monastic, cathedral, and college libraries, in the process making extensive notes on what he saw. However, attitudes to the religious medieval and therefore Catholic heritage were deeply ambivalent. When the first volume of William Dugdale's *Monasticon Anglicanum* appeared in 1655 it was seen by some as a 'covert plea for the revival of Catholicism'.[53] Quite apart from deliberate destruction and desecration for doctrinaire reasons, much of the fabric from the religious houses and shrines was simply left to crumble and decay, where it was not plundered for building materials. Except in the case of a narrow group of scholars and gentlemen, it is arguable that it was not until the perceived threat from a return to Catholicism was lifted, and that was probably not until after the second Jacobite rebellion of 1745, that the recreational potential of Gothic religious architecture could be unlocked.

The problem, however, was not simply one of religion. The medieval period in general was looked upon with disdain, as an era of backwardness and barbarity. As Rosemary Sweet has written, 'Eighteenth-century attitudes to the middle ages were complex, shifting and ambivalent, but the most straightforward reaction was one of distaste. The assumed barbarity of the middle ages acted as a foil to the polite and commercial society of eighteenth-century Britain.'[54] Not that the British were uninterested in recreational contact with the past, but this was largely a Classical and European past. The Grand Tour was, in theory, as much a journey in time as in space, an opportunity to enjoy close encounters with ancient Classical civilizations. How much this was *perceived* as a journey in time is difficult to say. Whilst it is true that illustrations of antiquities, such as those produced by Giovanni Batista Piranesi (1720–78) of Rome, which were widely bought by British travellers, contain elements of decay and nostalgia,[55] it is likely that tourists from Britain saw the remains not as images of the past but as models of modernity, to be replicated in their own building plans. Indeed, the Grand Tour was as much about viewing the Renaissance and the recent Classical heritage – about the 'modern' buildings of Paris and Rome – as it was about that the survivals of antiquity. The same focus on the contemporary could also be argued for the generality of early eighteenth-century travellers who toured around Britain. Daniel Defoe, in his popular guide, *A Tour Through the Whole Island of Great Britain* (1724–6), openly declared, 'I studiously avoid meddling with antiquity in these accounts, studying to give you the present state of the countries and towns through which I travel.'[56]

The 'popularisation' of antiquarianism in the late eighteenth century through 'the proliferation of printed media' and the broadening of subject matter and content, was indicative of a deepening and widening thirst for the past.[57] It coincided, as we have seen, with the revival of interest in folk idioms and historic national cultures in Britain as a whole, and the broader movements towards Romanticism and the discovery of nature. Investing the past and nature with a new significance, and fusing the two together, created an amalgam of time and space that was catalysed by the input of nationalist sentiments, and was to have considerable long-term implications. The revival of interest in Gothicism and the medieval period, traceable back at least to the mid-eighteenth century, broke the Classical hegemony and greatly expanded the material, particularly native heritage, that could be explored.[58] By the 1820s, and Walter Scott's novels *The Abbot* (1820) and *Kenilworth* (1821), the periodic threshold of what constituted heritage was being further stretched to include the first part of the early modern period, the so-called 'Olden Time', a period loosely located in the Tudor and early Stuart years. This not only increased the volume of heritage available, but also introduced a form of the past that was not ruinated and religiose, but intact, occupied, if only nominally, and unequivocally secular. Survivals of this type appealed particularly to the popular market, where people bought cheap fiction and prints depicting the colourful life of old

England, and engaged in what Peter Mandler has called 'the first age of mass visiting' of country houses.[59]

By the 1870s this first age was beginning to wane, as owners, facing economic and social pressures, closed, mothballed, or, in search of greater privacy, restricted access to their properties. But, as Paul Readman has argued, this did not signal a declining recreational interest in the past.[60] It was the late Victorian period which saw the full fusion of the three forces of history, nature, and nationalism. This added to the earlier wildernesses, such as the Lake District and the Scottish Border Country, a further tier of imagined countrysides, generally smaller in scale, more homely, and more accessible to the cities, like the Cotswolds, the Norfolk Broads, Poppyland, Shakespeareland, Boar's Hill, the Malverns, and Wessex. An artist, composer, or particularly a literary figure was usually crucial in shaping the character of these new Arcadia; for example, William Morris and J. Arthur Gibbs in the case of the Cotswolds, A. E. Housman in that of Wenlock Edge and Shropshire, Clement Scott in Poppyland (Norfolk), A. A. Milne in Ashdown Forest (Sussex), and Thomas Hardy (1840–1928) in Wessex.[61] Topography was fundamental to Hardy's literary work. It was the landscape as much as the characters which carried the meaning of his writing. Operating on the boundary between real and invented places, he re-cast the mental topography of a portion of Dorset, transforming it for tourists into what was effectively a literary theme park. Devotees of the author were already making pilgrimages to the area in the 1890s – the last of the major novels, *Jude the Obscure*, first began to appear in 1894 – and in 1905, to meet their needs, Herman Lea, a bicycling and automobile companion of Hardy, published with the latter's permission, *A Handbook to the Wessex Country of Thomas Hardy's Novels and Poems*. It was the beginning of a minor industry. In the following year B. C. A. Windle produced *The Wessex of Thomas Hardy*, introduced with the comment that 'Mr Hardy has annexed unto himself a small . . . stretch of country, and has steadily, in novel after novel, proceeded to people it with a new population . . . he has resuscitated, one even may say re-created, the old half-forgotten kingdom of Wessex.'[62]

The 're-creation' of a historic location reminds us that though these areas were predominantly rural they were also perceived to be 'old', repositories of what was felt to be by this period a rapidly disappearing national past.[63] In the late nineteenth century this past, as the choice of Wessex suggests, was primarily Roman, medieval, and 'Olden Time'. This was the historical bread and butter of the county antiquarian societies, and it was medieval, Tudor, and Jacobean properties that filled the early pages of *Country Life*, published from 1897.[64] Interest in the eighteenth century was beginning to stir, but it was not until the inter-war period that the Georgian era began to be woven properly into the national historic fabric.[65] The fashionable and elitist Georgian Group was only founded in 1938, and up until the Second World War a town such as Ludlow, despite its predominantly Georgian appearance, was primarily portrayed in guide literature as medieval and Tudor.[66] Though the rural and the historic were closely allied, it was perfectly possible to include towns in the notion of the past so long as they fitted the definition of that past and were not too engulfed in the trappings of modernity. Their credentials as historic centres were also strengthened if they were located within the newly invented countrysides, and could be perceived as 'country towns', and used as a (comfortable) base camp from which to explore the surrounding areas.

Bath was hardly a simple country town, but it did provide a touring base for the Cotswolds and the West Country. Moreover, it possessed a rich heritage of its own, Roman and Georgian, which it exploited in the twentieth century to offset the decline of its function as a spa and health centre. The years after the Second World War saw the destruction of several swathes of 'minor' eighteenth-century architecture in the city, what was later dubbed 'The Sack of Bath', in the interests of modernizing the landscape.[67] It was a process replicated in many towns at the time, as in the post-war era the past had to compete with a surge of enthusiasm for change. There was no necessary contradiction between the two. As was clear from at least the eighteenth century onwards, it was the very embracing of change that stimulated a counter and compensatory passion for the past. None the less, promoting the future and preserving the past were always likely to produce conflicts of interest, and in the 1950s and 1960s it was the future which tended to hold the upper hand.

By the 1970s a powerful reaction had set in, and, as in the late nineteenth century, there were cries of horror at the prospect of a vanishing heritage. At the same time the commodification of the past was ratcheted up to a new level to service an ever deepening market, and a bewildering range of areas of recreative consumption developed, not only tourism, but 'authentic'-style classical music, tribute bands, antique collecting, popular history and archaeology, not to mention shopping, increasingly accommodated in neo-Tudor and neo-Georgian shopping malls. Indoor and outdoor museums proliferated, as did high-tech historical attractions and theme parks, such as the Oxford Story, Yorvik (York), Celtica (Machynlleth), the Canterbury Tales, the Tales of Robin Hood (Nottingham), Camelot (Lancashire), and A Day at the Wells (Tunbridge Wells, Kent). By the 1990s the geographer David Lowenthal could claim, 'all at once heritage is everywhere . . . the whole world is lauding – or lamenting – some past, be it fact or fiction', the historian Stefan Collini could refer to 'the explosion of interest in recent decades in what can only be called "pastifying" ', and the archaeologist Peter Fowler could speculate, 'I doubt if anyone before this moment can have been subject to quite so much "pastness" as there is around now *and be so aware of it*'.[68] Nothing was more telling than the remarkable growth in the National Trust, from a quarter of a million members in 1970, to two million by 1990.[69] A critical factor behind the Trust's spiralling appeal was the emergence of the second age of mass visiting of country houses. This began in the 1950s, as more and more properties were opened to the public, but surged forward during the latter decades of the century as, in the 1980s, 'country-house mania' swept the nation.[70] Even a cursory glance at the maps in the National Trust handbook will reveal the concentration of properties in the south-east, the Home Counties, and in proximity to urban centres. Each house – and it is likely now to be as much the historic garden as the historic architecture that attracts the visitor – constitutes a time capsule into which those who inhabit Britain's urban conurbations can retreat temporarily. Each is a concentrated point of the past, embedded within the wider imagined countrysides and wildernesses established over three centuries.

9

CONCLUSION

'A BIT OTT?'

After 11 September 2001 we were told nothing would be the same again. As I complete this conclusion in summer 2005, less than a year after the re-election of the incumbent President for a second term, that seems a dubious conclusion. We were also told that the enormity of the events put everything into perspective. In particular the event drew a clear line between what mattered and what did not, between the real world of politics, religion, war, and human tragedy, and the 'glorious irrelevance' that constituted sport. Whether such a line really exists was doubtful at the time, and the writing of this book has made me even more sceptical. Visiting the USA for a conference on the future of social history on the eve of the 2004 Presidential election, during the climax of the electioneering, brought the matter home to me forcibly. Nobody at the conference was in any doubt that this was the most important election for decades and that the electorate was more politicized than at any point in recent history. Yet more than competing for attention with the Bush–Kerry contest in the talk around the conference bars was the recent victory of the Boston Red Sox over the New York Yankees, and the prospect of victory for the former in the curiously named World Series. What was striking was not only the passion aroused by the subject, but also the role, in this most technologically advanced and progressive of societies, of myth, memory, and magic. The Red Sox, 'baseball's perennial losers, reputedly cursed for almost a century by the misguided sale of the game's greatest player' (the fabled 'Babe' Ruth, to the Yankees, who subsequently won the World Series 26 times, while their Boston rivals failed to lift the trophy once), had now laid to rest the ghost, 'the curse of the Bambino', that haunted them. The victory that duly arrived in the World Series prompted a deeply nostalgic piece from the British-born historian and Red Sox supporter Simon Schama, concluding with the comment, 'now you know why I was up to 4am on Thursday morning watching every last pitch of the game with St Louis online; now you can measure the combination of ecstatic disbelief and narcotic jubilation coursing through my veins as our ace closer Keith Foulke made the last out. A bit OTT? Absolutely not . . .'.[1]

If there is a simple conclusion from this book it is that leisure matters and that it cannot be separated from the forces that drive the 'real' world. None the less, it remains central to the paradox that gives leisure its meaning and function that while being *of* the real world it should be *outside* it. That it should *appear* irrelevant. Operating at one remove from life, leisure allows emotions to be aroused and played with – Schama's 'ecstatic disbelief and narcotic jubilation' spring to mind – that would be inappropriate and simply too dangerous for the real world. Play, along with symbol and the 'other', are the three concepts used in the Introduction to define leisure. These will be returned to later. What is important is to have a workable definition of leisure that establishes its separate identity relative to other categories of human behaviour, and allows its special character, role, and significance to be assessed over a long period of time. The Introduction suggested six possible phases in the development of leisure since 1500. However, there should be no assumptions as to the timing or extent of change, or as to whether it predominated over the forces of continuity. These matters will be addressed in the following section. The approach adopted in this study has been largely a thematic as opposed to a chronological one. In part this reflects the limited volume of secondary literature directed specifically at the history of leisure in the pre-modern period, and the patchy nature of coverage of different aspects of leisure in general. But it also recognizes the pressing need to focus on analysis rather than description, themes rather than narrative; and above all, the importance of probing many of the assumptions that underpin the history of leisure, even if this does no more than raise further questions.

CONTINUITY AND CHANGE

By and large I have adopted a sceptical approach to assumptions of change and chronology. Historians have a professional interest in finding change since this helps to define and justify their mode of investigation. Moreover, within society at large there is the profoundly influential myth of progress. From a leisure perspective the book has challenged the notion of a 'great divide' at the time of the Industrial Revolution. It has posed the question: If historians are finding commercialization and a rising middle class at every period in the past, how viable are the concepts and the chronologies based upon them? Further, it has queried whether there was ever a time when there was no time: or, to be more specific, whether there was any period since the late middle ages when clock time was not a significant part of most people's lives. It has also suggested that task and cyclical time are still important elements in contemporary society.

However, it is no part of the agenda of this book to deny that change, and major change, have occurred over the last 500 years. It is perfectly credible to argue that clock time plays a much larger part in people's lives in 2000 than it did in 1500, and that the balance between clock and task time has changed. It would be difficult not to agree that the volume of commercialized leisure has expanded enormously over the period, though it is important to recognize that this was a phased process, and it remains an open question as to the extent to which the *proportion* of commercialized to non-commercialized leisure has changed. It is quite plausible to argue that proportionally the middle class is larger now than in the past, and that there have been periods when it has been more or less pleasure-orientated. It seems likely that a specific formulation of the working class emerged with rapid industrialization and urbanization in the late eighteenth century, and then declined with the changing character and overall erosion of the manufacturing sector in the mid-twentieth century. It is implausible to argue that the landed elite any longer hold the proportion of wealth, or wield the level of political and social influence that they did, say, in the seventeenth or even nineteenth centuries; but that is not to say that an upper order or class does not continue to exist. It seems likely that men's engagement with dancing declined in the eighteenth century, as did women's access to sport in the early nineteenth century, in the latter case only recovering for middle-class women in the late nineteenth century and then generally on very unequal terms. Over the 500-year period in question there have been enormous changes in the political configuration of what we now call Britain, and leisure has contributed to and reflected the shifting character of the pieces which constitute the national jigsaw. Southern Ireland's de-coupling from the British project was anticipated and reinforced by the formation of the Gaelic Athletic Association in 1884, and the development of a sporting agenda defined in specifically Irish-Celtic terms; on the other hand, Scotland's integration into the project can be seen in the evolution of the Highland recreational industry and the commercial and psychological investment from the late nineteenth century in soccer, though on the basis of a separate association. Perhaps the most sweeping changes identified in this book have been brought about by urbanization and industrialization. The shift from a predominantly rural and agrarian society to one overwhelmingly urban and industrial cannot be ignored, and resulted in a major re-orientation in the recreational perception and use of space, associated, for example, with the rise of the holiday away from home, and the creation of imagined wildernesses and countrysides.

Urbanization and industrialization return us to the problem of periodization. Both were very long-term processes, but both kicked in more dramatically at some point in the eighteenth or nineteenth century. Does this return us then to the 'great divide'? The Introduction suggested tentatively, in respect of leisure, something more nuanced – the existence of six phases of change between 1500 and 2000: 1350–1530, 1530–1660, 1660–1780, 1780–1870, 1870–1960, and 1960 to the present day. Each phase merges rather than abruptly transforms into the other, and may make little sense for particular forms of leisure. The scheme is proposed to counter the charge of being nihilistically a-historical and to offer at least a framework for debate. But some may argue that this is too fragmented. That there is/are a grander divide(s) to be discovered if we look and theorize hard enough. The Industrial Revolution used to be conceived of as such a watershed. However, that concept and the associated periodization have become unfashionable because of its associations with Marxism, class, and the notion that material change drives the cultural superstructure. What has been sought for, instead, is something within the superstructure itself; a cultural, as opposed to an economic driver. Chris Rojek has identified three basic 'social formations': capitalism, modernity, and postmodernity. These are social formations and not chronological phases, and it would seem that to some degree all three run concurrently. None the less, it is clear that a sort of time sequence is at the very least implied. Modernity is divided into Modernity 1 and Modernity 2, and the former 'refers to the general transformation of personality, economy and society which has its roots in the Renaissance and the Enlightenment but which crystallized with the industrial revolution'. That would give us dates for the genesis of Modernity 1 of somewhere between the fourteenth century (the origins of the Renaissance), the late seventeenth to early eighteenth century (the Enlightenment), and the late eighteenth to early nineteenth century (the Industrial Revolution). With its emphasis upon 'the disorder of things', the rise of the department store and the *flâneur*, Modernity 2 emerges in the late nineteenth century, whereas the transition to postmodernity, 'a generalized change in social conditions' which includes 'the collapse of the division between high (elite) and low (mass) culture; the replacement of a teleological view of history with a view that stresses discontinuity', would seem, in Rojek's anlaysis, to date from around the 1960s or 1970s.[2] Richard Giulianotti identifies three stages in the trajectory of football, the traditional or pre-modern, the modern, and the post-modern, the first lasting at least until the First World War, the second divided into early (early 1920s–45), intermediate (1945–early 1960s), and late modern (early 1960s–late 1980s), and the final stage running from 1990.[3] John Urry has written that 'Although there is much dispute about when the modern period began (the scientific revolutions of the sixteenth and seventeenth centuries, or the "enlightenment" of the eighteenth century, or the modern urban– industrial civilisation of the nineteenth century), it is widely agreed that modern societies are strikingly different from traditional or pre-modern societies.' Urry also introduces a contemporary postmodernist phase of 'de-differentiation', to contrast with the 'process of differentiation' which characterized modernism.[4]

It is clear from these three accounts by sociologists of leisure not only that there is limited consensus as to when the various phases began, though there is a broad agreement that postmodernism emerges in the late twentieth century, but also that chronology is not the principal concern. This may frustrate historians, but the riposte would be that it is social and cultural formations and processes that matter, and that overemphasis upon *when* change occurred deflects from adequate theorizing about *what* changes happened, and *why*. Moreover it could be argued that the disagreement about the timing of transition from one phase to another simply reflects the fact that there are no dramatic moments of transition, and that the seeds of one social form lie in another. None the less, there is a clearly articulated and agreed series of stages here, and one that it is temporally sequential; pre-modern, modern, and post-modern. And in this sequence the notion of 'great divides' is present; the one, occurring at some point between the fourteenth and nineteenth centuries, marking the transition from the pre-modern to the modern, the other, occurring at some point in the late twentieth century, the transition from modern to post-modern. The notion of three stages, and two great divides, is curiously reminiscent of the now unfashionable Marxist sequence of feudalism, capitalism, and communism. And just as that economically driven sequence proved stimulating but unsatisfactory as a meta-narrative, so the new, culturally driven model leaves doubts. It is not simply the imprecision over when the first great divide happened, nor the idea that the second great divide of the millennium should coincide providentially with the age in which contemporary academics live, but also the very notion of the 'great divide', that is disturbing. To what extent is it plausible to categorize the range of recreational experience in Britain between 1500 and 2000 in terms of three distinct social or cultural forms? Though three are identified, in practice it is the modern one which dominates, since it is this which is the one against which the other two are defined. Can all that happened before the modern be adequately swept into the bag labelled 'pre-modern'? Will all that transpires after the modern be encompassed by the post-modern? And, if a new social formation appears, what possibly can it be called?

SYMBOL, PLAY, AND 'OTHER'

It seems unlikely to this author that the basic mental and physical faculties that control how human beings sense the world and operate within it have changed over the last five centuries, though it is acknowledged that over many millennia of evolution such transformations have occurred. It is the element of continuity that provides the template upon which processes of change are played out. Continuity in the case of leisure was provided by the three elements that lie at the heart of its meaning: symbol, play, and 'other'. The human need for these three elements, and for their combination in a mode of activity called 'leisure', remains constant. Most forms of behaviour are to some degree symbolic, but it is the *intensity* of the symbolism that is crucial in the context of leisure. The anthropologist Victor Turner has argued that 'in a Ndembu ritual context, almost every article used, every gesture employed . . . every unit of space and time, by convention stands for something other than itself',[5] and it is the extent of the parallelism, and richness and complexity of the representation, that characterizes leisure. Many recreations, for example, involve journeys through space or time that can be seen to parallel journeys at work or through the human life-cycle. David Hamilton has written of golf, 'The links had from the start their "fairways" – the fisherman's term for a safe passage. Golf was a serious journey out and back, as unpleasant but rewarding as the winter deep-sea fishing of the towns. It was a voyage out and back in rough weather, and full of hazard.'[6] Much of the pleasure of recreational walking lies in the way that it captures in microcosm – with its mixture of rough and smooth terrain, its beginning, middle, and end, moments of tiredness and exhilaraton, and decisions over which route to follow – the larger journey through life. En route, forms in the landscape can be invested with human sentiments, such as national identity, awe, ruggedness, and beauty. Elements of racing, chasing, hunting, and fighting are present in many board and computer games, and the 'symbolic power relations' manifested during play tend, in Pierre Bourdieu's words, 'to reproduce and to reinforce the power relations which constitute the structure of social space'.[7] A medieval board game like merrills, of which there were many variants, such as fox and geese, just as much as modern games like Monopoly or Scrabble, can be fiercely competed over, allowing the participants to mimic wider conflicts for power and status in families and social groups. The same can be argued for hunting and horse racing. In both cases animals are used to stand in for human beings and are often, in the process, anthropomorphized, as in Richard Carew's account of a Tudor fox hunt:

> and if he [master Reignard] be so met as he find himself overmatched, he abideth and biddeth them [the hounds] battle . . . manfully closing at hand-blows with the sword of his teeth, not forgetting yet the whiles to make an honourable retreat with his face still turned towards the enemy; by which means, having once recovered his fortress, he then gives the *fico* [a vulgar gesture] to all that his adversaries can by siege, force, mine, sword, assault, or famine, attempt against him.[8]

Within leisure, symbolic acts invariably include a theatrical ingredient. Agents and observers are engaged in a *performance*. As Bill Murray argues, 'Football might not have the same emotional tensions generated by an operatic tenor or the depth of feeling of a soliloquy by Shakespeare, but it has its own dramatic tensions in a performance where the script is not written in advance, and comes to an unpredictable end only when the final whistle blows.'[9] In the case of leisure the histrionic takes the form of play, or as Clifford Geertz characterizes it in his investigation of the Balinese cockfight, 'deep play'. The juxtaposition of the two words captures the fundamental ambivalence of leisure, that it is both serious and superficial, real and unreal – a paradox that has been continually emphasized in this study. Geertz writes, 'It is this kind of bringing of assorted experiences of everyday life to a focus that the cockfight, set aside from that life as "only a game" and reconnected to it as "more than a game", accomplishes, and so creates . . . a paradigmatic human event.' 'Deep play' permits us to experience our darkest and brightest emotions free of the necessary constraints imposed by everyday life. But Geertz also emphasizes that 'cockfights are not merely reflections of a preexisting sensibility analogically represented; they are positive agents in the creation and maintenance of such a sensibility'.[10]

Play takes leisure beyond passive representation, so that it not only mirrors but also structures the way participants feel, and ultimately the forms of everyday life itself.

Yet there has to remain a gap between play and everyday life. Ben Malbon argues of clubbing that 'Playful vitality is found within a temporary world of the clubber's own construction in which the everyday is disrupted, the mundane is forgotten and the ecstatic becomes possible.'[11] Play permits access to the extraordinary, or as Robert Malcolmson has put it, 'Play has the power to create a coherent sense of experience which is radically different from that of everyday life.'[12] This study has highlighted and explored the role of 'otherness' in all types of leisure and at all periods. The disruption of the ordinary is obvious enough in the more bizarre forms of entertainment, such as the eighteenth-century fire-eater Powell, who for a finale 'made a composition of pitch, brimstone, and other combustibles . . . [which] he ate it in its state of liquefaction, and blazing furiously, without appearing to sustain the least injury', the practice of cheetah racing which took place on the greyhound track at Romford in the 1930s, and the recent fad for bog snorkelling in Llanwrtyd Wells.[13] Accounts of the abnormal and the exceptional, of murders and monsters, freaks, giants, heroes, movie stars, and sporting *galácticos* have been the stock-in-trade of popular literature and the press since their origins. And though some forms of leisure may stretch the boundaries of normality in a less outlandish way, it is access to other spaces and times that underpins the rise of the spa and seaside holiday, the emergence of the recreational countryside, and the expansion of tourism, popular history, and the heritage industry.

During the last five centuries the forms taken by the 'other' in Britain have varied hugely across place and time. Economic change and urban growth have, for example, reconfigured the countryside and the coast as 'exceptional' locations, though this redefinition of otherness has been far more marked amongst the inhabitants of the urban English 'core' than of the rural Celtic 'periphery'. A persistent form of otherness is the carnivalesque. Usually this is associated with early modern society and the temporary inversion of social norms that attended occasions in the festive calendar like Christmas, Shrove Tuesday, and May Day, or events such as parish wakes, funeral wakes, skimmingtons, executions, and elections.[14] Excessive drinking, loss of inhibition, sexual immorality, mock figures of authority (such as lords of misrule and boy bishops), cross-dressing, the donning of animal costume, discordant noise, have all been associated with carnival, whose character could be summed up in the phrase, 'the world turned upside down'. The volcanic character of carnival, the need for moments of cathartic disorder and excess, suggest an immature society in a state of transition from barbarity to civility, unable to establish the stable characteristics of modern, post-Enlightenment society. Yet there is plenty of evidence that carnival did not disappear with the arrival of industrialization and modernity. Popular culture in the nineteenth century was, in the words of Peter Bailey, 'a culture that trades in carnivalesque echoes of excess and inversion, grand utopian conceits of permanent democracy of pleasure and the emotionalised myths of melodrama'.[15] This was not only because traditional festivals, such as fairs and parish wakes, persisted well into the nineteenth century,[16] but also because the forms which carnival took mutated, in part to escape the restrictions imposed by the reformers, but also more importantly to meet the changing economic and social realities of the time.

Horse racing, conveniently protected by the aristocracy, provided a vehicle for carnivalesque behaviour among the lower orders.[17] In 1854 the Stirling races were denounced as an 'evil to which the violent and vicious look forward as to a carnival of the worst passions of human nature',[18] and Hippolyte Taine commented on how during Derby Day social distinctions were temporarily relaxed 'after the manner of the ancient saturnalia'.[19] Elements of carnival have been found in the behaviour of modern football supporters, particularly the Irish and Scots,[20] in classical and rock music festivals,[21] and beach culture and the seaside resort, the last of which John Walton described as 'a liminal environment . . . where the usual constraints on respectability and decorum in public behaviour might be pushed aside in the interests of holiday hedonism, and of carnivalesque escape from the petty restrictions of everyday life in displays of excess'.[22] It could be argued that so-called binge drinking, and the notion of a youth counter-culture, fall into the same category.[23] When an observer from *Mass Observation* ventured into Lambeth during the 1930s to explore the cultural context out of which the Lambeth Walk craze had emerged, what was discovered was a regime of adult, mixed sex, pub-based clubs holding uproarious late night parties, which included cross-dressing and animal mimicry. At one of the parties, held on the August Bank Holiday,

> two of the toughest men came in, some time after midnight, made up with red eyebrows and white cheeks, each wearing a woman's hat and dress. . . . One also had false breasts, the other a pregnant belly. A woman came up and kicked the belly, and the man with the false breasts made his wife hold them. One of the men made an appropriately lewd remark and there was some pantomiming of the kind which is usually classed as 'obscene'. . . . Finally the party broke up in the best of good temper, singing:
>
>> We play the Lambeth way,
>> Not like you but a bit more gay,
>> And when we have a bit of fun
>> Oh, boy – [24]

The persistence of carnival across the period covered by this study, albeit in regularly mutating forms, should remind us of the underlying need to express the 'other'. This is not only because paradoxically it proves an effective way of affirming the structures through which society operates – as Jean Baudrillard puts it, 'everything is metamorphosed into its opposite to perpetuate itself';[25] not only because those structures create pressures from which occasional release is a psychological imperative; but also because the existence of structure creates the opportunity for anti-structural behaviour, and the creativity, fun, and exhilaration associated with that. Like otherness, symbol and play are fundamental to the human condition, and their special combination in recreational activities has made the practice of leisure, if not the forms it takes, an historical constant across at least the last 500 years.

NOTES

PREFACE

1 *Guardian*, 15 September 2001, Sport, p. 2; 17 September, Sport, p. 32; *Observer*, 16 September 2001, p. 13.
2 E. Dunning and C. Rojek (eds), *Sport and Leisure in the Civilizing Process: Critique and Counter-Critique* (Basingstoke: Macmillan, 1992) p. xii.
3 *Guardian*, 6 June 2002, p. 17.
4 R. Hoggart, *The Uses of Literacy* (1st pub. 1957; Harmondsworth: Penguin, 1966); R. Williams, *Culture and Society, 1780–1950* (1st pub. 1958; Harmondsworth: Penguin, 1968); E. P. Thompson, *The Making of the English Working Class* (1st pub. 1963; Harmondsworth: Penguin, 1968).
5 P. Bourdieu, *In Other Words: Essays Towards a Reflexive Sociology* (Cambridge: Polity, 1990) p. 159.

1 INTRODUCTION

1 L. Haywood et al., *Understanding Leisure*, 2nd edn (Cheltenham: Stanley Thornes, 1995) p. 10; D. L. Sills (ed.), *International Encyclopedia of the Social Sciences* (New York: Macmillan and Free Press, 1979) vol. 9, p. 250.
2 Haywood et al., *Understanding Leisure*, p. 2; Sills, *Encyclopedia*, vol. 9, p. 250.
3 Sills, *Encyclopedia*, vol. 9, p. 250; A. and J. Kuper, *The Social Science Encyclopedia*, 2nd edn (London: Routledge, 1996) p. 920; K. Roberts, *Contemporary Society and the Growth of Leisure* (London: Longman, 1978) pp. 3–5.
4 T. DeNora, *Music in Everyday Life* (Cambridge: Cambridge University Press, 2000) pp. 104–5; R. Palmer, *The Sound of History: Song and Social Comment* (London: Pimlico, 1996) pp. 84–120; K. Dallas (ed.), *One Hundred Songs of Toil* (London: Wolfe Publishing, 1974).

5   Palmer, *Sound of History*, pp. 32–7; D. Johnson, *Music and Society in Lowland Scotland in the Eighteenth Century* (London: Oxford University Press, 1972) pp. 105–6.

6   DeNora, *Music*, p. 60.

7   W. H. Fraser, 'Developments in Leisure', in W. H. Fraser and R. J. Morris (eds), *People and Society in Scotland*, vol. 2: *1830–1914* (Edinburgh: John Donald, 1990) p. 240; P. Clark, *The English Alehouse: A Social History, 1200–1830* (London: Longman, 1983) pp. 139, 229–30; B. Harrison, *Drink and the Victorians: The Temperance Question in England, 1851–1872*, 2nd edn (Keele: Keele University Press, 1994) pp. 53, 56, 326; W. Lambert, *Drink and Sobriety in Victorian Wales, c.1820–c.1895* (Cardiff: University of Wales Press, 1983) pp. 42–3.

8   J. Urry, *The Tourist Gaze: Leisure and Travel in Contemporary Society* (London: Sage, 1990) p. 131.

9   J. Black, *The British and the Grand Tour* (London: Croom Helm, 1985) pp. 233–41; B. Dolan, *Ladies of the Grand Tour* (London: HarperCollins, 2001) pp. 17–54; C. Fiennes, *The Journeys of Celia Fiennes*, ed. C. Morris (London: Cresset Press, 1947) pp. 1–2.

10 W. Shaw, *The Three Choirs Festival* (Worcester and London: Ebenezer Baylis and Son, 1954) pp. 3–5; J. S. Smith, *The Story of Music in Birmingham* (Birmingham: Cornish Brothers, 1945) pp. 23–5.

11 D. A. Reid, 'Playing and Praying', in M. Daunton (ed.), *The Cambridge Urban History of Britain*, vol. 3: *1840–1950* (Cambridge: Cambridge University Press, 2000) p. 745; R. Holt, *Sport and the British: A Modern History* (Oxford: Oxford University Press, 1989) p. 262.

12 G. Ó Crualaoich, 'The "Merry Wake" ', in J. S. Donnelly and K. A. Miller (eds), *Irish Popular Culture, 1650–1850* (Dublin: Irish Academic Press, 1989) pp. 173–200; S. Ó Suilleabháin, *Irish Wake Amusements* (Dublin: Mercier Press, 1979); J. Brand, *Observations on Popular Antiquities, Including the Whole of Mr Bourne's Antiquitates Vulgares* (1st pub. 1777; London: William Baynes, *c*.1820) pp. 20–1.

13 H. Cunningham, *Leisure in the Industrial Revolution, c.1780–c.1880* (London: Croom Helm, 1980) pp. 20, 57; G. S. Jones, 'Working-Class Culture and Working-Class Politics in London, 1870–1900: Notes on the Remaking of a Working Class', *Journal of Social History*, 7 (1974) p. 492.

14 Sills, *Encyclopedia*, p. 251.

15 W. Outhwaite and T. Bottomore (eds), *The Blackwell Dictionary of Twentieth-Century Social Thought* (Oxford: Blackwell, 1993) p. 329.

16 R. Porter and M. M. Roberts (eds), *Pleasure in the Eighteenth Century* (Basingstoke: Macmillan, 1996).

17   R. Hutton, *The Stations of the Sun: A History of the Ritual Year in Britain* (Oxford: Oxford University Press, 1997) p. 157.

18   Cunningham, *Leisure in the Industrial Revolution*, p. 12.

19   Sills, *Encyclopedia*, pp. 249–50.

20   J. Clarke and C. Critcher, *The Devil Makes Work: Leisure in Capitalist Britain* (Basingstoke: Palgrave Macmillan, 1985) p. 58.

21   P. Bailey, *Leisure and Class in Victorian England: Rational Recreation and the Contest for Control, 1830–1885* (London: Routledge, 1978) p. 4; Fraser, 'Developments', p. 237.

22   Urry, *Tourist Gaze*, p. 102.

23   P. Burke, 'The Invention of Leisure in Early Modern Europe', *Past and Present*, 146 (1995) p. 137 and *passim*.

24   J. H. Plumb, *The Commercialization of Leisure in Eighteenth-century England* (Reading: University of Reading, 1973); Cunningham, *Leisure in the Industrial Revolution*, pp. 9–10; P. Bailey, 'The Politics and the Poetics of Modern British Leisure: a Late Twentieth-century Review', *Rethinking History*, 13 (1999) p. 137.

25   J. -L. Marfany and P. Burke, 'Debate: the Invention of Leisure in Early Modern Europe', *Past and Present*, 156 (1997) pp. 174–91.

26   Ibid., pp. 196–7.

27   Holt, *Sport and the British*, p. 367.

28   R. Hutton, *The Rise and Fall of Merry England: The Ritual Year, 1400–1700* (Oxford: Oxford University Press, 1996) p. 62.

29   Ibid., pp. 69–226.

30   Johnson, *Music*, pp. 8–10; Fraser, 'Developments', pp. 236–7.

31   K. Thomas, 'Work and Leisure in Pre-industrial Society', *Past and Present*, 29 (1964) pp. 58–9.

32   Hutton, *Merry England*, p. 261; Plumb, *Commercialization*; P. Borsay, *The English Urban Renaissance: Culture and Society in the Provincial Town, 1660–1770* (Oxford: Clarendon Press, 1989); P. Clark and R. Houston, 'Culture and Leisure, 1750–1840', in P. Clark (ed.), *Cambridge Urban History of Britain*, vol. 2: *1540–1840* (Cambridge: Cambridge University Press, 2000) pp. 575–613.

33   Cunningham, *Leisure in the Industrial Revolution*, p. 22; A. Harvey, *The Beginnings of a Commercial Sporting Culture in Britain, 1793–1850* (Aldershot: Ashgate, 2004).

34   Bailey, 'Politics', p. 132.

35   Cunningham, *Leisure in the Industrial Revolution*, pp. 14, 140.

36   N. Tranter, *Sport, Economy and Society in Britain, 1750–1914* (Cambridge: Cambridge University Press, 1997) p. 13; Holt, *Sport and the British*, p. 135; see also T. Mason (ed.), *Sport in Britain: A Social*

History (Cambridge: Cambridge University Press, 1989), where most of the essays point to the origins of modern sport in the later nineteenth century.

37 Bailey, 'Politics', p. 135.
38 A. Marwick, *The Sixties: Cultural Revolution in Britain, France, Italy and the United States, c.1958–1974* (Oxford: Oxford University Press, 1999) p. 5; A. Marwick, *Culture in Britain since 1945* (Oxford: Basil Blackwell, 1991) pp. 67–72; J. Green, *All Dressed Up: The Sixties and the Counterculture* (London: Pimlico, 1999) p. xiii.

2 ECONOMY

1 W. Vamplew, *Pay Up and Play the Game: Professional Sport in Britain, 1875–1914* (Cambridge: Cambridge University Press, 2004) pp. 11–14.
2 D. Levinson and K. Christensen (eds), *Encyclopedia of World Sport from Ancient Times to the Present* (Oxford: ABC-Clio, 1996) p. 80.
3 Plumb, *Commercialization*.
4 J. Brewer, ' "The Most Polite Age and the Most Vicious": Attitudes towards Culture as a Commodity, 1660–1800', in A. Bermingham and J. Brewer (eds), *The Consumption of Culture, 1600–1800: Image, Object, Text* (London: Routledge, 1997) pp. 342–5.
5 J. Brewer, *The Pleasures of the Imagination: English Culture in the Eighteenth Century* (London: HarperCollins, 1997) pp. xvii, 92, 362; W. Weber, *The Rise of the Musical Classics in Eighteenth-century England: A Study in Canon, Ritual, and Ideology* (Oxford: Clarendon Press, 1996) pp. 17–19; L. Lippincott, 'Expanding on Portraiture: the Market, the Public, and the Hierarchy of Genres in Eighteenth-century Britain', in Bermingham and Brewer, *Consumption*, pp. 75–88; L. Lippincott, *Selling Art in Georgian London: The Rise of Arthur Pond* (New Haven, CT: Yale University Press, 1983).
6 Clark and Houston, 'Culture and Leisure', p. 583.
7 Brewer, *Pleasures*, pp. 164–6, 515–16; Borsay, *Urban Renaissance*, pp. 219–21.
8 D. Solkin, *Painting for Money: The Visual Arts and the Public Sphere in Eighteenth-century England* (New Haven, CT: Yale University Press, 1992) p. 274.
9 S. McVeigh, *Concert Life in London from Mozart to Haydn* (Cambridge: Cambridge University Press, 1993) pp. 4–6; Cunningham, *Leisure in the Industrial Revolution*, p. 35; Harvey, *Beginnings*.
10 M. Huggins, *Flat Racing and British Society, 1790–1914: A Social and Economic History* (London: Frank Cass, 2000) pp. 13, 15.

11 P. Horn, *Pleasures and Pastimes in Victorian Britain* (Stroud: Alan Sutton, 1999) p. 1; J. Walvin, *Leisure and Society, 1830–1950* (London: Longman, 1978) p. 62; Cunningham, *Leisure in the Industrial Revolution*, p. 174.

12 Bailey, *Leisure and Class*, pp. 147–52; D. Kift, *The Victorian Music Hall: Culture, Class and Conflict*, trans. R. Kift (Cambridge: Cambridge University Press, 1996) pp. 17–35.

13 W. Donaldson, *Popular Literature in Victorian Scotland: Language, Fiction and the Press* (Aberdeen: Aberdeen University Press, 1986) p. ix; D. Vincent, *Literacy and Popular Culture: England, 1750–1914* (Cambridge: Cambridge University Press, 1989) pp. 210–26.

14 Vamplew, *Pay Up*, p. 52; Holt, *Sport and the British*, p. 145; Tranter, *Sport, Economy and Society*, p. 16.

15 S. G. Jones, *Workers at Play: A Social and Economic History of Leisure, 1918–1939* (London: Routledge and Kegan Paul, 1986) pp. 3, 35.

16 J. McAleer, *Popular Reading and Publishing in Britain, 1914–50* (Oxford: Clarendon Press, 1992) p. 7.

17 Ibid., p. 42.

18 Hoggart, *Uses of Literacy*, chapters 7–8, especially p. 211.

19 R. Holt and T. Mason, *Sport in Britain, 1945–2000* (Oxford: Blackwell, 2000) p. 107; D. Russell, *Football and the English: A Social History of Association Football in England, 1863–1995* (Preston: Carnegie, 1997) pp. 156–234.

20 R. H. Britnell, *The Commercialization of English Society, 1000–1500*, 2nd edn (Manchester: Manchester University Press, 1996).

21 J. M. Carter, *Medieval Games: Sports and Recreations in Feudal Society* (London: Greenwood Press, 1992) p. 133.

22 M. Spufford, *Small Books and Pleasant Histories: Popular Fiction and Its Readership in Seventeenth-century England* (Cambridge: Cambridge University Press, 1981); A. Fox, *Oral and Literate Culture in England, 1500–1700* (Oxford: Clarendon Press, 2000) pp. 14–16; J.-C. Agnew, *Worlds Apart: The Market and the Theater in Anglo-American Thought, 1550–1750* (Cambridge: Cambridge University Press, 1986); A. Gurr, *Playgoing in Shakespeare's London*, 3rd edn (Cambridge: Cambridge University Press, 2004); Clark, *English Alehouse*, pp. 64–144.

23 J. Boulton, 'London, 1540–1700', in Clark, *Cambridge Urban History*, vol. 2, p. 316.

24 J. Benson, *The Rise of a Consumer Society in Britain, 1880–1980* (London: Longman, 1994) p. 12.

25 See Vamplew, *Pay Up*, pp. 14–17, and Benson, *Consumer Society*, pp. 11–55, for the application of such a model.

26 Vamplew, *Pay Up*, p. 53.

27   A. Davies, *Leisure, Gender and Poverty: Working Class Culture in Salford and Manchester, 1900–1939* (Buckingham: Open University Press, 1992) pp. 14–29.

28   A. Davies, 'Cinema and Broadcasting', in P. Johnson (ed.), *Twentieth-century Britain: Economic, Social and Cultural Change* (Harlow: Longman, 1994) p. 264; B. S. Rowntree and G. R. Lavers, *English Life and Leisure* (London: Longmans, Green, 1951) p. 123.

29   Benson, *Consumer Society*, pp. 1–27.

30   D. Defoe, *A Tour Through the Whole Island of Great Britain* (1st pub. 1724–6), ed. G. D. H. Cole and D. C. Browning, 2 vols (London: Everyman, 1962) vol. 2, p. 34.

31   P. Hembry, *The English Spa, 1560–1815: A Social History* (London: Athlone Press, 1990); P. Hembry, *British Spas from 1815 to the Present: A Social History*, ed. and compiled by L. W. and E. E. Cowie (London: Athlone Press, 1997); J. K. Walton, *The English Seaside Resort: A Social History, 1750–1914* (Leicester: Leicester University Press, 1983) pp. 5–44; J. K. Walton, *The British Seaside: Holidays and Resorts in the Twentieth Century* (Manchester: Manchester University Press, 2000) pp. 51–70; P. Borsay, 'Health and Leisure Resorts, 1700–1840', in Clark, *Cambridge Urban History*, vol. 2, pp. 776–84; A. J. Durie, *Scotland for the Holidays: Tourism in Scotland, c.1780–1939* (East Linton: Tuckwell Press, 2003) pp. 65–108.

32   J. Lowerson, *Sport and the English Middle Classes, 1870–1914* (Manchester: Manchester University Press, 1993).

33   N. McKendrick, J. Brewer, and J. H. Plumb, *The Birth of a Consumer Society: The Commercialization of Eighteenth-century England* (London: Hutchinson, 1983) p. 1; J. Brewer and R. Porter (eds), *Consumption and the World of Goods* (London: Routledge, 1994); Bermingham and Brewer, *Consumption*; C. Campbell, *The Romantic Ethic and the Spirit of Modern Consumerism* (Oxford: Blackwell, 1987); D. Andrew and R. McGowen, *The Perreaus and Mrs Rudd: Forgery and Betrayal in Eighteenth-century London* (Berkeley: University of California Press, 2001) pp. 112–35; M. Berg, *Luxury and Pleasure in Eighteenth-century Britain* (Oxford: Oxford University Press, 2005).

34   W. H. Fraser, *The Coming of the Mass Market, 1850–1914* (London: Macmillan, 1981) especially p. x; T. Richards, *The Commodity Culture of Victorian England: Advertising and Spectacle, 1851–1914* (London: Verso, 1991) p. 1; Benson, *Consumer Society*.

35   S. Bowden, 'The New Consumerism', in Johnson, *Twentieth-century Britain*, pp. 242–62.

36   Walvin, *Leisure and Society*, pp. 63, 153.

37 Urry, *Tourist Gaze*, p. 14.

38 Benson, *Consumer Society*, pp. 2–4; N. Cox, *The Complete Tradesman: A Study of Retailing, 1550–1820* (Aldershot: Ashgate, 2000) pp. 2–5.

39 Cox, *Complete Tradesman*, pp. 139–45; V. C. E. Morgan, 'Producing Consumer Space in Eighteenth-century England: Shops, Shopping and the Provincial Town' (unpub. Ph.D. thesis, Coventry University, 2003) pp. 151, 207–8, 217–20; A. Hann and J. Stobart, 'Sites of Consumption: the Display of Goods in Provincial Shops in Eighteenth-century England', *Cultural and Social History*, 2 (2005) pp. 181–6; J. K. Walton, 'Towns and Consumerism', in M. Daunton (ed.), *The Cambridge Urban History of Britain*, vol. 3: *1840–1950* (Cambridge: Cambridge University Press, 2000) pp. 723–4; E. D. Rappaport, *Shopping for Pleasure: Women in the Making of London's West End* (Princeton, NJ: Princeton University Press, 2000); Haywood et al., *Understanding Leisure*, pp. 108–10; R. Shields, 'Spaces for the Subject of Consumption', in R. Shields (ed.), *Lifestyle Shopping: The Subject of Consumption* (London: Routledge, 1992) p. 6.

40 D. Defoe, *The Complete English Tradesman* (1st pub. 1725 and 1727, reprinted; New York: Burt Franklin, 1970) p. 61.

41 DeNora, *Music*, p. 36.

42 T. Herbert, 'Nineteenth-century Brass Bands', in T. Herbert (ed.), *Bands: The Brass Band Movement in the 19th and 20th Centuries* (Buckingham: Open University Press, 1991) pp. 17–20; Tranter, *Sport, Economy and Society*, p. 33; Mason, *Sport in Britain*, pp. 193–5; Durie, *Scotland for the Holidays*, p. 121; K. McCrone, *Sport and the Physical Emancipation of English Women, 1870–1914* (London: Routledge, 1988) pp. 177–84.

43 Borsay, *Urban Renaissance*, p. 217; Vamplew, *Pay Up*, p. 47; W. Vamplew, *The Turf: A Social and Economic History of Horse Racing* (London: Allen Lane, 1976) pp. 29–37; D. C. Itzkowitz, *Peculiar Privilege: A Social History of English Fox-Hunting, 1753–1885* (Hassocks: Harvester Press, 1977) pp. 50–66; R. Carr, *English Fox Hunting: A History* (London: Weidenfeld and Nicolson, 1976) pp. 106–10; A. Hignell, *A 'Favourit' Game: Cricket in South Wales before 1914* (Cardiff: University of Wales Press, 1992) pp. 42–7, 88–91.

44 M. R. Booth, *Theatre in the Victorian Age* (Cambridge: Cambridge University Press, 1991) pp. 12–16, 18–21.

45 G. Williams, *Valleys of Song: Music and Society in Wales, 1840–1914* (Cardiff: University of Wales Press, 1998) p. 42.

46 Black, *British and the Grand Tour*, pp. 1–87; J. Towner, *A Historical Geography of Recreation and Tourism in the Western World, 1540–1940* (Chichester: Wiley, 1996) pp. 106–15.

47 M. Morgan, *National Identities and Travel in Victorian Britain* (Basingstoke: Palgrave Macmillan, 2001) pp. 9–45; S. O'Connell, *The Car and British Society: Class, Gender and Motoring, 1896–1939* (Manchester: Manchester University Press, 1998) pp. 77–111.

48 Walton, *English Seaside Resort*, p. 22; J. K. Walton, 'Railways and Resort Development in North-west England, 1830–1914', in E. M. Sigsworth (ed.), *Ports and Resorts in the Regions* (Hull: Hull College of Higher Education, for Conference of Regional and Local History Tutors in Tertiary Education (CORAL), 1980) pp. 120–37.

49 B. Reay, *Popular Cultures in England 1550–1750* (London: Longman, 1998) pp. 47–50; Spufford, *Small Books*; Fox, *Oral and Literate Culture*; B. Capp, *Astrology and the Popular Press: English Almanacs, 1500–1800* (London: Faber, 1979).

50 G. A. Cranfield, *The Development of the Provincial Newspaper, 1700–1760* (Westport, CT: Greenwood Press, 1962) pp. 212–14, 217–18; R. M. Wiles, *Freshest Advices: Early Provincial Newspapers in England* (Columbus, OH: Ohio University Press, 1965) pp. 152, 183; R. M. Wiles, 'Crowd-Pleasing Spectacles in Eighteenth-century England', *Journal of Popular Culture*, 1 (1967) pp. 90–105.

51 Holt, *Sport and the British*, pp. 306–26; Holt and Mason, *Sport in Britain*, pp. 93–120; J. Hill, *Sport, Leisure and Culture in Twentieth-century Britain* (Basingstoke: Palgrave Macmillan, 2002) pp. 43–58; Russell, *Football*, pp. 103–13, 138–44, 181–209, 213–15.

52 P. Borsay, *The Image of Georgian Bath: Towns, Heritage, and History* (Oxford: Oxford University Press, 2000) pp. 117–23.

53 E. Swinglehurst, *Cook's Tours: The Story of Popular Travel* (Poole: Blandford Press, 1980).

54 S. Rosenfeld, *Strolling Players and Drama in the Provinces, 1660–1765* (Cambridge: Cambridge University Press, 1939); Brewer, *Pleasures*, pp. 384–91; C. Chinn, *Better Betting with a Decent Feller: Bookmaking, Betting and the British Working Class, 1750–1980* (London: Harvester Wheatsheaf, 1991); R. Munting, *An Economic and Social History of Gambling in Britain and the USA* (Manchester: Manchester University Press, 1996) pp. 89–115.

55 Clark, *English Alehouse*, pp. 41–4; Harrison, *Drink and the Victorians*, p. 304.

56 Clark, *English Alehouse*, pp. 145–60, 222–42, 306–26; A. Everitt, 'The English Urban Inn, 1560–1760', in A. Everitt (ed.), *Perspectives in English Urban History* (London: Macmillan, 1973) pp. 113–19; Borsay, *Urban Renaissance*, pp. 144–5, 157, 175–7, 179, 214, 218; Harrison, *Drink and the Victorians*, pp. 50–5; D. B. Smith, *Curling: An Illustrated*

History (Edinburgh: John Donald, 1981) pp. 192–5; Mason, *Sport in Britain*, pp. 24–9; D. Underdown, *Start of Play: Cricket and Culture in Eighteenth-century England* (London: Allen Lane, 2000) pp. 108, 111, 126–30; Bailey, *Leisure and Class*, pp. 27–8; Tranter, *Sport, Economy and Society*, p. 60; D. A. Reid, 'Interpreting the Festive Calendar: Wakes and Fairs as Carnivals', in R. D. Storch (ed.), *Popular Culture and Custom in Nineteenth-century England* (London: Croom Helm, 1982) pp. 127, 135; A. Croll, *Civilizing the Urban: Popular Culture and Public Space in Merthyr, c.1870–1914* (Cardiff: University of Wales Press, 2000) pp. 151–4.

57   Borsay, *Urban Renaissance*, pp. 214–15, 218–19; P. Borsay, 'Politeness and Elegance: the Cultural Re-fashioning of Eighteenth-century York', in M. Hallett and J. Rendall (eds), *Eighteenth-century York: Culture, Space and Society*, Borthwick Text and Calendar 30 (York: University of York, 2003) pp. 5–7; J. Burnett, *Riot, Revelry and Rout: Sport in Lowland Scotland before 1860* (East Linton: Tuckwell Press, 2000) p. 22.

58   Walton, *English Seaside Resort*, pp. 128–55; J. D. Marshall, 'Two Railway Resorts: Grange and Seascale', in J. D. Marshall, *Old Lakeland: Some Cumbrian Social History* (Newton Abbot: David and Charles, 1971) pp. 184–95.

59   *Guardian*, 12 August 2002, Sport, p. 19.

60   Mason, *Sport in Britain*, pp. 40, 64–7, 124, 211; Holt and Mason, *Sport in Britain*, pp. 109–10, 112–13; 165–6; G. Moorhouse, *A People's Game: The Centenary History of Rugby League Football, 1895–1995* (London: Hodder and Stoughton, 1995) pp. 278–81.

61   *Financial Times*, 5 August 2003, p. 10.

62   J. K. Walton, *The Blackpool Landlady: A Social History* (Manchester: Manchester University Press, 1978); J. K. Walton, 'The Blackpool Landlady Revisited', *Manchester Regional History Review*, 8 (1996) pp. 23–31; J. K. Walton, *Fish and Chips and the British Working Class, 1870–1940* (Leicester: Leicester University Press, 1992).

63   Borsay, *Urban Renaissance*, pp. 183–5; Vamplew, *Turf*, pp. 45–6.

64   Bailey, *Leisure and Class*, pp. 147–50; Kift, *Victorian Music Hall*, pp. 33–5.

65   Hill, *Sport, Leisure and Culture*, pp. 62–3; Davies, 'Cinema and Broadcasting', pp. 269–70; A. Eyles, *Old Cinemas* (Princes Risborough: Shire Publications, 2001) pp. 8–11.

66   Munting, *Gambling*, pp. 96–100; M. Clapson, *A Bit of a Flutter: Popular Gambling and English Society, c.1823–1961* (Manchester: Manchester University Press, 1992) pp. 68–72.

67   Urry, *Tourist Gaze*, pp. 48–9.

68 S. Dobson and J. Goddard, *The Economics of Football* (Cambridge: Cambridge University Press, 2001) pp. 23–4.

69 Holt and Mason, *Sport in Britain*, p. 62; Hill, *Sport Leisure and Culture*, pp. 140–4; M. Polley, *Moving the Goalposts: A History of Sport and Society since 1945* (London: Routledge, 1998) pp. 114–27.

70 Mason, *Sport in Britain*, pp. 158–63.

71 K. A. P. Sandiford, *Cricket and the Victorians* (Aldershot: Scolar, 1994) pp. 83–4; G. Williams, *1905 and All That* (Llandysul: Gomer, 1991) pp. 140–71; Vamplew, *Pay Up*, pp. 199–203.

72 D. Birley, *A Social History of English Cricket* (London: Aurum Press, 1999) pp. 148, 159–60.

73 Brewer, *Pleasures*, pp. 325–423, 531–72; Borsay, *Urban Renaissance*, pp. 124–5.

74 McVeigh, *Concert Life*, pp. 4–6, 32–4; Bailey, *Leisure and Class*, pp. 30, 150–1; Herbert, 'Nineteenth-century Brass Bands', pp. 33–7; Hoggart, *Uses of Literacy*, p. 153.

75 G. Torkildsen, *Leisure and Recreation Management*, 4th edn (London: E & FN Spon, 1999) pp. 283–313; Hill, *Sport, Leisure and Culture*, pp. 95–146.

76 Quoted in Urry, *Tourist Gaze*, p. 75.

77 Bailey, 'Politics', pp. 142–3.

78 R. Giulianotti, *Football: A Sociology of the Global Game* (Cambridge: Polity, 1999) pp. 112–13; Russell, *Football*, pp. 45–52.

79 Tranter, *Sport, Economy and Society*, pp. 71–4; Holt, *Sport and the British*, pp. 281–7; Lowerson, *Sport*, pp. 240–51.

80 Mason, *Sport in Britain*, pp. 227–9; Vamplew, *Turf*, p. 182.

81 Sandiford, *Cricket*, p. 65; T. Mason, 'Sport and Recreation', in Johnson, *Twentieth-century Britain*, p. 119.

82 *Guardian*, 29 November 2002, p. 34.

83 Walton, *English Seaside Resort*, pp. 221–2; Urry, *Tourist Gaze*, p. 53.

84 Brewer, *Pleasures*, pp. 325–32.

85 Rosenfeld, *Strolling Players*.

86 Borsay, *Urban Renaissance*, p. 160.

87 Quoted in Brewer, *Pleasures*, pp. 24–5.

88 Weber, *Musical Classics*, p. 47.

89 E. Cumming and W. Kaplan, *The Arts and Crafts Movement* (London: Thames and Hudson, 1991) pp. 9–28; F. MacCarthy, *The Simple Life: C. R. Ashbee in the Cotswolds* (London: Lund Humphries, 1988).

90 F. MacCarthy, *William Morris: A Life for Our Time* (London: Faber and Faber, 1994) pp. 394–5, 429–35, 445, 452, 457–8.

3 STATE

1 Brand, *Observations*, p. iii.

2 Vamplew, *Turf*, p. 98; D. Birley, *Sport and the Making of Britain* (Manchester: Manchester University Press, 1996) p. 229.

3 R. Holt, 'Sport and History: the State and the Subject in Britain', *Twentieth Century British History*, 7 (1996) p. 231; Holt, *Sport and the British*, p. 270.

4 J. Hill, *Sport, Leisure and Culture*, p. 165.

5 Bailey, *Leisure and Class*, p. 39; Durie, *Scotland for the Holidays*, p. 129.

6 Towner, *Historical Geography*, pp. 60–2; D. P. Mackaman, 'Competing Visions of Urban Grandeur: Planning and Developing Nineteenth-century Spa Towns in France', and J. Steward, 'The Spa Town of the Austro-Hungarian Empire and the Growth of Tourist Culture: 1860–1914', both in P. Borsay, G. Hirschfelder and R.-E. Mohrmann (eds), *New Directions in Urban History: Aspects of European Art, Health, Tourism and Leisure since the Enlightenment* (Munster: Waxmann, 2000) pp. 41–61, 91–2.

7 Jones, *Workers at Play*, p. 108; R. McKibbin, *Classes and Cultures: England, 1918–1951* (Oxford: Oxford University Press, 1998) p. 380; Holt, 'Sport and History', p. 240; J. Williams, *Cricket and England: A Cultural and Social History of the Inter-War Years* (London: Frank Cass, 1999) p. 41.

8 Polley, *Moving the Goalposts*, p. 17; Holt and Mason, *Sport in Britain*, pp. 21–2, 146–67; A. Blake, *The Land without Music: Music, Culture and Society in Twentieth-century Britain* (Manchester: Manchester University Press, 1997) pp. 58–60; Hill, *Sport, Leisure and Culture*, pp. 149–63.

9 Rowntree and Lavers, *English Life and Leisure*, pp. 138, 191–8; Clarke and Critcher, *Devil Makes Work*, p. 87.

10 K. Roberts, in C. Critcher, P. Bramham and A. Tomlinson (eds), *Sociology of Leisure: A Reader* (London: E & FN Spon, 1999) p. 11; Haywood et al., *Understanding Leisure*, pp. 178–80.

11 *Guardian*, G2, 5 January 2004, p. 3.

12 Bailey, 'Politics', pp. 143–5.

13 H. Cunningham, 'Leisure and Culture', in F. M. L. Thompson (ed.), *The Cambridge Social History of Britain*, vol. 2: *The People and Their Environment* (Cambridge: Cambridge University Press, 1990), p. 325.

14 Clark and Houston, 'Culture and Leisure', p. 592.

15 Hutton, *Merry England*, especially p. 262.

16 F. P. Magoun, *History of Football: From the Beginnings to 1871* (Bochum-Langendreer: Verlag Heinrich Pöppinghas O. H. G., 1938) p. 5;

O. M. Geddes, *A Swing Through Time: Golf in Scotland, 1457–1743* (Edinburgh: HMSO, 1992) p. 1; T. Henricks, *Disputed Pleasures: Sport and Society in Pre-industrial England* (New York: Greenwood Press, 1991) pp. 44–68; Birley, *Sport and the Making*, pp. 27–45.

17 Clark, *English Alehouse*, pp. 166–87; E. Malcolm, 'The Rise of the Pub: a Study in the Disciplining of Popular Culture', in Donnelly and Miller, *Irish Popular Culture*, pp. 55–64.

18 R. Grassby, 'The Decline of Falconry in Early Modern England', *Past and Present*, 157 (1997) pp. 58–60; J. Cannon (ed.), *The Oxford Companion to British History* (Oxford: Oxford University Press, 1997) p. 401; Henricks, *Disputed Pleasures*, pp. 16–22, 44–51, 77–81, 118–22; P. B. Munsche, *Gentlemen and Poachers: The English Game Laws, 1671–1831* (Cambridge: Cambridge University Press, 1981) pp. 8–27.

19 T. Williamson, *Polite Landscapes: Gardens and Society in Eighteenth-century England* (Stroud: Alan Sutton, 1995) p. 136.

20 P. W. White, *Theatre and Reformation: Protestantism, Patronage and Playing in Tudor England* (Cambridge: Cambridge University Press, 1992) pp. 1–66; A. Fox, 'Religious Satire in English Towns, 1570–1640', in P. Collinson and J. Craig (eds), *The Reformation in English Towns, 1500–1640* (Basingstoke: Macmillan, 1998) pp. 222–4.

21 White, *Theatre*, pp. 163–74; J.-C. Agnew, *Worlds Apart: The Market and the Theater in Anglo-American Thought, 1550–1750* (Cambridge: Cambridge University Press, 1986) pp. 125–48; L. Hotson, *The Commonwealth and Restoration Stage* (New York: Russell and Russell, 1962) pp. 3–59; T. L. G. Burley, *Playhouses and Players of East Anglia* (Norwich: Jarrold and Sons, 1928) pp. 165–6; K. Barker, *Bristol at Play: Five Centuries of Live Entertainment* (Bradford-on-Avon; Moonraker Press, 1976) pp. 3–4; L. Fox, *The Borough Town of Stratford-upon-Avon* (Stratford: Corporation of Stratford-upon-Avon, 1953) pp. 143–4; W. T. MacCaffrey, *Exeter, 1540–1640: The Growth of an English County Town* (Cambridge, MA: Harvard University Press, 1975) p. 271.

22 C. Durston, 'Puritan Rule and the Failure of Cultural Revolution, 1645–1660', in C. Durston and J. Eales (eds), *The Culture of English Puritanism, 1560–1700* (Basingstoke: Macmillan, 1996) pp. 210–33.

23 J. Brewer, *Pleasures*, p. 383; Borsay, *Urban Renaissance*, pp. 183–4, 303–5; V. J. Liesenfeld, *The Licensing Act of 1737* (Madison: University of Wisconsin Press, 1984).

24 Booth, *Theatre*, p. 6.

25 Carr, *English Fox Hunting*, pp. 224–5.

26 J. Greenway, *Drink and British Politics since 1830: A Study in Policy Making* (Basingstoke: Palgrave Macmillan, 2003).

27 Munting, *Gambling*, pp. 6–88, 144–68; Clapson, *Bit of a Flutter*, pp. 1–78, 108–37, 187–206.

28 White, *Theatre*, pp. 56–7, 164–5, 173–4.

29 J. Summerson, *Inigo Jones* (Harmondsworth: Penguin, 1996) pp. 21–3, 59–60.

30 P. May, *The Changing Face of Newmarket: A History from 1600 to 1760* (Newmarket: Peter May Publications, 1984) pp. 3–5, 23–5; R. Onslow, *The Heath and the Turf: A History of Newmarket* (London: Arthur Barker, 1971) pp. 19–24; R. Longrigg, *A History of Horse Racing* (London: Macmillan, 1972) pp. 32–55.

31 J. Hook, *The Baroque Age in England* (London: Thames and Hudson, 1976) pp. 68–92; M. Foss, *The Age of Patronage: The Arts in Society, 1660–1750* (London: Hamish Hamilton, 1971) pp. 110–61.

32 Brewer, *Pleasures*, pp. 235, 364.

33 D. Watkin, 'George III and the Culture of the Enlightenment', *The Georgian* (Spring 2004) pp. 6–9; D. Watkin, *The Architect King: George III and the Culture of the Enlightenment* (London: Royal Collections Enterprises, 2004).

34 R. Whalley, 'Royal Victoria Park', *Bath History*, 5 (1994) p. 153; R. Bearman, 'Bishopton Spa, Stratford-upon-Avon', *Warwickshire History*, 2:6 (1974/75) p. 20; R. Chaplin, 'The Rise of Royal Leamington Spa', *Warwickshire History*, 2:2 (1972/3) p. 24.

35 Smith, *Curling*, pp. 113–18.

36 L. Colley, *Britons: Forging the Nation, 1707–1837* (New Haven, CT: Yale University Press, 1992) pp. 233, 235.

37 G. Jarvie, *Highland Games: The Making of the Myth* (Edinburgh: Edinburgh University Press, 1991) pp. 43–70.

38 Cunningham, 'Leisure and Culture', p. 321.

39 Vamplew, *Turf*, pp. 192–6.

40 Hill, *Sport, Leisure and Culture*, pp. 165–78; Cunningham, 'Leisure and Culture', pp. 322–3; Polley, *Moving the Goalposts*, pp. 25–7; Mason, *Sport in Britain*, pp. 64–7.

41 D. Eastwood, *Government and Community in the English Provinces, 1700–1870* (Basingstoke: Macmillan, 1997) p. 19; R. Price, *British Society, 1680–1880: Dynamism, Containment and Change* (Cambridge: Cambridge University Press, 1999) pp. 155–91.

42 C. Dyer, 'Small Towns, 1270–1540', in D. Palliser (ed.), *The Cambridge Urban History of Britain*, vol. 1: *600–1540* (Cambridge: Cambridge University Press, 2000) p. 531; Malcolm, 'Rise of the Pub', p. 56.

43 Hutton, *Merry England*, pp. 111–99.

44 J. Strutt, *Glig-Gamena Angel-Deod, or The Sports and Pastimes of the People of England* (1st pub. 1801; 2nd edn, London: White, 1810) p. 251.

45 Vamplew, *Turf*, pp. 86–7; Borsay, *Urban Renaissance*, p. 119.

46 Bailey, *Leisure and Class*, pp. 20–1; R. D. Storch, ' "Please to Remember the Fifth of November": Conflict, Solidarity and Public Order in Southern England, 1851–1900', in Storch, *Popular Culture*, pp. 90–3, 95.

47 Davies, *Leisure*, pp. 144–52; Chinn, *Better Betting*, pp. 222–7, 236–41.

48 G. Waterfield (ed.), *Palaces of Art: Art Galleries in Britain, 1750–1990* (London: Dulwich Picture Art Galleries in association with Lund Humphries, 1991) p. 21; E. P. Hennock, *Fit and Proper Persons: Ideas and Reality in Nineteenth-century Urban Government* (London: Edward Arnold, 1973) p. 77; J. Kite, ' "A Good Bargain": the Struggle for a Public Library', *Bath History*, 4 (1992) pp. 136–54.

49 D. Russell, *Popular Music in England, 1840–1914: A Social History* (Manchester: Manchester University Press, 1987) pp. 37–40.

50 McKibbin, *Classes and Cultures*, p. 423; D. Berry, *Wales and the Cinema: The First Hundred Years* (Cardiff: University of Wales Press, 1995) pp. 184–5.

51 Polley, *Moving the Goalposts*, p. 21.

52 Vamplew, *Turf*, p. 226.

53 McKibbin, *Classes and Cultures*, p. 424.

54 Hill, *Sport, Leisure and Culture*, pp. 95–111; McKibbin, *Classes and Cultures*, pp. 457–76.

55 Hutton, *Merry England*, pp. 111–52.

56 T. C. Curtis and W. A. Speck, 'The Societies for the Reformation of Manners: a Case Study in the Theory and Practice of Moral Reform', *Literature and History*, 3 (1976) pp. 45–64; R. B. Shoemaker, 'Reforming the City: the Reformation of Manners Campaign in London, 1690–1738', in L. Davison et al. (eds), *Stilling the Grumbling Hive: The Response to Economic and Social Problems in England, 1689–1750* (Stroud: Alan Sutton, 1992) pp. 99–120.

57 L. Bland, *Banishing the Beast: English Feminism and Sexual Morality, 1885–1914* (Harmondsworth: Penguin, 1995) p. 109; Chinn, *Better Betting*, pp. 217–27.

58 Hill, *Sport, Leisure and Culture*, p. 130; Holt, 'Sport and History', p. 241.

59 P. Clark, *British Clubs and Societies, 1580–1800: The Origins of an Associational World* (Oxford: Clarendon Press, 2000).

60 M. Schaich, 'A War of Words? Old and New Perspectives on the Enlightenment', *German Historical Institute London Bulletin*, 24 (2002) p. 44.

61 Williams, *Cricket*, p. 41.

62 Williams, *Cricket*, p. 23; R. Mortimer, *The Jockey Club* (London: Cassell, 1958) pp. 10, 20–34; Vamplew, *Turf*, pp. 77–8, 108–9; C. R. Hill, *Horse Power: The Politics of the Turf* (Manchester: Manchester University Press, 1987) p. 147.

63 J. Jenkins and P. James, *From Acorn to Oak Tree: The Growth of the National Trust, 1895–1994* (London: Macmillan, 1994) pp. 24–31.

64 R. Morris, 'Voluntary Societies and British Urban Elites, 1780–1850: An Analysis', in P. Borsay (ed.), *The Eighteenth-century Town: A Reader in English Urban History, 1688–1820* (Harlow: Longman, 1990) p. 366.

65 Clarke and Critcher, *Devil Makes Work*, pp. 122–34.

66 A. C. Reeves, *Pleasures and Pastimes in Medieval England* (Stroud: Sutton, 1995), pp. 103–10; Henricks, *Disputed Pleasures*, pp. 16–22; Cannon, *Oxford Companion*, p. 388.

67 R. B. Manning, *Hunters and Poachers: A Cultural and Social History of Unlawful Hunting in England, 1485–1640* (Oxford: Clarendon Press, 1993) pp. 198–209.

68 Durie, *Scotland for the Holidays*, p. 115.

69 Onslow, *Heath*, pp. 19–24; R. Onslow, *Royal Ascot* (Marlborough: Crowood Books, 1990) pp. 8–10.

70 McKibbin, *Classes and Cultures*, pp. 427–31; Hill, *Sport, Leisure and Culture*, p. 70.

71 C. Phythian-Adams, 'Ceremony and the Citizen: the Communal Year at Coventry, 1450–1550', and D. Palliser, 'The Trade Gilds of York', both in P. Clark and P. Slack (eds), *Crisis and Order in English Towns, 1500–1700: Essays in Urban History* (London: Routledge and Kegan Paul, 1972) pp. 57–85, 97, 103, 110.

72 M. Berlin, 'Civic Ceremony in Early Modern London', *Urban History Yearbook* (1986) pp. 15–27.

73 B. Mackerell, 'Account of the Company of St George in Norwich', *Norfolk Archaeology*, 3 (1852) p. 363.

74 J. Brand, *The History and Antiquities of the Town and County of Newcastle Upon Tyne*, 2 vols (Newcastle upon Tyne, 1789), vol. 2, p. 516.

75 H. Meller, *Leisure and the Changing City, 1870–1914* (London: Routledge and Kegan Paul, 1976) pp. 48–71.

76 Fraser, 'Developments', pp. 258–9; B. Holcomb, 'Revisioning Place: De- and Re-Constructing the Image of the Industrial City', in G. Kearns and C. Philo (eds), *Selling Places: The City as Cultural Capital, Past and Present* (Oxford: Pergamon Press, 1993) pp. 133–43; T. Hall, *Urban Geography* (London: Routledge, 1998) pp. 112–14.

77 Croll, *Civilizing the Urban*.

78 Cunningham, *Leisure in the Industrial Revolution*, pp. 20–2.

79 13 Geo II, c. 19, 'An act to restrain and prevent the excessive increase of horse races . . .' (1740).

80 R. W. Malcolmson, *Popular Recreations in English Society, 1700–1850* (Cambridge: Cambridge University Press, 1973) pp. 98–9, 146–52.

81 C. Langhamer, *Women's Leisure in England, 1920–60* (Manchester: Manchester University Press, 2000) pp. 19–20.

82 Quoted in H. Sul, 'The King's Book of Sports: the Nature of Leisure in Early Modern England', *International Journal of the History of Sport*, 17 (2000) p. 168.

83 York City Archives, House Book, 1 Nov. 1708, 22 Sept. 1739.

84 Walton, *English Seaside Resort*, pp. 128–55; J. K. Walton, *Blackpool* (Edinburgh: Edinburgh University Press, 1998) pp. 80–4, 126–30. On investment strategy and 'municipal economism' see J. Hassan, *The Seaside, Health and the Environment in England and Wales since 1800* (Aldershot: Ashgate, 2003) pp. 69–70; N. J. Morgan and A. Pritchard, *Power and Politics at the Seaside: The Development of Devon's Seaside Resorts in the Twentieth Century* (Exeter: Exeter University Press, 1999) pp. 155–78.

85 B. A. Thomas, *Penarth: The Garden by the Sea* (Machynlleth: Barry A. Thomas, 1997) pp. 1–93.

86 Reeves, *Pleasures and Pastimes*, pp. 116–22; Henricks, *Disputed Pleasures*, pp. 25–9; T. McLean, *The English at Play in the Middle Ages* (Windsor: Kensall Press, 1983) pp. 60–76; Manning, *Hunters and Poachers*, pp. 41–56.

87 Russell, *Football*, pp. 69–72, 237; G. Vinnai, *Football Mania. The Players and the Fans: The Mass Psychology of Football* (London: Ocean Books, 1973).

88 Vamplew, *Turf*, pp. 36, 45, 99.

89 Magoun, *History of Football*, p. 16; Holt and Mason, *Sport in Britain*, pp. 124–6, 158–9.

90 E. Le Roy Ladurie, *Carnivals in Romans: A People's Uprising at Romans, 1579–1580*, trans. M. Feeney (Harmondsworth: Penguin, 1981).

91 P. Collinson, *The Birthpangs of Protestant England: Religious and Cultural Change in the Sixteenth and Seventeenth Centuries* (New York: St Martin's Press, 1988) p. 41; Brewer, *Pleasures*, p. 37.

92 R. Poole, *Time's Alteration: Calendar Reform in Early Modern England* (London: University College London Press, 1998) pp. 167–71.

93 Malcolmson, *Popular Recreations*, pp. 39–40.

94 Longrigg, *Horse Racing*, pp. 44–5.

95 A. Ó. Maolfabhail, 'Hurling: an Old Game in a New World', in G. Jarvie (ed.), *Sport in the Making of Celtic Cultures* (Leicester: Leicester

University Press, 1999) pp. 149–65; W. R. Wilde, *Irish Popular Superstitions* (1st pub. 1852; reprinted, Shannon: Irish University Press, 1972) pp. 82–3.

96 R. A. N. Jones, 'Popular Culture, Policing and the "Disappearance" of the *Ceffyl Pren* in Cardigan, *c.*1837–1850', *Ceredigion*, 11 (1988–9) pp. 19–40; D. V. Jones, *Rebecca's Children: A Study of Rural Society, Crime and Protest* (Oxford: Oxford University Press, 1989) pp. 196–8, 267, 286, 297–8, 312.

97 Henricks, *Disputed Pleasures*, pp. 55–8; McLean, *English at Play*, pp. 2–3, 11–17.

98 Quoted in Birley, *Sport and the Making*, p. 37.

99 J. Thirsk, *Horses in Early Modern England: For Service, for Pleasure, for Power* (Reading: University of Reading, 1978) pp. 12, 22; Mason, *Sport in Britain*, p. 231.

100 D. Birley, *Land of Sport and Glory: Sport and British Society, 1887–1910* (Manchester: Manchester University Press, 1995) p. 230; Bailey, *Leisure and Class*, pp. 125–8; Holt, 'Sport and History', pp. 239–40.

101 Lowerson, *Sport*, pp. 285–94; Hill, *Sport, Leisure and Culture*, pp. 152–3; Vamplew, *Turf*, pp. 64–6; Holt, *Sport and the British*, pp. 276–7.

102 S. Inwood, *A History of London* (Basingstoke: Macmillan, 1998) pp. 927–30.

103 Hutton, *Merry England*, pp. 111–99, especially pp. 168–9, 190–3, 197; Hutton, *Stations of the Sun*, pp. 253–7, 323–4.

104 C. Whitfield (ed.), *Robert Dover and the Cotswold Games* (London: Henry Sotherson, 1962) pp. 1–29.

105 Cunningham, *Leisure in the Industrial Revolution*, pp, 46–51; Malcolmson, *Popular Recreations*, pp. 144–5.

106 Thompson, *Making of the English Working Class*, p. 443.

107 Underdown, *Start of Play*, pp. 59–63; A. J. Kettle, 'Lichfield Races', *Transactions of the Lichfield and South Staffordshire Archaeological Society*, 6 (1964–5) pp. 39–41.

108 Weber, *Musical Classics*, pp. 23–74.

109 Kift, *Victorian Music Hall*, pp. 80–114.

110 See, for example, Morgan and Pritchard, *Power and Politics at the Seaside*.

111 P. Weideger, *Gilding the Acorn: Behind the Façade of the National Trust* (London: Simon & Schuster, 1994) pp. 136–54, 189–91, 195.

4 CLASS

1 F. Drake, *Eboracum: Or, the History and Antiquities of the City of York* (1st pub. 1736; reprinted, East Ardsley: E.P. Publishing, 1978) p. 241.

2 For a survey of the historiography of popular culture, and one that argues that the 'role of politics, power and social inequality have been neglected', see E. Griffin, 'Popular Culture in Industrializing England', *Historical Journal*, 45 (2002) pp. 619–35.

3 For a survey of the modern historiography of class in Britain, see D. Cannadine, *Class in Britain* (Harmondsworth: Penguin, 2000) and for the changing historiography of leisure, see Bailey, 'Politics', pp. 131–75.

4 Holt, *Sport and the British*, p. 348.

5 Clarke and Critcher, *Devil Makes Work*, p. 190.

6 E. P. Thompson, 'Patrician Society, Plebeian Culture', *Journal of Social History*, 7 (1974) pp. 382–405; E. P. Thompson, 'Eighteenth-century English Society: Class Struggle without Class?', *Social History*, 3 (1978) p. 151; P. Burke, *Popular Culture in Early Modern Europe* (London: Temple Smith, 1979) pp. 23–9. In Burke's formulation (p. 28) the 'two cultural traditions in early modern Europe . . . did not correspond symmetrically to the two main social groups, the elite and the common people. The elite participated in the little tradition, but the common people did not participate in the great tradition.'

7 P. Joyce, *Visions of the People: Industrial England and the Question of Class, 1848–1914* (Cambridge: Cambridge University Press, 1994) p. 9.

8 Cannadine, *Class*, p. 15; R. Morris, in Cannon, *Oxford Companion to British History*, p. 217; J. M. Golby and A. W. Purdue, *The Civilisation of the Crowd: Popular Culture in England, 1750–1900* (London: Batsford, 1984) p. 195; revised edn (Stroud: Sutton, 1999) p. 7.

9 Hutton, *Merry England*, pp. 72–3; J. Barry, 'Popular Culture in Seventeenth-century Bristol', in B. Reay (ed.), *Popular Culture in Seventeenth-Century England* (London: Routledge, 1988) pp. 80–1; T. Harris, 'Problematising Popular Culture', in T. Harris (ed.), *Popular Culture in England, c.1500–1850* (Basingstoke: Macmillan, 1995) pp. 14–20; Fox, *Oral and Literate Culture*, pp. 406–9.

10 Croll, *Civilizing the Urban*, p. 218; M. Johnes, *Soccer and Society: South Wales, 1900–1939* (Cardiff: University of Wales Press, 2002) p. 209.

11 Introduction, in S. L. Kaplan (ed.), *Understanding Popular Culture: Europe from the Middle Ages to the Nineteenth Century* (Berlin: Mouton, 1984) p. 5; Reay, *Popular Cultures in England*, p. 1; see also P. Bailey, *Popular Culture and Performance in the Victorian City* (Cambridge: Cambridge University Press, 1998) pp. 10–11.

12 Cannadine, *Class*, pp. 19–20.

13 Huggins, *Flat Racing*, p. 15; Mason, 'Sport and Recreation', pp. 111–14; Malcolmson, *Popular Recreations*, p. 165.

14 Cannadine, *Class*, pp. 164, 166.

15   P. Laslett, *The World We Have Lost* (London: Methuen, 1968) p. 22.

16   T. Veblen, *The Theory of the Leisure Class* (1st pub. 1899; London: Unwin Books, 1970) pp. 41, 46, 51, 71.

17   K. Thomas, 'Work and Leisure in Pre-industrial Society', *Past and Present*, 29 (1964) p. 57; Cunningham, 'Leisure and Culture', p. 291.

18   D. Selwyn, *Jane Austen and Leisure* (London: Hambledon Press, 1999) pp. xiii–xiv.

19   Quoted in Strutt, *Glig-Gamena*, pp. xvii–xviii.

20   Black, *British and the Grand Tour*, especially pp. 134–58; Towner, *Historical Geography*, p. 132; A. Wilton and I. Bignamini (eds), *Grand Tour: The Lure of Italy in the Eighteenth Century* (London: Tate Gallery, 1996).

21   *Richard Creed's Journal of the Grand Tour, 1699–1700*, transcribed by A. Thomas (Oundle: Oundle Museum, 2002) p. 2.

22   N. Cox, *The Gentleman's Recreation* (1st pub. 1677; reprinted, East Ardsley: E.P. Publishing, 1973) p. 1.

23   McLean, *English at Play*, pp. 36–59; Henricks, *Disputed Pleasures*, pp. 16–24, 44–51, 77–81, 118–22; Manning, *Hunters and Poachers*; Grassby, 'Decline of Falconry', pp. 37–62; F. Heal and C. Holmes, *The Gentry in England and Wales, 1500–1700* (Basingstoke: Macmillan, 1994), pp. 289–93; Itzkowitz, *Peculiar Privilege*; Carr, *English Fox Hunting*; R. Longrigg, *The History of Foxhunting* (Basingstoke: Macmillan, 1975); J. R. and M. M. Gold, *Imagining Scotland: Tradition, Representation and Promotion in Scottish Tourism since 1750* (Aldershot: Scolar, 1995) pp. 109–12; Durie, *Scotland for the Holidays*, pp. 111–23.

24   M. Girouard, *The Return to Camelot: Chivalry and the English Gentleman* (New Haven, CT: Yale University Press, 1981).

25   Williamson, *Polite Landscapes*, pp. 133–4; Durie, *Scotland for the Holidays*, p. 121.

26   Manning, *Hunters and Poachers*, pp. 35–56.

27   L. Barker-Jones, *Princelings, Privilege and Power: The Tivyside Gentry in Their Community* (Llandysul: Gomer Press, 1999) p. 185.

28   E. P. Thompson, *Whigs and Hunters: The Origin of the Black Act* (London: Allen Lane, 1975); Carr, *English Fox Hunting*, pp. 68–86; Durie, *Scotland for the Holidays*, p. 112; Gold and Gold, *Imagining Scotland*, pp. 108–12.

29   E. Waterhouse, *Painting in Britain, 1530 to 1790*, 4th edn (Harmondsworth: Penguin, 1978) pp 297–305; S. Deuchar, *Sporting Art in Eighteenth-century England: A Social and Political History* (New Haven, CT: Yale University Press, 1988) pp. 86–91.

30   Longrigg, *Horse Racing*, pp. 57–63; D. Craig, *Horse-Racing: The Breeding of Thoroughbreds and a Short History of the English Turf* (Harmondsworth: Penguin, 1949) pp. 35–93, especially pp. 88–93.

31   Borsay, *Urban Renaissance*, pp. 262–3.

32   A. Bryson, *From Courtesy to Civility: Changing Codes of Conduct in Early Modern England* (Oxford: Clarendon Press, 1998).

33   A. Dain, 'Assemblies and Politeness, 1660–1840' (unpub. Ph.D. thesis, University of East Anglia, 2001) pp. 108–202; A.-I. Tardiff, 'A Cultural History of Social Dancing among the Upper Ranks in Eighteenth-century England' (unpub. Ph.D. thesis, University of Cambridge, 2002) pp. 38–66.

34   Johnson, *Music*, pp. 33–43, 188.

35   Weber, *Musical Classics*, pp. 20, 167; see also McVeigh, *Concert Life*, pp. 7, 11–12, 20–1, 44–9.

36   Hoggart, *Uses of Literacy*, pp. 22, 32.

37   Ibid., pp. 72–166.

38   Clark, *English Alehouse*, pp. 123–65.

39   Davies, *Leisure*, pp. 14–81.

40   Thompson, *Making of the English Working Class*, pp. 456–69; Williams, *Culture and Society*, pp. 312–13.

41   T. M. Owen, *The Customs and Traditions of Wales* (Cardiff: University of Wales Press and the Western Mail, 2000) pp. 50–5.

42   Johnes, *Soccer*, p. 130.

43   McKibbin, *Classes and Cultures*, p. 382; T. Mason, *Association Football and English Society, 1863–1915* (Brighton: Harvester, 1980) pp. 238–41; Mason, *Sport in Britain*, pp. 24–9; C. Bevan, 'Brass Band Contests: Art or Sport?', in Herbert, *Bands*, p. 116.

44   For a perspective which stresses the discontinuity between traditional rowdiness and modern hooliganism see M. Johnes, 'Hooligans and Barrackers: Crowd Disorder and Soccer in South Wales, *c*.1906–39', *Soccer and Society*, 1 (2000) pp. 19–35.

45   R. McKibbin, 'Working-Class Gambling in Britain, 1880–1939', *Past and Present*, 82 (1979), especially pp. 165–71.

46   G. S. Holmes, *Augustan England: Professions, State and Society, 1680–1730* (London: George Allen & Unwin, 1982); P. Langford, *A Polite and Commercial People: England, 1727–1783* (Oxford: Clarendon Press, 1989); P. Earle, *The Making of the English Middle Class: Business, Society and Family Life in London, 1660–1730* (London: Methuen, 1989); Berg, *Luxury and Pleasure*, pp. 199–246.

47   J. Barry and C. Brooks (eds), *The Middling Sort of People: Culture, Society and Politics in England, 1550–1800* (Basingstoke: Macmillan, 1994); Reay, *Popular Cultures in England*, pp. 202–4; K. Wrightson, *Earthly Necessities: Economic Lives in Early Modern Britain* (London: Penguin, 2002) pp. 289–306.

48 J. C. D. Clark, *Revolution and Rebellion: State and Society in England in the Seventeenth and Eighteenth Centuries* (Cambridge: Cambridge University Press, 1986) p. 166.

49 McKendrick, Brewer and Plumb, *Birth of a Consumer Society*; Golby and Purdue, *Civilisation of the Crowd*, p. 162; Cunningham, 'Leisure and Culture', pp. 296–7.

50 F. M. L. Thompson, *The Rise of Respectable Society: A Social History of Victorian Britain, 1830–1900* (London: Fontana, 1988) p. 260; G. Cross, *A Social History of Leisure since 1600* (State College, PA: Venture Publishing, 1990) pp. 193–6.

51 Borsay, *Urban Renaissance*, pp. 119, 123, 127, 265–6; Weber, *Musical Classics*, p. 137.

52 D. S. Macleod, *Art and the Victorian Middle Class: Money and the Making of Cultural Identity* (Cambridge: Cambridge University Press, 1996) pp. 1–2.

53 Bailey, *Leisure and Class*, pp. 65–72; Bailey, *Popular Culture*, pp. 13–29.

54 Lowerson, *Sport*, pp. 17–21.

55 Towner, *Historical Geography*, pp. 97–8; Walton, *British Seaside*, p. 53; Durie, *Scotland for the Holidays*, p. 70; Benson, *Consumer Society*, pp. 98–101.

56 Huggins, *Flat Racing*, pp. 4–5; M. Huggins and J. A. Mangan (eds), *Disreputable Pleasures: Less Virtuous Victorians at Play* (London: Frank Cass, 2004).

57 Bourdieu, *In Other Words*, pp. 156–7.

58 *Financial Times*, 30/31 March 2002, p. XXII.

59 Levinson and Christensen, *Encyclopedia*, pp. 6–8.

60 McKibbin, *Classes and Cultures*, p. 382; Hill, *Sport, Leisure and Culture*, pp. 132, 140–1; Reid, 'Playing and Praying', pp. 783–4; Lowerson, *Sport*, pp. 21–4, 95–124; Holt and Mason, *Sport in Britain*, p. 49.

61 D. Cannadine, *The Decline and Fall of the British Aristocracy* (London: Macmillan, 1996).

62 Russell, *Football*, pp. 229–34; Mason, *Sport in Britain*, pp. 179–80; Giulianotti, *Football*, pp. 147–52.

63 Borsay, *Urban Renaissance*, pp. 243–8; W. Weber, *Music and the Middle Class: The Social Structure of Concert Life in London, Paris and Vienna* (London: Croom Helm, 1975); Holt, *Sport and the British*, pp. 109–12; L. Davidoff, *The Best Circles: Society, Etiquette and the Season* (1st pub. 1973; London: Hutchinson, 1986) p. 36; Carr, *English Fox Hunting*, p. 242.

64 R. Wilson and A. Mackley, *Creating Paradise: The Building of the English Country House, 1660–1800* (London: Hambledon and London, 2000)

pp. 92, 240; Manning, *Hunters and Poachers*, p. 55; Carr, *English Fox Hunting*, pp. 181–4.

65 Borsay, 'Health and Leisure Resorts', pp. 792–3; J. A. R. Pimlott, *The Englishman's Holiday: A Social History* (1st pub. 1947; Hassocks: Harvester, 1976) pp. 40–3.

66 J. A. Sharpe, *Early Modern England: A Social History, 1550–1760*, 2nd edn (London: Edward Arnold, 1997) p. 205.

67 R. Roberts, *The Classic Slum: Salford Life in the First Quarter of the Century* (Harmondsworth: Penguin, 1974) p. 13.

68 Sandiford, *Cricket*, pp. 25–7; Mason, *Association Football*, pp. 89–92, 157; Holt, *Sport and the British*, pp. 159–60; Johnes, *Soccer*, pp. 115–16; Russell, *Popular Music*, pp. 170–4; Herbert, 'Nineteenth-century Brass Bands', pp. 37–44.

69 Roberts, *Classic Slum*, pp. 38–9, 183–4; Reay, *Popular Culture in Seventeenth-century England*, pp. 12–13.

70 P. Joyce, *Work, Society and Politics: The Culture of the Factory in Late Victorian England* (Brighton: Harvester, 1980) pp. 284–5.

71 Bailey, *Popular Culture*, pp. 30–46.

72 Quoted in Williams, *Valleys of Song*, p. 178; see also Walton, *English Seaside Resort*, p. 190.

73 Jones, *Workers at Play*, pp. 66–7; Vamplew, *Pay Up*, p. 254.

74 D. Vaisey (ed.), *The Diary of Thomas Turner, 1754–1765* (Oxford: Oxford University Press, 1984).

75 Cannadine, *Class*, p. 121.

76 Walton, *British Seaside*, pp. 169–92; Borsay, *Image of Georgian Bath*, p. 312.

77 Weber, *Music and the Middle Class*, pp. 56–7.

78 Holt, *Sport and the British*, p. 95.

79 Lowerson, *Sport*, pp. 181–6.

80 Blake, *Land Without Music*, pp. 54–64.

81 Urry, *Tourist Gaze*, pp. 88–9; J. Urry, *Consuming Places* (London: Routledge, 1995) pp. 225–7.

82 F. M. L. Thompson, *Gentrification and the Enterprise Culture: Britain, 1780–1980* (Oxford: Oxford University Press, 2001) pp. 98–121.

83 Bailey, *Leisure and Class*, pp. 154–5; Kift, *Victorian Music Hall*, pp. 62–8; Russell, *Popular Music*, pp. 66–72, 199–210; Golby and Purdue, *Civilisation of the Crowd*, p. 106; Langhamer, *Women's Leisure*, p. 64; Russell, *Football*, pp. 55–7; Clapson, *Bit of a Flutter*, p. 174; Donaldson, *Popular Literature*, p. x.

84 A. Gurr, 'The Theatre and Society', in J. Morrill (ed.), *The Oxford Illustrated History of Tudor and Stuart Britain* (Oxford: Oxford University

Press, 1996) p. 158; L. Klein, 'Politeness for Plebs: Consumption and Social Identity in Early Eighteenth Century England', in Bermingham and Brewer, *Consumption*, pp. 362–82.

85   B. Lemire, 'Consumerism in Preindustrial and Early Industrial England: the Trade in Secondhand Clothes', *Journal of British Studies*, 27 (1989) pp. 1–24.

86   McLean, *English at Play*, pp. 70, 118; Manning, *Hunters and Poachers*, p. 235; Hutton, *Stations of the Sun*, pp. 264–6; S. W. Mintz, 'The Changing Roles of Food in the Study of Consumption', in Brewer and Porter, *Consumption*, pp. 263–7.

87   Fraser, 'Developments in Leisure', p. 245; Burnett, *Riot, Revelry and Rout*, pp. 35–6; D. Smith and G. Williams, *Fields of Praise: The Official History of the Welsh Rugby Union, 1881–1981* (Cardiff: University of Wales Press, 1980) pp. 20–8; Holt, *Sport and the British*, pp. 71–2.

88   Walton, *English Seaside Resort*, pp. 5, 216; Benson, *Consumer Society*, pp. 98–105.

89   Brewer and Porter, *Consumption*, pp. 40–2, 208, 274–7, 294; Bermingham and Brewer, *Consumption*, pp. 12–13; Tranter, *Sport, Economy and Society*, pp. 26–31.

90   Towner, *Historical Geography*, pp. 267–9.

91   H. Smith, 'Billiards Snookered: the Decline of Professional Billiards in England', *British Society of Sports Bulletin*, 18 (2001) p. 27.

92   Burke, *Popular Culture*, pp. 3–22, 281–6; Johnson, *Music*, pp. 130–49; R. Sweet, *Antiquaries: The Discovery of the Past in Eighteenth-century England* (London: Hambledon and London, 2004) pp. 334–9.

93   M. Hughes and R. Stradling, *The English Musical Renaissance, 1840–1940: Constructing a National Music*, 2nd edn (Manchester: Manchester University Press, 2001) pp. 77–81, 98–9, 174–5; Blake, *Land Without Music*, pp. 44–7.

94   McLean, *English at Play*, pp. 11–17, 82–4; Henricks, *Disputed Pleasures*, pp. 58–60, 81–3, 136–8, 140–2; Underdown, *Start of Play*, pp. 15–16; Carr, *English Fox Hunting*, pp. 21–30.

95   Hutton, *Merry England*, p. 72: Hutton, *Stations of the Sun*, pp. 112–23, 271–3; J. M. Golby and A. W. Purdue, *The Making of Modern Christmas* (London: Batsford, 1986) pp. 41–80.

96   T. Harrison and C. Madge, *Britain by Mass Observation* (1st pub. 1939; London: Century Hutchinson, 1986) p. 174.

97   Thompson, *Respectable Society*, p. 324; J. Richards, *The Age of the Dream Palace: Cinema and Society in Britain, 1930–1939* (London: Routledge and Kegan Paul, 1989) pp. 15–16; Hill, *Sport, Leisure and Culture*, pp. 106–8.

98 Burke, *Popular Culture*, p. 58; Kaplan, *Understanding*, p. 12; Johnson, *Music*, chapters 6–10.

99 S. Barton, *Working-Class Organizations and Popular Tourism, 1840–1970* (Manchester: Manchester University Press, 2005), especially pp. 216–18; Holt, *Sport and the British*, p. 135.

100 J. Goulstone, 'The Working-Class Origins of Modern Football', *International Journal of the History of Sport*, 17 (2000) pp. 135–43; A. Harvey, 'Football's Missing Link: the Real Story of the Evolution of Modern Football', in J. A. Mangan (ed.), *Sport in Europe: Politics, Class, Gender* (London: Frank Cass, 1999) p. 114.

101 Moorhouse, *People's Game*, pp. 28–45; Holt, *Sport and the British*, pp. 152–3.

102 Lowerson, *Sport*, pp. 24–6, 106–7.

103 Cunningham, *Leisure in the Industrial Revolution*, pp. 90–2, 99–107, 123–7; Bailey, *Leisure and Class*; Fraser, 'Developments', pp. 243–8, 250–1, 258–60; Holt, *Sport and the British*, pp. 136–48; Golby and Purdue, *Civilisation of the Crowd*, pp. 88–110; A. Delves, 'Popular Recreations and Social Conflict in Derby, 1800–1850', in E. and S. Yeo (eds), *Popular Culture and Class Conflict, 1590–1914: Explorations in the History of Labour and Leisure* (Brighton: Harvester, 1981) pp. 115–16: Cross, *Social History of Leisure*, pp. 99–101.

104 Burke, *Popular Culture*, especially pp. 23–9, 270–81.

105 Brand, *Observations*, preface to Bourne, p. xi.

106 Hutton, *Merry England*, pp. 241–6; M. Ingram, 'Ridings, Rough Music, and the "Reform of Popular Culture" in Early Modern England', *Past and Present*, 15 (1984) pp. 79–113; Reay, *Popular Cultures in England*, pp. 210–12; 216–18; P. Jenkins, *The Making of a Ruling Class: The Glamorgan Gentry, 1640–1790* (Cambridge: Cambridge University Press, 1983) pp. 205–8.

107 Jenkins, *Making of a Ruling Class*, pp. 268–71; R. Suggett, 'Festivals and Social Structures in Early Modern Wales', *Past and Present*, 152 (1996) p. 85.

108 S. Connolly, ' "Ag Déanamh *Commanding*": Elite Responses to Popular Culture, 1660–1850', in Donnelly and Miller, *Irish Popular Culture*, pp. 11–17; K. Whelan, 'An Underground Gentry? Catholic Middlemen in Eighteenth-Century Ireland', in ibid, p. 160; S. Ó. Maitiú, *The Humours of Donnybrook: Dublin's Famous Fair and Its Suppression* (Blackrock: Irish Academic Press, 1996) pp. 37–8.

109 Golby and Purdue, *Civilisation of the Crowd*, p. 200; see also Cunningham, 'Leisure and Culture', pp. 319–20.

110 Hoggart, *Uses of Literacy*, p. 342; Cannadine, *Class*, p. 131; D. Russell, 'Football and Society in the North West, 1919–1939', *Journal of the*

North West Labour History Group, 24 (1999/2000) p. 13; Hill, *Sport, Leisure and Culture*, pp. 63, 65, 79, 104; Blake, *Land Without Music*, pp. 90–5.

111   Bailey, *Popular Culture*, pp. 10–11.

112   Fraser, 'Developments', p. 257; Kift, *Victorian Music Hall*, p. 175.

113   Underdown, *Start of Play*, pp. 66–71; Williams, *Cricket*, pp. 15–16, 45; Huggins, *Flat Racing*, pp. 9, 15; Itzkowitz, *Peculiar Privilege*, pp. 26, 105, 176–7; Carr, *English Fox Hunting*, pp. 49, 155.

114   Roberts, *Classic Slum*, p. 163.

115   Smith and Willams, *Fields of Praise*, p. 195; D. Hamilton, *The Scottish Golf Guide*, 2nd edn (Edinburgh: Canongate Books, 1995) pp. 7, 12.

116   Geddes, *Swing Through Time*, p. 58; Birley, *Land of Sport and Glory*, p. 103; Holt, *Sport and the British*, p. 72; J. Lowerson, 'Golf and the Making of Myth', in G. Jarvie and G. Walker (eds), *Scottish Sport and the Making of a Nation: Ninety Minute Patriots?* (Leicester: Leicester University Press, 1994) pp. 75–90; *Observer*, 21 July 2000.

117   Reay, *Popular Cultures in England*, p. 213.

118   Vamplew, *Turf*, especially pp. 77–8, 130–1, 178–9; Borsay, *Urban Renaissance*, pp. 183–5, 304–5; Burnett, *Riot, Revelry and Rout*, pp. 101–38.

119   Mason, *Association Football*, pp. 223–42.

120   Brewer, *Pleasures*, pp. 342–8, 561–5; D. Burrows and R. Dunhill (eds), *Music and Theatre in Handel's World: The Family Papers of James Harris, 1732–1780* (Oxford: Oxford University Press, 2002) p. xxviii and *passim*.

121   Clapson, *Bit of a Flutter*, pp. 138–41; Mason, *Sport in Britain*, pp. 15–16.

122   Booth, *Theatre*, p. 2; Gurr, *Playgoing*, pp. 14–38.

123   D. Höher, 'The Composition of Music Hall Audiences', in P. Bailey (ed.), *Music Hall: The Business of Pleasure* (Milton Keynes: Open University Press, 1986) pp. 86–8.

124   Richards, *Age of the Dream Palace*, pp. 16–17, 24–5, 28; Langhamer, *Women's Leisure*, pp. 60–1.

5   IDENTITIES

1   McKibbin, *Classes and Cultures*, p. 342.

2   McCrone, *Sport*, especially pp. 283–5.

3   DeNora, *Music*, p. 49; B. Malbon, *Clubbing: Dancing, Ecstasy and Vitality* (London: Routledge, 1999) p. 126; J. Dumazedier, *Sociology of Leisure* (Amsterdam: Elsevier, 1974) p. 71.

4   I. Watts, *The Rise of the Novel* (Harmondsworth: Penguin, 1966), especially chapter 2; Brewer, *Pleasures*, pp. 192–7, 540.

5   P. Borsay, 'The Culture of Improvement', in P. Langford (ed.), *The Short Oxford History of the British Isles: The Eighteenth Century* (Oxford: Oxford University Press, 2002) p. 190.

6   Cunningham, *Leisure in the Industrial Revolution*, p. 76; Critcher et al., *Sociology of Leisure*, p. 11; Urry, *Consuming Places*, p. 217.

7   Urry, *Tourist Gaze*, pp. 45–6; Urry, *Consuming Places*, p. 197.

8   D. Hollett, *The Pioneer Ramblers, 1850–1914* (North Wales Area of the Ramblers' Association, 2002).

9   R. Carew, *The Survey of Cornwall* (1st pub. 1602; reprinted, Redruth: Tamar Books, 2000) p. 89; *Bamford's Passages in the Life of a Radical, and Early Days*, ed. H. Dunckley, 2 vols (London: T. Fisher Unwin, 1905) vol. 1, p. 131.

10 M. Crang, *Cultural Geography* (London: Routledge, 1998) pp. 60–2; Black, *British and the Grand Tour*, p. 239.

11 Langhamer, *Women's Leisure*, pp. 1, 18; Haywood et al., *Understanding Leisure*, pp. 2, 7, 243–53; Hill, *Sport, Leisure and Culture*, pp. 8–9.

12 Holt, *Sport and the British*, p. 173.

13 A. Shepard, *Meanings of Manhood in Early Modern England* (Oxford: Oxford University Press, 2003) pp. 2–3.

14 Reay, *Popular Cultures in England*, p. 27; E. A. Foyster, *Manhood in Early Modern England: Honour, Sex and Marriage* (London: Longman, 1999) p. 22; T. Hitchcock, *English Sexualities, 1700–1800* (Basingstoke: Macmillan, 1997) pp. 58–75.

15 Levinson and Christensen, *Encyclopedia*, pp. 152–3.

16 Walton, *Blackpool*, pp. 146–8; Walton, *British Seaside*, pp. 161–2.

17 E. Dunning, 'Sport as a Male Preserve: Notes on the Social Sources of Masculine Identity and Its Transformations', *Theory, Culture and Society*, 3 (1986) pp. 79–90; Holt, *Sport and the British*, p. 8; Lowerson, *Sport*, pp. 64–94; Polley, *Moving the Goalposts*, pp. 104–10; Williams, *Cricket*, pp. 93–4; Giulianotti, *Football*, pp. 154–7.

18 J. A. Mangan, *Athleticism in the Victorian and Edwardian Public School* (Cambridge: Cambridge University Press, 1981); T. Money, *Manly and Muscular Diversions: Public Schools and the Nineteenth-century Sporting Revival* (London: Duckworth, 2001), especially pp. 66–9.

19 M. Cronin, *Sport and Nationalism in Ireland: Gaelic Games, Soccer and Irish Identity since 1884* (Dublin: Four Courts Press, 1999) p. 22.

20 For the debate on the subject see Levinson and Christensen, *Encyclopedia*, pp. 240–1.

21 Mason, *Sport in Britain*, p. 38; McKibbin, *Classes and Cultures*, pp. 356–7.

22 Clark, *British Clubs*, pp. 2–3, 22, 24, 84, 122, 130–1; Cunningham, 'Leisure and Culture', p. 295; S. Rigby, *English Society in the Later Middle*

Ages: Class, Status and Gender (Basingstoke: Macmillan, 1995), p. 276; H. Leyser, *Medieval Women: A Social History of Women in England, 450–1500* (London: Phoenix, 2004) p. 161.

23 T. Collins and W. Vamplew, *Mud, Sweat and Beers: A Cultural History of Sport and Alcohol* (Oxford: Berg, 2000).

24 Clark, *English Alehouse*, pp. 78–9, 82–4, 131–2, 147–51, 235–6; Malcom, 'Rise of the Pub', pp. 51, 55–6; J. D. Melville, 'The Use and Organization of Domestic Space in Late Seventeenth-century London' (unpub. Ph.D. thesis, University of Cambridge, 1999) pp. 239–53.

25 Fraser, 'Developments', p. 243; Davies, *Leisure*, pp. 30, 61–73; Rowntree and Lavers, *English Life and Leisure*, pp. 165, 175.

26 M. Hunter, *Science and Society in Restoration England* (Cambridge: Cambridge University Press, 1981) pp. 59–86.

27 Blake, *Land without Music*, pp. 67–8.

28 O'Connell, *Car*, pp. 43–76.

29 J. Williams, *A Game for Rough Girls? A History of Women's Football in Britain* (London: Routledge, 2003) pp. 25–44, 181–8; Mason, *Sport in Britain*, pp. 178–9.

30 Lowerson, *Sport*, pp. 215–19; Lowerson, 'Golf and the Making of a Myth', p. 85; McCrone, *Sport*, pp. 166–77; Durie, *Scotland for the Holidays*, p. 125; *Guardian*, 16 July 2002, G2, pp. 2–3; 27 March 2003, pp. 35–6; 20 May 2003, G2, pp. 4–5.

31 R. Ryan, 'The Emergence of Middle-class Yachting in the North-west of England from the Later Nineteenth Century', in S. Fisher (ed.), *Recreation and the Sea* (Exeter: Exeter University Press, 1997) p. 171.

32 Johnes, *Soccer*, pp. 117–19; Giulianotti, *Football*, pp. 153–4, 157–9; Clapson, *Bit of a Flutter*, p. 174; Holt and Mason, *Sport in Britain*, pp. 104, 114.

33 Langhamer, *Women's Leisure*, pp. 29–44.

34 Owen, *Customs and Traditions*, p. 37.

35 Davidoff, *Best Circles*, pp. 56–7; B. Hill, *Women Alone: Spinsters in England, 1660–1850* (New Haven, CT: Yale University Press, 2001) pp. 173–4.

36 A. Vickery, 'Women and the World of Goods: a Lancashire Consumer and Her Possessions', in Brewer and Porter, *Consumption*, p. 280; A. Vickery, *The Gentleman's Daughter: Women's Lives in Georgian England* (New Haven, CT: Yale University Press, 1998) pp. 183–94. But see also the case for men as consumers, in Berg, *Luxury*, pp. 236–46.

37 Rappaport, *Shopping*, p. 220; Walton 'Towns and Consumerism', pp. 723–4; Reid, 'Playing and Praying', p. 783.

38 B. Caine, *English Feminism, 1780–1980* (Oxford: Oxford University Press, 1997) pp. 131–47; K. Gleadle, *British Women in the Nineteenth Century* (Basingstoke: Palgrave Macmillan, 2001) pp. 178–9, 184.

39 Benson, *Consumer Society*, pp. 180–203; S. Bruely, *Women in Britain since 1900* (Basingstoke: Macmillan, 1999) pp. 72–3.

40 Tardiff, 'Social Dance', pp. 135–79.

41 E. Casciani, *Oh, How We Danced! A History of Ballroom Dancing in Scotland* (Edinburgh: Mercat Press, 1994) pp. 40–65.

42 Harrison and Madge, *Mass Observation*, p. 177; Rowntree and Lavers, *English Life and Leisure*, p. 283.

43 Borsay, *Urban Renaissance*, pp. 243–8; M. Girouard, *The English Town* (New Haven, CT: Yale University Press, 1990) pp. 132–3; Dain, 'Assemblies', pp. 255–71.

44 Haywood et al., *Understanding Leisure*, pp. 129–33; Critcher et al., *Sociology of Leisure*, pp. 134–9.

45 Davies, *Leisure*, pp. 55–61.

46 Lowerson, *Sport*, p. 208; McCrone, *Sport*, pp. 195–215, 257–67; J. Hargreaves, 'The Victorian Cult of the Family and the Early Years of Female Sport', in E. G. Dunning, J. A. Maguire, and R. E. Pearton (eds), *The Sports Process: A Comparative and Developmental Approach* (Champaign, IL: Human Kinetics, 1993) pp. 75, 78, 80.

47 Brand, *Observations*, p. 255; Wilde, *Superstitions*, pp. 31–70; Hutton, *Stations of the Sun*, pp. 226–43.

48 Dolan, *Ladies of the Grand Tour*, p. 11.

49 Swingelhurst, *Cook's Tours*, p. 35.

50 Borsay, 'Health and Leisure Resorts', pp. 795–6.

51 S. Skedd, 'Women Teachers and the Expansion of Girls' Schooling in England, *c*.1760–1820', in H. Barker and E. Chalus (eds), *Gender in Eighteenth-century England: Roles, Representations and Responsibilities* (Harlow: Longman, 1997) pp. 102–25; Golby and Purdue, *Civilisation of the Crowd*, pp. 148–9; K. Flint, *The Woman Reader, 1837–1914* (Oxford: Clarendon Press, 1993) p. 330.

52 Spufford, *Small Books*, pp. 34–6, 62–4; Fox, *Oral and Literate Culture*, pp. 18–19, 58, 407–9.

53 McAleer, *Popular Reading*, especially pp. 246–7, 250–1; McKibbin, *Classes and Cultures*, pp. 471–2, 486–96, 508.

54 Manning, *Hunters and Poachers*, pp. 5, 194; McLean, *English at Play*, pp. 50–6; Grassby, 'Decline of Falconry', p. 49.

55 Carr, *English Fox Hunting*, pp. 71, 242; Itzkowitz, *Peculiar Privilege*, pp. 48–9, 55–8.

56 McCrone, *Sport*, pp. 154–91; Lowerson, *Sport*, pp. 203–20.

57   Clark and Houston, 'Culture and Leisure', pp. 581–2; McVeigh, *Concert Life*, pp. 53–6; Strutt, *Glig-Gamena*, p. 254.

58   Hutton, *Stations of the Sun*, pp. 61–2; Johnson, *Music*, pp. 181–3; Russell, *Popular Music*, pp. 199–211; Williams, *Valleys of Song*, pp. 62, 108; Fraser, 'Developments', p. 244.

59   Kift, *Victorian Music Hall*, pp. 45–53, 62–8, 72–3: Croll, *Civilizing the Urban*, p. 198.

60   R. Leppert, *Music and Image: Domesticity, Ideology and Socio-Cultural Formations in Eighteenth-century England* (Cambridge: Cambridge University Press, 1988); Johnson, *Music*, pp. 23–4; H. D. Johnstone and R. Fiske (eds), *The Blackwell History of Music in Britain*; vol. 4: *The Eighteenth Century* (Oxford: Blackwell, 1990) pp. 5–9.

61   Herbert, 'Nineteenth-century Brass Bands', pp. 46–9; D. Russell, ' "What's Wrong with Brass Bands?" Cultural Change and the Band Movement, 1918–c.1964', in Herbert, *Bands*, pp. 65–6.

62   N. Cook, *Music: A Very Short Introduction* (Oxford: Oxford University Press, 1998) pp. 109–10.

63   S. Frith, 'Towards an Aesthetic of Popular Music', in R. Leppert and S. McClary (eds), *Music and Society: The Politics of Composition, Performance and Reception* (Cambridge: Cambridge University Press, 1987) pp. 146–8.

64   Clarke and Critcher, *Devil Makes Work*, pp. 81–2.

65   Holt, *Sport and the British*, pp. 15, 19; Burnett, *Riot, Revelry and Rout*, pp. 221–4; 232; Carter, *Medieval Games*, pp. 83–5; McLean, *English at Play*, pp. 50–6; Sandiford, *Cricket*, p. 28; Tranter, *Sport, Economy and Society*, p. 78; Underdown, *Start of Play*, pp. 81, 85, 111–12.

66   Sandiford, *Cricket*, pp. 42–8; McCrone, *Sport*, pp. 141–8.

67   R. Porter, *London: A Social History* (London: Hamish Hamilton, 1994) p. 132.

68   J. Black, *Modern British History since 1900* (Basingstoke: Macmillan, 2000) pp. 22–4; T. Kushner, 'Immigration and "Race Relations" in Postwar British Society', in Johnson, *Twentieth-century Britain*, pp. 411–26.

69   Henricks, *Disputed Pleasures*, p. 149; McKibbin, *Classes and Cultures*, p. 366; Mason, *Sport in Britain*, pp. 99–105.

70   Clapson, *Bit of a Flutter*, pp. 116–17; Davies, *Leisure*, pp. 126–9; Kift, *Victorian Music Hall*, pp. 45–6.

71   Blake, *Land without Music*, pp. 103–4, 116–19.

72   M. Pittock, *Celtic Identity and the British Image* (Manchester: Manchester University Press, 1999); D. Outram, *The Enlightenment* (Cambridge: Cambridge University Press, 1995) pp. 63–79.

73   Urry, *Tourist Gaze*, pp. 142–3.

74   Hill, *Sport, Leisure and Culture*, p. 139.

75   Holt and Mason, *Sport in Britain*, p. 86.

76   Polley, *Moving the Goalposts*, pp. 154–6; Giulianotti, *Football*, pp. 162–3; N. Evans and P. O'Leary, 'Playing the Game: Sport and Ethnic Minorities in Wales', in C. Williams, N. Evans, and P. O'Leary (eds), *A Tolerant Nation? Exploring Ethnic Diversity in Wales* (Cardiff: University of Wales Press, 2003) p. 121.

77   Holt and Mason, *Sport in Britain*, p. 132; *Guardian*, 13 May 2002, p. 22; *Observer*, Sport, 19 September 2004, pp. 8–9.

78   R. Rapoport and R. N. Rapoport, *Leisure and the Family Life Cycle* (London: Routledge and Kegan Paul, 1978); Langhamer, *Women's Leisure*.

79   P. Thane, *Old Age in English History: Past Experiences, Present Issues* (Oxford: Oxford University Press, 2000) is a revealing study of the history of old age, though there is relatively little discussion of leisure as such.

80   Haywood et al., *Understanding Leisure*, pp. 140–3; Clarke and Critcher, *Devil Makes Work*, pp. 153–5; Critcher et al., *Sociology of Leisure*, pp. 78–87.

81   K. Thomas, *Age and Authority in Early Modern England* (London: British Academy, 1976) pp. 5, 12, 44.

82   H. Cunningham, *Children and Childhood in Western Society since 1500* (Harlow: Longman, 1995) p. 1.

83   P. Ariès, *Centuries of Childhood* (1st pub. 1960; Harmondsworth: Penguin, 1979) p. 68.

84   J. H. Plumb, 'The New World of Children in the Eighteenth Century', *Past and Present*, 67 (1975) pp. 64–95; Cunningham, *Children*, pp. 41–78; C. Heywood, *Children and Childhood in the West from Medieval to Modern Times* (Cambridge: Polity, 2001) pp. 19–31.

85   J. Street, 'Youth Culture', in Johnson, *Twentieth-century Britain*, pp. 460–75; Hill, *Sport, Leisure and Culture*, pp. 114–28; Blake, *Land without Music*, pp. 94–102; G. Mungham and G. Pearson (eds), *Working Class Youth Culture* (London: Routledge and Kegan Paul, 1976).

86   Rowntree and Lavers, *English Life and Leisure*, pp. 230–1, 280; Richards, *Age of the Dream Palace*, pp. 14, 67–85; McKibbin, *Classes and Cultures*, pp. 394, 419–20; Davies, *Leisure*, pp. 82–108, 170–1; Langhamer, *Women's Leisure*, especially pp. 56–7.

87   Walton, 'Towns and Consumerism', pp. 740–1; Heywood, *Children and Childhood*, pp. 29–30.

88   B.A. Hanawalt, *Growing Up in Medieval London: The Experience of Childhood in History* (Oxford: Oxford University Press, 1993) p. 7; Cunningham, *Children*, pp. 13–15, 30–4; Heywood, *Children and Childhood*, pp. 12–18.

89   McLean, *English at Play*, pp. 85–6; Reeves, *Pleasures and Pastimes*, pp. 73–4; Strutt, *Glig-Gamena*, pp. 335–53.

90   Hutton, *Stations of the Sun*, pp. 163–6, 237, 247; Wilde, *Superstitions*, pp. 47, 52, 63; Bamford, *Early Days*, in *Bamford's Passages*, vol. 1, pp. 137–9; T. Owen, *Welsh Folk Customs* (Llandysul: Gomer Press, 1987) pp. 86, 133–4.

91   P. F. Radford, 'Escaping Philippedes Connection: Death, Injury and Illness in 18th Century Sport in Britain', in T. Terrret (ed.), *Sport and Health in History* (Sankt Augustin: Academia Verlag, 1999) p. 91.

92   I. and P. Opie, *The Lore and Language of Schoolchildren* (1st pub. 1959; Oxford: Clarendon Press, 1967) pp. 1–2.

93   Brand, *Observations*, p. 271; Malcolmson, *Popular Recreations*, pp. 55–6.

94   Bamford, *Early Days*, in *Bamford's Passages*, vol. 1, p. 85.

95   Shepard, *Meanings of Manhood*, pp. 96–113; Clark, *English Alehouse*, p. 127.

96   G. Rosser and E. P. Dennison, 'Urban Culture and the Church, 1300–1540', in Palliser, *Cambridge Urban History*, vol. 1, pp. 358–9; Hanawalt, *Growing Up*, pp. 11, 114–18.

97   Malcolm Bradbury, quoted in Green, *All Dressed Up*, p. 2.

98   On youth culture, see Hill, *Sport, Leisure and Culture*, pp. 114–25; J. Croft, 'Youth Culture and Style', in M. Story and P. Childs (eds), *British Cultural Identities*, 2nd edn (London: Routledge; 2002) pp. 139–73; Cross, *Social History of Leisure*, pp. 206–16.

99   Marwick, *Sixties*, p. 11.

100 S. Cohen, *Folk Devils and Moral Panics: The Creation of the Mods and Rockers* (1st pub. 1972; Oxford: Blackwell, 1993).

101 Quoted in Hanawalt, *Growing Up*, p. 125; A. Ross (ed.), *A Selection from The Tatler and The Spectator of Steele and Addison* (Harmondsworth: Penguin, 1982) p. 303; J. Hoppit, *Land of Liberty? England, 1689–1727* (Oxford: Clarendon Press, 2000) p. 439; Clapson, *Bit of a Flutter*, pp. 79–81.

102 Sharpe, *Early Modern England*, pp. 56–76.

103 P. Borsay, 'Childhood, Adolescents, and Fashionable Urban Society in Eighteenth-century England', in A. Müller (ed.), *Fashioning Childhood in the Eighteenth Century* (Aldershot: Ashgate, forthcoming).

104 Golby and Purdue, *Civilisation of the Crowd*, pp. 145–7; L. Davidoff and C. Hall, *Family Fortunes: Men and Women of the English Middle Class, 1780–1850* (London: Hutchinson, 1988) pp. 357–96.

105 Hutton, *Stations of the Sun*, pp. 113–14; Owen, *Welsh Folk Customs*, p. 35.

106 Hutton, *Stations of the Sun*, p. 426.

107 Walton, *English Seaside Resort*, p. 41.

108 Benson, *Consumer Society*, pp. 86–95; Clarke and Critcher, *Devil Makes Work*, pp. 170–3.

109 Haywood et al., *Understanding Leisure*, pp. 107–8; Hill, *Sport, Leisure and Culture*, pp. 109–10.

110 Mangan, *Athleticism*, p. 146.

111 Malcolmson, *Popular Recreations*, p. 37; T. Wright, *The History and Antiquities of Ludlow* (1st pub. 1826; reprinted, Manchester: E. J. Morton, 1972) pp. 193–4.

112 Carew, *Survey of Cornwall*, p. 80.

113 Owen, *Customs and Traditions*, pp. 43–4.

114 Owen, *Customs and Traditions*, pp. 64–6; Jones, 'Popular Culture', pp. 19–40.

115 Wilde, *Superstitions*, p. 48.

116 Davies, *Leisure*, pp. 124–30.

117 J. K. Walton and R. Poole, 'The Lancashire Wakes in the Nineteenth Century', in Storch, *Popular Culture*, p. 114.

118 B. Harrison, 'Pubs', in H. J. Dyos and M. Wolff (eds), *The Victorian City: Image and Realities*, 2 vols (London: Routledge and Kegan Paul, 1973) vol. 1, pp. 169–70.

119 Roberts, *Classic Slum*; M. Young and P. Willmott, *Family and Kinship in East London* (London: Routledge and Kegan Paul, 1957).

120 Clark, *British Clubs*; Morris, 'Voluntary Societies', pp. 338–66; Tranter, *Sport, Economy and Society*, pp. 22–4; Cunningham, 'Leisure and Culture', pp. 325–6; Bailey, 'Politics', p. 145.

121 Russell, *Football*, pp. 14–17; Williams, *Valleys of Song*, pp. 133, 143.

122 Brewer, *Pleasures*, p. 50, who uses the phrase to describe clubs rather than newspapers and periodicals.

123 Cranfield, *Newspaper*, pp. 99, 101, 105–6; Wiles, *Freshest Advices*, pp. 173–4, 243, 322.

124 Ross, *Selections*, pp. 24, 144–7.

125 Spufford, *Small Books*, pp. 224–32; Burke, *Popular Culture*, pp. 149–77.

126 Brewer, *Pleasures*, pp. 334–48; P. M. Young, *Handel* (London: Dent, 1979) pp. 45, 57–8; Burrows and Dunhill, *Music*, pp. 9–10, 20; C. Black, *The Linleys of Bath* (London: Martin Secker, 1911) pp. 28–118; K. James, 'Venanzio Rauzzini and the Search for Musical Perfection', *Bath History*, 3 (1990) pp. 90–113; E. D. Mackerness, *A Social History of English Music* (London: Routledge and Kegan Paul, 1964) pp. 95–6.

127 Holt, *Sport and the British*, p. 21; Birley, *Sport and the Making*, pp. 109, 118–19, 123, 155–6, 165; Underdown, *Start of Play*, p. 157.

128 Golby and Purdue, *Civilisation of the Crowd*, p. 76.

129 Lowerson, *Sport*, pp. 69–72.

130 *Observer*, 25 May 2003, Review, p. 1.

131 Holt, *Sport and the British*, p. 23; Evans and O'Leary, 'Playing the Game', p. 113.

132 Smith and Williams, *Fields of Praise*, pp. 74–6; R. Holt, 'The King Over the Border: Dennis Law and Scottish Football', in Jarvie and Walker, *Scottish Sport*, pp. 61, 71.

133 McKibbin, *Classes and Cultures*, p. 437.

134 J. Simpson and S. Roud, *A Dictionary of English Folklore* (Oxford: Oxford University Press, 2001) pp. 286–7.

135 'Account of the Company of St George in Norwich', *Norfolk Archaeology*, 3 (1852) pp. 363–4; Wilde, *Superstitions*, pp. 64–5.

136 *Observer Sport Monthly*, September 2002; *Observer*, 25 May 2003, Review, p. 1.

137 *Guardian*, Sport, 11 October 2004, pp. 2–3.

138 K. Thomas, *Man and the Natural World: Changing Attitudes in England, 1500–1800* (Harmondsworth: Penguin, 1984) pp. 92–191.

139 Brand, *Observations*, p. 379.

140 J. Bale, *Landscapes of Modern Sport* (Leicester: Leicester University Press, 1994) pp. 61–2.

6 PLACE

1   Williams, *Valleys of Song*, pp. 39–53.

2   Burke, *Popular Culture*, pp. 116–48; Reay, *Popular Cultures in England*, pp. 164–5.

3   Hutton, *Merry England*, p. 46.

4   R. Bushaway, *By Rite: Custom, Ceremony and the Community in England, 1700–1880* (London: Junction Books, 1982) pp. 34–48.

5   See, for example, Hutton, *Merry England*, pp. 31, 99–100; Hutton, *Stations of the Sun*, pp. 201–3, 211; Carew, *Survey of Cornwall*, p. 86.

6   Burnett, *Riot, Revelry and Rout*, pp. 84, 93–4; Owen, *Customs and Traditions*, pp. 71–2; Ó Crualaoich, 'Merry Wake', p. 194.

7   D. Underdown, *Revel, Riot and Rebellion: Popular Politics and Culture in England, 1603–1660* (Oxford: Oxford University Press, 1987) pp. 73–7; Underdown, *Start of Play*, pp. 11–14.

8   Williams, *Cricket*, pp. 27–35.

9   Walton, *English Seaside Resort*, pp. 28–34; Walton, *British Seaside*, pp. 51–2.

10 Roberts, *Classic Slum*, p. 156.

11 Burnett, *Riot, Revelry and Rout*, pp. 61–2.

12 Croll, *Civilizing the Urban*, pp. 121, 123, 131–6; Williams, *Valleys of Song*, p. 94.

13 Crang, *Cultural Geography*, p. 61.

14 R. Suggett, 'Festivals and Social Structures in Early Modern Wales', *Past and Present*, 152 (1996) p. 103.

15 A. Winchester, *Discovering Parish Boundaries* (Princes Risborough: Shire, 2000) pp. 39–40.

16 Malcolmson, *Popular Recreations*, pp. 35, 37, 44; Burnett, *Riot, Revelry and Rout*, p. 52; Hutton, *Stations of the Sun*, p. 235.

17 Suggett, 'Festivals', pp. 102–5.

18 P. Borsay, ' "All the Town's a Stage": Urban Ritual and Ceremony, 1660–1800', in P. Clark (ed.), *The Transformation of English Provincial Towns* (London: Hutchinson, 1984) pp. 228–34, 237–8.

19 Johnes, *Soccer*, pp. 132–4, 160–9.

20 Russell, 'Football and Society', pp. 11–13.

21 Simpson and Roud, *Dictionary*, p. 271; Harrison and Madge, *Mass Observation*, pp. 185–97.

22 Borsay, *Urban Renaissance*, pp. 6–8, 29–30, 139–40, 188–93, 202–3.

23 Burnett, *Riot, Revelry and Rout*, p. 96; W. H. Quarrell and M. Mare (eds), *London in 1710: From the Travels of Zacharias Von Uffenbach* (London: Faber & Faber, 1934) p. 49.

24 Underdown, *Start of Play*, pp. 83–4; Sandiford, *Cricket*, pp. 112–13; Williams, *Cricket*, pp. 132–3; McKibbin, *Classes and Cultures*, p. 333.

25 Hutton, *Stations of the Sun*, p. 83.

26 Russell, 'Football and Society', p. 13; D. Russell, 'Music and Northern Identity, 1890–*c*.1965', in N. Kirk (ed.) *Northern Identities: Historical Interpretation of the 'North' and 'Northernness'* (Aldershot: Ashgate, 2000) pp. 23–46.

27 M. Huggins, 'Sport in the Social Construction of Identity in North-east England, 1800–1914', in Kirk, *Northern Identities*, pp. 132–62.

28 B. Anderson, *Imagined Communities: Reflections on the Origins and Spread of Nationalism*, revised edn (London: Verso, 1991) pp. 5–7.

29 Burke, *Popular Culture*, pp. 11–14.

30 J. Black and R. Porter (eds), *The Penguin Dictionary of Eighteenth-century History* (Harmondsworth: Penguin, 1996) pp. 494–5; Levinson and Christensen, *Encyclopedia*, pp. 290–2.

31 Tranter, *Sport, Economy and Society*, p. 18; H. S. Altham and E. W. Swanton, *A History of Cricket*, 2nd edn (London, 1938) pp. 144–8; Moorhouse, *People's Game*, pp. 70–115.

32 Holt, *Sport and the British*, p. 272.

33 Hutton, *Stations of the Sun*, pp. 215–17, 393–9; Mackerell, 'Account', p. 363; D. Cressy, *Bonfires and Bells: National Memory and the Protestant Calendar in Elizabethan and Stuart England* (Stroud: Sutton, 2004).

34 Owen, *Welsh Folk Customs*, pp. 123, 140–1; R. Palmer, *The Folklore of Radnorshire* (Woonton Almeley: Logaston Press, 2001) p. 67.

35 G. H. Jenkins, *The Foundations of Modern Wales, 1642–1780* (Oxford: Oxford University Press, 1993) pp. 213–53.

36 P. Morgan, 'From a Death to a View: the Hunt for the Welsh Past', in E. Hobsbawm and T. Ranger (eds), *The Invention of Tradition* (Cambridge: Cambridge University Press, 1992) p. 99.

37 P. Morgan, *New History of Wales: The Eighteenth Century Renaissance* (Llandybie: Christopher Davies, 1981) pp. 56–62; E. Jones, 'The Age of Societies', in E. Jones (ed.), *The Welsh in London, 1500–2000* (Cardiff: University of Wales Press, 2001) pp. 66–83.

38 Quoted in Williams, *Valleys of Song*, p. 82.

39 Croll, *Civilizing the Urban*, pp. 112, 122.

40 Williams, *1905*, p. 85; Smith and Williams, *Fields of Praise*, p. 171.

41 Johnes, *Soccer*, pp. 172–201; Hignell, *'Favourit' Game*, pp. 209–11; Williams, *1905*, pp. 169–71; Mason, *Sport in Britain*, pp. 314–18; Evans and O'Leary, 'Playing the Game', pp. 111–12.

42 *Western Mail*, 10 September 2002, Sport, p. 16.

43 Mason, *Sport in Britain*, p. 179.

44 Mason, *Sport in Britain*, pp. 318–20.

45 Jarvie and Walker, *Scottish Sport*, pp. 3–8, from the *Herald*, 24 April 1992.

46 *Guardian*, 14 June 2002, p. 5.

47 A. Bairner, 'Football and the Idea of Scotland', in Jarvie and Walker, *Scottish Sport*, pp. 9–26; W. Murray, *The Old Firm: Sectarianism, Sport and Society in Scotland*, revised edn (Edinburgh: John Donald, 2000).

48 Smith, *Curling*, pp. 10–11, 31–4.

49 Burnett, *Riot, Revelry and Rout*, pp. 198–205.

50 *Guardian*, 22 February 2002, G2, pp. 2–3.

51 Jarvie, *Highland Games*, p. 105.

52 Fraser, 'Developments', p. 257.

53 Donaldson, *Popular Literature*, especially pp. 26, 29–34, 87, 149–50.

54 E. Malcolm, 'Popular Recreations in Nineteenth-Century Ireland', in O. MacDonagh, W. F. Mandle, and P. Travers (eds), *Irish Culture and Nationalism, 1750–1950* (Basingstoke: Macmillan, 1985) p. 49.

55 S. Connolly (ed.), *The Oxford Companion to Irish History* (Oxford: Oxford University Press, 1998) pp. 536–7.

56 J. Ryan, 'Nationalism and Irish Music', in G. Gillen and H. White (eds), *Irish Musical Studies,* vol. 3: *Music and Irish Cultural History* (Blackrock: Irish Academic Press, 1995) p. 102.

57 For the case of Scottish music, see Johnson, *Music,* pp. 130–49, 187–200.

58 R. U. Ógaín, 'Traditional Music and Irish Cultural History', in Gillen and White, *Irish Musical Studies,* pp. 84–5.

59 Ryan, 'Nationalism', pp. 101–15; H. White, in Connolly, *Oxford Companion to Irish History,* p. 373.

60 Jarvie, *Sport in the Making of Celtic Cultures,* essays by Bairner, de Búrca, and Ó Maolfabhai, pp. 112–25, 100–11, 149–65; Birley, *Sport and the Making,* pp. 276–82; Holt, *Sport and the British,* pp. 238–46; N. Garnham, *The Origins and Development of Football in Ireland* (Belfast: Ulster Historical Foundation, 1999) pp. 9–21.

61 W. F. Mandle, 'The Gaelic Athletics Association and Popular Culture, 1884–1924', in MacDonagh et al., *Irish Culture,* pp. 104–21; M. de Búrca, *The GAA: A History,* 2nd edn (Dublin: Gill and Macmillan, 2000), especially pp. 200–5; *Guardian,* 22 August 2002, G2, p. 4; *Observer,* 17 April 2005, Sport, p. 4.

62 Cronin, *Sport,* pp. 20–1.

63 *Guardian,* 24 May 2002, p. 32.

64 Pittock, *Celtic Identity,* pp. 24–34; Spufford, *Small Books,* pp. 182–4.

65 Brewer, *Pleasures,* pp. 472–80.

66 C. Deelman, *The Great Shakespeare Jubilee* (London: Michael Joseph, 1964).

67 Fox, *Borough Town of Stratford,* pp. 151–9; L. Fox, *The Shakespeare Birthplace Trust: A Personal Memoir* (Stratford-upon-Avon: Shakespeare Birthplace Trust, 1997) pp. 3–45.

68 Weber, *Musical Classics,* pp. 223–42.

69 Hughes and Stradling, *Musical Renaissance*; Blake, *Land without Music,* pp. xi–xiv, 37–47.

70 J. N. Moore, *Edward Elgar: A Creative Life* (Oxford: Oxford University Press, 1999); B. Smith, *Peter Warlock: The Life of Philip Heseltine* (Oxford: Oxford University Press, 1994); S. Banfield, *Gerald Finzi: An English Composer* (London: Faber & Faber, 1998).

71 R. Colls, *Identity of England* (Oxford: Oxford University Press, 2002) p. 122; Birley, *Land of Sport and Glory,* pp. 269–71; Sandiford, *Cricket,* pp. 162–5; Williams, *Cricket,* pp. 1–17.

72 N. Cardus, *English Cricket* (London: Collins, 1947), p. 7: Altham and Swanton, *History of Cricket,* p. 436.

73 Russell, *Football,* pp. 106–7, 118–23.

74 Holt and Mason, *Sport*, pp. 133, 171–2.

75 Pittock, *Celtic Identity*, pp. 134–41.

76 Holt and Mason, *Sport in Britain*, pp. 140–5.

77 P. Borsay, 'Metropolis and Enlightenment: the British Isles, 1660–1800', *Journal for the Study of British Cultures*, 10 (2003) pp. 149–70.

78 McKibbin, *Classes and Cultures*, pp. 457–76; Holt and Mason, *Sport in Britain*, pp. 94–102.

79 McKibbin, *Classes and Cultures*, pp. 8–9.

80 Colley, *Britons*, pp. 195–236; D. Cannadine, 'The Context, Performance and Meaning of Ritual: the British Monarchy and the "Invention of Tradition", *c.*1820–1977', in Hobsbawm and Ranger, *Invention of Tradition*, pp. 108–32.

81 Gold and Gold, *Imagining Scotland*, pp. 71–81; Jarvie, *Highland Games*, pp. 59–70.

82 Quoted in Williams, *Valleys of Song*, p. 129, and n. 50, p. 216.

83 Evans and O'Leary, 'Playing the Game', p. 114; Williams, *1905*, pp. 81–2.

84 Russell, *Popular Music*, pp. 117–19; J. M. Mackenzie, 'Empire and Metropolitan Cultures', in A. Porter (ed.), *The Oxford History of the British Empire*, vol. III: *The Nineteenth Century* (Oxford: Oxford University Press, 1999) pp. 277–80; McAleer, *Popular Reading*, p. 253.

85 Booth, *Theatre*, p. 21.

86 Mangan, *Athleticism*, pp. 179–206; J. A. Mangan, *The Games Ethic and Imperialism: Aspects of the Diffusion of an Ideal* (Harmondsworth: Viking, 1986); Sandiford, *Cricket*, pp. 144–60; Williams, *Cricket*, pp. 12–14.

87 B. Stoddart, 'Sport, Cultural Imperialism, and Colonial Response in the British Empire', *Comparative Studies in Society and History*, 30 (1988) pp. 649–73; Holt, *Sport and the British*, pp. 204–23.

88 Birley, *Land without Music*, p. 168.

89 See C. Eisenberg, 'The Rise of Internationalism in Sport', in M. H. Geyer and J. Paulmann (eds), *The Mechanics of Internationalism: Culture, Society and Politics from the 1840s to the First World War* (Oxford: German Historical Institute and Oxford University Press, 2001) pp. 385–8.

90 T. Devine, *The Scottish Nation, 1700–2000* (Harmondsworth: Penguin, 2000) p. 289.

91 K. Robbins, 'The United Kingdom as a Multi-national State', in J. G. Beramendi, R. Máiz, and X. M. Núñez (eds), *Nationalism in Europe Past and Present* (Santiago de Compostela: University of Santiago de Compostela, 1994) vol. 2, p. 315.

7 SPACE

1 R. Tannahill, *Food in History* (Harmondsworth: Penguin, 1988) pp. 242, 267–9, 274–6; M. Snodin (ed.), *Rococo: Art and Design in Hogarth's England* (London: Trefoil Books and the Victoria and Albert Museum, 1984), especially pp. 271–6; C. S. Smith, *Eighteenth Century Decoration: Design and the Domestic Interior in England* (London: Weidenfeld and Nicolson, 1993) pp. 134, 140–1, 143–5, 307, 244; Berg, *Luxury*, pp. 46–84; D. Jacques, *Georgian Gardens: The Reign of Nature* (London: Batsford, 1990) pp. 43–7.

2 M. Hadfield, *A History of British Gardening* (London: Hamlyn, 1969); C. Thacker, *The Genius of Gardening: The History of Gardening in Britain and Ireland* (London: Weidenfeld and Nicolson, 1994); B. Elliott, *Victorian Gardens* (London: Batsford, 1990), especially pp. 28–32, 65–6.

3 Thomas, *Natural World*, pp. 277–8; Cannon, *Oxford Companion to British History*, pp. 1015–16.

4 J. Harley, *Music in Purcell's London: The Social Background* (London: Dennis Dobson, 1968) pp. 152–60; C. Ehrlich, *The Music Profession in Britain since the Eighteenth Century* (Oxford: Clarendon Press, 1985) pp. 16–19.

5 Reeves, *Pleasures and Pastimes*, pp. 174–82.

6 E. Hobsbawm, *Labouring Men: Studies in the History of Labour* (London: Weidenfeld and Nicolson, 1968) p. 34; Barton, *Working-class Organizations*, pp. 23–7; D. H. Morgan, 'The Place of Harvesters in Nineteenth-century Village Life', in R. Samuel (ed.), *Village Life and Labour* (London: Routledge and Kegan Paul, 1975) pp. 50–2; A. A. C. Hedges, *Yarmouth is an Ancient Town* (Yarmouth: Great Yarmouth Corporation, 1973) pp. 20–1.

7 Towner, *Historical Geography*.

8 A. van Gennep, *The Rites of Passage*, trans. M. B. Vizedom and G. L. Caffee (1st pub. 1909; London: Routledge and Kegan Paul, 1977), especially pp. 184–5.

9 Pimlott, *Englishman's Holiday*, p. 265.

10 Urry, *Consuming Places*, pp. 201–2.

11 S. McIntyre, 'Bath: the Rise of a Resort Town, 1660–1800', in P. Clark (ed.), *Country Towns in Pre-industrial England* (Leicester: Leicester University Press, 1981) p. 210.

12 *Richard Creed's Journal*, pp. 23–4.

13 *The Times Higher Educational Supplement*, 26 July 2002, p. 16.

14 Barton, *Working-class Organizations*, p. 140; Walton, *English Seaside Resort*, pp. 33–4; Walton, *Blackpool*, p. 69.

15   Walton, *Blackpool Landlady*, pp. 80, 93–4, 116, 122, 196.

16   C. Rojek, *Ways of Escape: Modern Transformations in Leisure and Travel* (London: Macmillan, 1993) p. 188.

17   Urry, *Consuming Places*, p. 177; Crang, *Cultural Geography*, pp. 113–14.

18   See, for example, B. Mitchell and H. Penrose (eds), *Letters from Bath, 1766–1767, by the Rev. John Penrose* (Gloucester: Sutton, 1983).

19   Borsay, 'Health and Leisure Resorts', pp. 787, 799–800.

20   J. Ellis, *The Georgian Town* (Basingstoke: Palgrave Macmillan, 2001) pp. 80–1; Vickery, *Gentleman's Daughter*, pp. 225–84.

21   Gold and Gold, *Imagining Scotland*, pp. 109–12; Durie, *Scotland for the Holidays*, pp. 110–23.

22   Hassan, *Seaside*, especially pp. 78–82.

23   Rojek, *Ways of Escape*, p. 175.

24   Black, *British and the Grand Tour*, pp. 109–16; R. Pearsall, *The Worm in the Bud: The World of Victorian Sexuality* (Harmondsworth: Penguin, 1971) pp. 319–31; T. C. Smout, 'Aspects of Sexual Behaviour', in A. A. MacLaren (ed.), *Social Class in Scotland: Past and Present* (Edinburgh: John Donald) p. 61.

25   Walton, *British Seaside*, p. 4.

26   Walton, *English Seaside Resort*, pp. 192–3; Walton, *British Seaside*, pp. 98–102; J. Travis, 'Continuity and Change in English Sea Bathing', in Fisher, *Recreation*, pp. 8–30; C. Ryan, 'Memories of the Beach', in C. Ryan (ed.), *The Tourist Experience: A New Introduction* (London: Cassell, 1998) pp. 155, 159–61; Rojek, *Ways of Escape*, pp. 189–91.

27   *The Times Higher Educational Supplement*, 23 August 2002, p. 21.

28   H. and A. Gernsheim, *A Concise History of Photography* (London: Thames & Hudson, 1971) pp. 36, 48–52; P. Holland, ' "Sweet It Is to Scan . . .": Personal Photographs and Popular Photography', in L. Wells (ed.), *Photography: A Critical Introduction* (London: Routledge, 1997) pp. 127–31.

29   A. Scharf (ed.), *Pioneers of Photography: An Album of Pictures and Words* (London: BBC, 1975) p. 16.

30   J. Lees-Milne and D. Ford, *Images of Bath* (Richmond-upon-Thames: Saint Helena Press, 1982), Gallery.

31   C. Christie, *The British Country House in the Eighteenth Century* (Manchester: Manchester University Press, 2000) p. 282; G. Jackson-Stops, *Blickling Hall* (National Trust, 1980) pp. 27–8.

32   Fiennes, *Journeys*, pp. 133–4; T. B. Burr, *The History of Tunbridge Wells* (London, 1766) p. 101; M. A. V. Gill, *Tunbridge Ware* (Princes Risborough: Shire, 1985).

33 Christie, *British Country House*, pp. 181–8; Wilton and Bignamini, *Grand Tour*, pp. 203–303; Wilson and Mackley, *Creating Paradise*, pp. 66–79; Waterfield, *Palaces of Art*, pp. 18, 24.

34 Hutton, *Stations of the Sun*, pp. 332–47; Bushaway, *By Rite*, pp. 107–38; Malcolmson, *Popular Recreations*, pp. 60–2.

35 Samuel, *Village Life*, pp. 7–8; Owen, *Customs and Traditions*, pp. 4–6.

36 H. Bourne, in Brand, *Observations*, p. 282; Owen, *Customs and Traditions*, p. 17; Hutton, *Stations of the Sun*, pp. 327–31.

37 Burke, *Popular Culture*, p. 33.

38 J. Langton, 'Urban Growth and Economic Change: from the Late Seventeenth Century to 1841', in Clark, *Cambridge Urban History*, vol. 2, p. 463.

39 Burnett, *Riot, Revelry and Rout*, pp. 169–70.

40 Collinson, *Birthpangs*, p. 53.

41 Strutt, *Glig-Gamena*, pp. 315–16; Hutton, *Stations of the Sun*, pp. 226–43; R. Judge, *The Jack-in-the-Green: A May Day Custom* (Ipswich: D. S. Brewer and Rowman & Littlefield, for the Folklore Society, 1979).

42 C. Phythian-Adams, 'Milk and Soot: the Changing Vocabulary of a Popular Ritual in Stuart and Hanoverian London', in D. Fraser and A. Sutcliffe (eds), *The Pursuit of Urban History* (London: Edward Arnold, 1983) p. 104.

43 Phythian-Adams, 'Ceremony', pp. 57–85; Reay, *Popular Cultures in England*, pp. 143–51; Borsay, ' "All the Town's a Stage" ', pp. 228–58.

44 Figures for 1500–1890 from J. de Vries, *European Urbanization, 1500–1800* (London: Methuen, 1984), pp. 39, 45–7; figures for 1951 calculated from L. H. Lees, 'Urban Networks', in Daunton, *Cambridge Urban History*, vol. 3, p. 70; Irish figures for 1951 calculated from W. E. Vaughan and A. J. Fitzpatrick (eds), *Irish Historical Statistics: Population, 1821–1871* (Dublin: Royal Irish Academy, 1978) pp. 327–48.

45 Palliser, *Cambridge Urban History*, vol. 1, pp. 741–2; Langton, 'Urban Growth', p. 462; P. Clark, 'Small Towns, 1700–1840', in Clark, *Cambridge Urban History*, vol. 2, p. 736; P. Corfield, *The Impact of English Towns, 1700–1800* (Oxford: Oxford University Press, 1982) p. 9. Langton calculates 40 per cent for 1700; the combination of Clark and Corfield is 31 per cent.

46 Corfield, *Impact*, p. 9; Lees, 'Urban Networks', p. 70; Irish figures calculated from Vaughan and Fitzpatrick, *Irish Historical Statistics*, pp. 2–3, 27–48; Connolly, *Oxford Companion*, pp. 161, 454; and D. Dickson, 'Death of a Capital: Dublin and the Consequences of

Union', in P. Clark and R. Gillespie (eds), *Two Capitals: London and Dublin, 1500–1840* (Oxford: Oxford University Press, 2001) p. 118.

47 Meller, *Leisure*, p. 2.

48 A. Howkins, *The Death of Rural England: A Social History of the Countryside since 1900* (London: Routledge, 2003); R. Williams, *The Country and the City* (London: Chatto & Windus, 1973) p. 248.

49 Palliser, *Cambridge Urban History*, vol. 1, p. 400; Clark, *Cambridge Urban History*, vol. 2, pp. 316, 650; Black and Porter, *Dictionary*, p. 117.

50 P. Borsay, 'London, 1660–1800: a Distinctive Culture?', in P. Clark and R. Gillespie (eds), *Two Capitals: London and Dublin, 1500–1840* (Oxford: Oxford University Press for the British Academy, 2001), pp. 170–8; Borsay, 'Metropolis', pp. 157–9.

51 Bryson, *From Courtesy to Civility*, especially pp. 128–42; Borsay, *Urban Renaissance*, pp. 262–3; Ross, *Selection*, pp. 100–2, 216–50.

52 J. Rosenheim, *The Emergence of a Ruling Order: English Landed Society, 1650–1750* (Harlow: Longman, 1998) pp. 215–52; S. Whyman, *Sociability and Power in Late Stuart England: The Cultural World of the Verneys, 1660–1720* (Oxford: Oxford University Press, 2002).

53 Howkins, *Death of Rural England*, p. 25.

54 M. Bunce, *The Countryside Ideal: Anglo-American Images of Landscape* (London: Routledge, 1994).

55 L. Williams, 'Rus in Urbe: the Greening of English Towns, 1660–1760' (unpub. Ph.D. thesis, University of Wales, 1998); L. Williams ' "To Recreate and Refresh Their Dulled Spirites in the Sweet and Wholesome Ayre": Green Space and the Growth of the City', in J. F. Merritt (ed.), *Imagining Early Modern London: Perceptions and Portrayals of the City from Stowe to Strype, 1598–1720* (Cambridge: Cambridge University Press, 2001) pp. 185–213; P. Borsay, 'The Rise of the Promenade: the Social and Cultural Use of Space in the English Provincial Town, c.1660–1800', *British Journal for Eighteenth-century Studies*, 9 (1986) pp. 125–40.

56 T. Longstaffe-Gowan, *The London Town Garden, 1740–1840* (New Haven, CT: Yale University Press, 2001); Thomas, *Man and the Natural World*, pp. 229–30, 234–6, 270; W. Wroth, *The London Pleasure Gardens of the Eighteenth Century* (London: Macmillan, 1896); M. Ogborn, *Spaces of Modernity: London Geographies, 1680–1780* (New York: Guilford Press, 1998) pp. 116–57; R. E. Duthie, 'English Florists' Societies and Feasts in the Seventeenth and First Half of the Eighteenth Centuries', *Garden History*, 10 (1983) pp. 17–35.

57 Cunningham, *Leisure in the Industrial Revolution*, pp. 92–7; Reid, 'Playing and Praying', pp. 762–6; Bunce, *Countryside Ideal*, pp. 141–53.

58 J. A. Patmore, *Land and Leisure in England and Wales* (Newton Abbot: David and Charles, 1970) pp. 48, 50, 52, 55.

59 McLean, *English at Play*, p. 4.

60 Underdown, *Start of Play*, pp. xviii, 151.

61 G. B. Buckley, *Fresh Light on 18th Century Cricket* (Birmingham: Cotterell, 1935) p. 38; G. B. Buckley, *Fresh Light on Pre-Victorian Cricket* (Birmingham: Cotterell, 1937) pp. 3–4; Birley, *Cricket*, pp. 44–6; Williams, *Cricket*, pp. 27–35.

62 Hignell, *'Favourit' Game*, pp. 12–31, 42, 72.

63 Burnett, *Riot, Revelry and Rout*, p. 27; Borsay, *Urban Renaissance*, p. 185.

64 Vamplew, *Turf*, pp. 38–48; R. Munting, *Hedges and Hurdles: A Social and Economic History of National Hunt Racing* (London: J. A. Allen, 1987) p. 40.

65 C. Estabrook, *Urbane and Rustic England: Cultural Ties and Social Spheres in the Provinces, 1660–1780* (Manchester: Manchester University Press, 1998) p. 267.

66 Bunce, *Countryside Ideal*, pp. 153–70.

67 R. Samuel, ' "Quarry Roughs": Life and Labour in Headington Quarry, 1860–1920. An Essay in Oral History', in Samuel, *Village Life*, pp. 139–263.

68 N. MacMaster, 'The Battle for Mousehold Heath, 1857–1884: "Popular Politics" and the Victorian Public Park', *Past and Present*, 127 (1990) pp. 117–54.

69 A. Sutcliffe, *Towards the Planned City: Germany, Britain, the United States and France, 1780–1914* (Oxford: Blackwell, 1981) pp. 64–8; H. Meller, *Towns, Plans and Society in Modern Britain* (Cambridge: Cambridge University Press, 1997) pp. 35–9.

70 Holt, *Sport and the British*, pp. 124–8; Lowerson, *Sport*, pp. 95–153; Bale, *Landscapes*, pp. 53–8.

71 Meller, *Towns*, pp. 56, 65; P. Hall, *Urban and Regional Planning* (London: Routledge, 1994) pp. 74–5, 82–3.

72 Howkins, *Death of Rural England*; J. Burchardt, *Paradise Lost: Rural Idyll and Social Change since 1800* (London: I. B. Tauris, 2002).

73 D. Matless, *Landscape and Englishness* (London: Reaktion, 1998) pp. 70–3.

74 Itzkowitz, *Peculiar Privilege*, pp. 50–66; Carr, *English Fox Hunting*, pp. 106–10.

75 H. J. Dyos and D. H. Aldcroft, *British Transport: An Economic Survey from the Seventeenth Century to the Twentieth* (Harmondsworth: Penguin, 1974) pp. 117–54, 168–9; K. Hudson, *A Social History of Archaeology: The British Experience* (London: Macmillan, 1981) pp. 44, 46–7, 62.

76 R. Shoesmith, *Alfred Watkins: A Herefordshire Man* (Woonton Almeley: Logaston Press, 1990) p. 108.

77 Holt, *Sport and the British*, p. 195.

78 Matless, *Landscape*, pp. 64–5; H. V. Morton, *In Search of England*, 26th edn (London: Methuen, 1939) p. 2.

79 See, for example, C. Scott, *Poppy-Land: Papers Descriptive of Scenery on the East Coast* (London: Carson and Comerford, 1886); T. Williamson, *The Norfolk Broads: A Landscape History* (Manchester: Manchester University Press, 1997) pp. 154–65; J. Taylor, *A Dream of England: Landscape, Photography and the Tourist's Imagination* (Manchester: Manchester University Press, 1994) pp. 64–119.

80 I. Ousby (ed.), *James Plumptre's Britain: The Journals of a Tourist in the 1790s* (London: Hutchinson, 1992) pp. 118, 126.

81 F. D. Klingender, *Art and the Industrial Revolution*, ed. A. Elton (London: Paladin, 1972); P. Lord, *The Visual Culture of Wales: Industrial Society* (Cardiff: University of Wales Press, 1998) pp. 21–33.

82 Clark and Houston, 'Culture and Leisure', pp. 583, 603–4; Clark, 'Small Towns', p. 758: Ellis, *Georgian Town*, p. 122.

83 Williamson, *Polite Landscapes*, pp. 77–99, 141–59.

84 J. Macve, *The Hafod Landscape: An Illustrated History and Guide* (Ystrad-Meurig: Hafod Trust, 2004) pp. 1–25; G. Cumberland, *An Attempt to Describe Hafod* (1st pub. 1796; reprinted and ed. J. Macve and A. Scalter, Hafod Trust, 1996).

85 Hollett, *Pioneer Ramblers, passim*; R. M. Jones, 'The Mountaineering of Wales', *Welsh History Review*, 19 (1998) pp. 44–67; Durie, *Scotland for the Holidays*, pp. 109–24.

86 W. Wordsworth, *Topographical Description of the Country of the Lakes in the North of England*, reprinted in W. M. Merchant (ed.), *Wordsworth: Poetry and Prose* (London: Rupert Hart-Davis, 1969) p. 740.

87 Patmore, *Land and Leisure*, pp. 193–207.

88 Borsay, 'Health and Leisure Resorts', pp. 775–803.

89 A. Corbin, *The Lure of the Sea: The Discovery of the Seaside in the Western World, 1750–1840*, trans. J. Phelps (Cambridge: Polity, 1994).

90 C. Hemming, *British Painters of the Coast and Sea: A History and Gazetteer* (London: Victor Gollancz, 1988); C. Hemming, *British Landscape Painters: A History and Gazetteer* (London: Victor Gollancz, 1989).

8 TIME

1 M. Perkins, *The Reform of Time: Magic and Modernity* (London: Pluto, 2001) p. 12; Urry, *Consuming Places*, p. 4.

2 Cunningham, 'Leisure and Culture', pp. 280–1; Davies, 'Cinema and Broadcasting', p. 264.
3 Rowntree and Lavers, *English Life and Leisure*, p. 123.
4 Reid, 'Playing and Praying', p. 750.
5 G. S. Bain, R. Bacon, and J. Pimlott, 'The Labour Force', in A. H. Halsey, *Trends in British Society since 1900* (London: Macmillan, 1974) pp. 104–5, 120.
6 Torkildsen, *Leisure*, pp. 86–7; Cross, *Leisure*, pp. 119–20.
7 Sharpe, *Early Modern England*, p. 214.
8 R. W. Malcolmson, *Life and Labour in England, 1700–1800* (London: Hutchinson, 1981) p. 37.
9 Thompson, *Respectable Society*, p. 272.
10 K. Thomas (ed.), *The Oxford Book of Work* (Oxford: Oxford University Press, 1999) p. 244.
11 Langhamer, *Women's Leisure*, pp. 171–2.
12 Quoted in A. Laurence, *Women in England, 1500–1760* (London: Weidenfeld and Nicolson, 1995) p. 112.
13 E. P. Thompson, *Customs in Common* (Harmondsworth: Penguin, 1993) pp. 352–403.
14 Rosser and Dennison, 'Urban Culture', pp. 344–5; J. Schofield and G. Stell, 'The Built Environment, 1300–1540', in Palliser, *Cambridge Urban History*, vol. 1, p. 392; L. Colchester, *Wells Cathedral* (London: Unwin Hyman, 1987) pp. 116–20.
15 Thomas, *Oxford Book of Work*, p. 61.
16 Thompson, *Customs*, pp. 370–8.
17 Clark and Houston, 'Culture and Leisure', pp. 589–90.
18 Poole, *Time's Alteration*, pp. 19–23; Perkins, *Reform of Time*, pp. 5–12; C. J. Sommerville, *The Secularization of Early Modern England: From Religious Culture to Religious Faith* (New York and Oxford: Oxford University Press, 1992) pp. 33–43.
19 *The New Bath Guide* (Bath: J. Savage, 1809) p. 21; J. Wood, *A Description of Bath*, 2nd edn (1749, reissued 1765; reprinted, Bath: Kingsmead, 1969) p. 443.
20 Magoun, *History of Football*, pp. 55, 70.
21 Malcolmson, *Popular Recreations*, pp. 37, 47.
22 Carew, *Survey of Cornwall*, p. 89; Malcolmson, *Popular Recreations*, p. 37.
23 Thompson, *Customs*, pp. 382–6; S. Pollard, *The Genesis of Modern Management: A Study of the Industrial Revolution in Great Britain* (Harmondsworth: Penguin, 1968) pp. 213–17.
24 For contemporary accounts, see Brand, *Observations*; Bamford, *Early Days* in *Bamford's Passages*, vol. 1, pp. 119–39; for modern accounts,

see Hutton, *Stations of the Sun*; Cressy, *Bonfires*, pp. 1–33; Owen, *Welsh Folk Customs*; Burnett, *Riot, Revelry and Rout*, pp. 81–7; Reay, *Popular Cultures in England*, pp. 132–67; Bushaway, *By Rite*, pp. 34–57; M. Lynch (ed.), *The Oxford Companion to Scottish History* (Oxford: Oxford University Press, 2001) pp. 60–4.

25 Simpson and Roud, *Dictionary*, pp. 44–5.

26 Phythian-Adams, 'Ceremony', p. 79; C. Phythian-Adams, *Local History and Folklore: A New Framework* (London: Bedford Square Press, 1975) pp. 21–5.

27 Reid, 'Playing and Praying', pp. 754–5.

28 Croll, *Civilizing the Urban*, p. 201; Davies, *Leisure*, pp. 124–30.

29 *The Diaries of Samuel Bamford*, ed. M. Hewitt and R. Poole (Stroud: Sutton, 2000) p. 241; Hoggart, *Uses of Literacy*, p. 68; Hutton, *Stations of the Sun*, p. 427.

30 Cressy, *Bonfires*, pp. 4–10.

31 Hutton, *Stations of the Sun*, pp. 25–33; Burnett, *Riot, Revelry and Rout*, pp. 81–3; Lynch, *Oxford Companion to Scottish History*, pp. 62–3; Fraser, 'Developments', pp. 236–7; Durston, 'Puritan Rule', pp. 211–14.

32 Golby and Purdue, *Christmas*; Hutton, *Stations of the Sun*, pp. 112–23; Owen, *Welsh Folk Customs*, pp. 27–69; Poole, *Time's Alteration*, pp. 152–7.

33 P. Collinson, 'Elizabethan and Jacobean Puritanism as a Form of Popular Religious Culture', in Durston and Eales, *English Puritanism*, p. 44; Cressy, *Bonfires*.

34 Connolly, *Oxford Companion to Irish History*, pp. 19, 20.

35 Borsay, *Urban Renaissance*, pp. 139–44, 154.

36 Davidoff, *Best Circles*, p. 30.

37 Williams, *Valleys of Song*, p. 133.

38 Walton, *Fish and Chips*, p. 140; N. Hornby, *Fever Pitch* (London: Indigo, 1996) p. 18.

39 D. Reid, 'The Decline of St Monday, 1766–1876', *Past and Present*, 71 (1976) pp. 76–101.

40 D. Brailsford, *Sport, Time and Society: The British at Play* (London: Routledge, 1991) pp. 79–82, 100–10.

41 Davies, *Leisure*, pp. 130–8.

42 Mason, *Sport in Britain*, p. 21.

43 C. Hill, *Society and Puritanism in Pre-Revolutionary England* (London: Panther, 1969) pp. 141–211.

44 Hutton, *Merry England*, pp. 171, 173, 189, 232–3.

45 Malcolmson, *Popular Recreations*, pp. 104–5.

46 Brailsford, *Sport, Time and Society*, pp. 115–22; Reid, 'Playing and Praying', pp. 751–4; for the tendency of weddings to re-locate from

Monday to Saturday and especially Sunday, see D. A. Reid, 'Weddings, Weekdays, Work and Leisure in Urban England 1791–1911: the Decline of St Monday Revisited', *Past and Present*, 152 (1996) pp. 135–63.

47 DeNora, *Music*, pp. 139–40.

48 Burke, *Popular Culture*, p. 124.

49 Johnson, *Music*, pp. 14–15.

50 Williams, *1905; Guardian*, 15 July 2002, Football Special, p. 8.

51 Mason, 'Sport and Recreation', p. 120.

52 Quoted in Smith, *Curling*, pp. 10–11.

53 G. Parry, 'Dugdale, Sir William', *Oxford Dictionary of National Biography* (Oxford: Oxford University Press, 2004); G. Parry, *The Trophies of Time: English Antiquarians of the Seventeenth Century* (Oxford: Oxford University Press, 1995) pp. 227–8.

54 Sweet, *Antiquaries*, p. 231.

55 Wilton and Bignamini, *Grand Tour*, pp. 75, 170–5: Black, *British and the Grand Tour*, p. 215.

56 Defoe, *Tour*, vol. 1, p. 263.

57 Sweet, *Antiquaries*, pp. 309–43.

58 K. Clark, *The Gothic Revival: An Essay in the History of Taste* (Harmondsworth: Penguin, 1964); *A Gothick Symposium* (Georgian Group, 1983).

59 P. Mandler, *The Fall and Rise of the Stately Home* (New Haven, CT: Yale University Press, 1997) pp. 21–106.

60 P. Readman, 'The Place of the Past in English Culture, *c.*1890–1914', *Past and Present*, 186 (2005) pp. 147–99.

61 MacCarthy, *William Morris*, especially pp. 311–16, 679–80; J. A. Gibbs, *A Cotswold Village* (1st pub. 1898; reprinted, Hemel Hempstead: Dog Ear Books, 1983); K. Jebb, *A. E. Housman* (Bridgend: Seren Books, 1992) pp. 73–94; Scott, *Poppy-Land*.

62 H. Lea, *The Hardy Guides*, ed. G. S. Cox, 2 vols (Harmondsworth: Penguin, 1986); B. C. A. Windle, *The Wessex of Thomas Hardy* (reprinted, East Ardsley: E. P. Publishing, 1978) pp. 5–6; S. Trezise, *The West Country as a Literary Invention: Putting Fiction in Its Place* (Exeter: Exeter University Press, 2000) pp. 139–71.

63 P. H. Ditchfield and F. Roe, *Vanishing England* (1st pub. 1910; reprinted, London: Studio Editions, 1993) especially pp. 1–14.

64 J. Cornforth, *The Search for a Style: Country Life and Architecture, 1897–1935* (New York: W. W. Norton, 1989); J. Cornforth, *The Inspiration of the Past: Country House Taste in the Twentieth Century* (Harmondsworth: Viking, 1985) pp. 20–46.

65 Cornforth, *Inspiration*, pp. 47–84.

66 G. Stamp, 'Origins of the Group', *Architectural Journal*, 175: 13 (1982) pp. 35–8.

67 Borsay, *Image of Georgian Bath*, pp. 168–84.

68 D. Lowenthal, *The Heritage Crusade and the Spoils of History* (London: Viking, 1997) p. ix; S. Collini, *English Pasts: Essays in History and Culture* (Oxford: Oxford University Press, 1999) pp. 94–5; P. J. Fowler, *The Past in Contemporary Society: Then, Now* (London: Routledge, 1992) p. xvii.

69 P. Weideger, *Gilding the Acorn: Behind the Façade of the National Trust* (London: Simon & Schuster, 1994) p. 180.

70 Mandler, *Fall and Rise of the Stately Home*, p. 411.

9 CONCLUSION

1 Levinson and Christensen, *Encyclopedia*, pp. 35–40; *Financial Times*, 5 August 2003, p. 5; *Guardian*, 29 October 2004, G2, pp. 6–7.

2 C. Rojek, *Decentring Leisure: Rethinking Leisure Theory* (London: Sage 1998) pp. 36, 79, 88, 90–2, 129–30; see also Rojek, *Ways of Escape*, pp. 97–135.

3 Giulianotti, *Football*, pp. xiii–xv, 166–9.

4 Urry, *Consuming Places*, p. 212: J. Urry, *Tourist Gaze*, p. 84.

5 V. W. Turner, *The Ritual Process: Structure and Anti-Structure* (Chicago: Aldine, 1969) p. 15.

6 Quoted in Burnett, *Riot, Revelry and Rout*, p. 66.

7 McLean, *English at Play*, p. 102; Bourdieu, *In Other Words*, p. 135.

8 Carew, *Survey of Cornwall*, p. 38; R. Scruton, *On Hunting* (London: Yellow Jersey Press, 1998) p. 91.

9 Murray, *Old Firm*, p. 300.

10 C. Geertz, *The Interpretation of Cultures* (London: Fontana, 1993) pp. 450–1.

11 Malbon, *Clubbing*, p. 164.

12 Malcolmson, *Popular Recreations*, p. 75.

13 Strutt, *Glig-Gamena*, pp. 213–14; *Financial Times*, 5 August 2003, p. 12; *Western Mail*, 17 February 2003.

14 Burke, *Popular Culture*, pp. 178–204; Hutton, *Merry England*, pp. 9–12, 30–1, 53–4, 90–1, 116–17; Hutton, *Stations of the Sun*, pp. 95–111, 151–68, 206–13, 247–50, 252, 259, 381; Reay, *Popular Cultures in England*, pp. 133, 151–61, 166–7; Phythian-Adams, *Local History*, pp. 23, 26; M. D. Bristol, *Carnival and Theater: Plebeian Culture and the Structure of Authority in Renaissance England* (New York: Methuen,

1989); Ó Crualaoich, 'Merry Wake', pp. 183–7, 193–4; Jones, 'Popular Culture', pp. 22–7; T. Laquer, 'Crowds, Carnival and the State in English Executions, 1604–1868', in D. Cannadine and J. M. Rosenheim (eds), *The First Modern English Society* (Cambridge: Cambridge University Press, 1989) pp. 305–55; F. O'Gorman, 'Campaign Rituals and Ceremonies: the Social Meaning of Elections in England, 1780–1860', *Past and Present*, 135 (1992) pp. 85, 108–9.

15 Bailey, *Popular Culture*, p. 11.

16 Reid, 'Festive Calendar', pp. 133–4.

17 Burnett, *Riot, Revelry and Rout*, pp. 169–73; Huggins, *Flat Racing*, p. 13.

18 Quoted in Tranter, *Sport, Economy and Society*, p. 38.

19 Quoted in Cunningham, *Leisure in the Industrial Revolution*, p. 124.

20 Russell, *Football*, pp. 98–102; Giulianotti, *Football*, pp. 59–61; Cronin, *Sport*, p. 22.

21 Blake, *Land without Music*, pp. 179–94.

22 Walton, *British Seaside*, p. 96; Urry, *Tourist Gaze*, p. 31; C. Ryan, 'Memories of the Beach', in C. Ryan, *The Tourist Experience: A New Introduction* (London: Cassell, 1997) pp. 159–61.

23 P. Borsay, 'Bingeing Britain', *BBC History Magazine*, 6: 7 (2005) pp. 44–8.

24 Harrison and Madge, *Mass Observation*, p. 147.

25 J. Baudrillard, *Simulacra and Simulation*, trans. S. F. Glaser (Ann Arbor: University of Michigan Press, 1994) p. 19.

SELECT BIBLIOGRAPHY

Anderson, B., *Imagined Communities: Reflections on the Origin and Spread of Nationalism*, revised edn (London: Verso, 1991).

Bailey, P., *Leisure and Class in Victorian England: Rational Recreation and the Contest for Control, 1830–1885* (London: Routledge, 1978).

Bailey, P., *Popular Culture and Performance in the Victorian City* (Cambridge: Cambridge University Press, 1998).

Bailey, P., 'The Politics and the Poetics of Modern British Leisure: a Late Twentieth-century Review', *Rethinking History*, 3 (1999) pp. 131–75.

Bale, J., *Landscapes of Modern Sport* (Leicester: Leicester University Press, 1994).

Bamford's Passages in the Life of an Early Radical, and Early Days, ed. H. Dunckley, 2 vols (London: T. Fisher Unwin, 1905).

Barton, S., *Working-Class Organizations and Popular Tourism, 1840–1870* (Manchester: Manchester University Press, 2005).

Baudrillard, J., *Simulacra and Simulation*, trans. S. F. Glaser (Ann Arbor: University of Michigan Press, 1994).

Benson, J., *The Rise of a Consumer Society in Britain, 1880–1980* (London: Longman, 1994).

Berg, M., *Luxury and Pleasure in Eighteenth-century Britain* (Oxford: Oxford University Press, 2005).

Bermingham, A. and Brewer, J. (eds), *The Consumption of Culture, 1600–1800: Image, Object, Text* (London: Routledge, 1997).

Berry, D., *Wales and the Cinema: The First Hundred Years* (Cardiff: University of Wales Press, 1995).

Birley, D., *Land of Sport and Glory: Sport and British Society, 1887–1910* (Manchester: Manchester University Press, 1995).

Birley, D., *Playing the Game: Sport and British Society, 1910–1945* (Manchester: Manchester University Press, 1995).

Birley, D., *Sport and the Making of Britain* (Manchester: Manchester University Press, 1996).

Birley, D., *A Social History of English Cricket* (London: Aurum, 1999).

Black, J., *The British and the Grand Tour* (London: Croom Helm, 1985).

Black, J. and Porter, R. (eds), *The Penguin Dictionary of Eighteenth-century History* (Harmondsworth: Penguin, 1996).

Blake, A., *The Land without Music: Music, Culture and Society in Twentieth-century Britain* (Manchester: Manchester University Press, 1997).

Booth, M. R., *Theatre in the Victorian Age* (Cambridge: Cambridge University Press, 1991).

Borsay, P., ' "All the Town's a Stage": Urban Ritual and Ceremony 1660–1800', in P. Clark (ed.), *The Transformation of English Provincial Towns, 1600–1800* (London: Hutchinson, 1984) pp. 228–58.

Borsay, P., *The English Urban Renaissance: Culture and Society in the Provincial Town, 1660–1770* (Oxford: Clarendon Press, 1989).

Borsay, P., *The Image of Georgian Bath: Towns, Heritage, and History* (Oxford: Oxford University Press, 2000).

Borsay, P., 'Health and Leisure Resorts, 1700–1840', in P. Clark (ed.), *Cambridge Urban History of Britain*, vol. 2: *1540–1840* (Cambridge: Cambridge University Press, 2000) pp. 775–803.

Borsay, P., 'Metropolis and Enlightenment: the British Isles, 1660–1800', *Journal for the Study of British Cultures*, 10 (2003) pp. 149–70.

Borsay, P., Hirschfelder, G., and Mohrmann, R.-E. (eds), *New Directions in Urban History: Aspects of European Art, Health, Tourism and Leisure since the Enlightenment* (Munster: Waxmann, 2000).

Bourdieu, P., *In Other Words: Essays towards Reflexive Sociology* (Cambridge: Polity, 1990).

Brailsford, D., *Sport, Time and Society: The British at Play* (London: Routledge, 1991).

Brand, J., *Observations on Popular Antiquities, Including the Whole of Mr Bourne's Antiquitates Vulgares* (1st pub. 1777; London: William Baynes, [c.1820]).

Brewer, J., *The Pleasures of the Imagination: English Culture in the Eighteenth Century* (London: HarperCollins, 1997).

Brewer, J. and Porter, R. (eds), *Consumption and the World of Goods* (London: Routledge, 1994).

Bryson, A., *From Courtesy to Civility: Changing Codes of Conduct in Early Modern England* (Oxford: Clarendon Press, 1998).

Bunce, M., *The Countryside Ideal: Anglo-American Images of Landscape* (London: Routledge, 1994).

Burchardt, J., *Paradise Lost: Rural Idyll and Social Change since 1800* (London: I. B. Tauris, 2002).

Burke, P., *Popular Culture in Early Modern Europe* (London: Temple Smith, 1979).

Burke, P., 'The Invention of Leisure in Early Modern Europe', *Past and Present*, 146 (1995) pp. 136–50.

Burnett, J., *Riot, Revelry and Rout: Sport in Lowland Scotland before 1860* (East Linton: Tuckwell Press, 2000).

Burrows, D. and Dunhill, R. (eds), *Music and Theatre in Handel's World: The Family Papers of James Harris, 1732–1780* (Oxford: Oxford University Press, 2002).

Bushaway, R., *By Rite: Custom, Ceremony and Community in England, 1700–1880* (London: Junction Books, 1982).

Cannadine, D., *Class in Britain* (Harmondsworth: Penguin, 2000).

Cannon, J. (ed.), *The Oxford Companion to British History* (Oxford: Oxford University Press, 1997).

Carew, R., *The Survey of Cornwall* (1st pub. 1602; Redruth: Tamar Books, 2000).

Carr, R., *English Fox Hunting: A History* (London: Weidenfeld and Nicolson, 1976).

Carter, J. M., *Medieval Games: Sports and Recreations in Feudal Society* (London: Greenwood Press, 1992).

Chinn, C., *Better Betting with a Decent Feller: Bookmaking, Betting and the British Working Class, 1750–1990* (London: Harvester Wheatsheaf, 1991).

Christie, C., *The British Country House in the Eighteenth Century* (Manchester: Manchester University Press, 2000).

Clapson, M., *A Bit of a Flutter: Popular Gambling and English Society, c.1823–1961* (Manchester: Manchester University Press, 1992).

Clark, P., *The English Alehouse: A Social History, 1200–1830* (London: Longman, 1983).

Clark, P., *British Clubs and Societies, 1580–1800: The Origins of an Associational World* (Oxford: Clarendon Press, 2000).

Clark, P. (ed.), *The Cambridge Urban History of Britain*, vol. 2: *1540–1840* (Cambridge: Cambridge University Press, 2000).

Clark, P. and Houston, R., 'Culture and Leisure, 1750–1840', in P. Clark (ed.), *Cambridge Urban History of Britain*, vol. 2: *1540–1840* (Cambridge: Cambridge University Press, 2000) pp. 575–613.

Clarke, J. and Critcher, C., *The Devil Makes Work: Leisure in Capitalist Britain* (Basingstoke: Palgrave Macmillan, 1985).

Colley, L., *Britons: Forging the Nation, 1707–1837* (New Haven, CT: Yale University Press, 1992).

Collinson, P., *The Birthpangs of Protestant England: Religious and Cultural Change in the Sixteenth and Seventeenth Centuries* (New York: St Martin's Press, 1988).

Connolly, S. (ed.), *The Oxford Companion to Irish History* (Oxford: Oxford University Press, 1998).

Corbin, A., *The Lure of the Sea: The Discovery of the Seaside in the Western World, 1750–1840*, trans. J. Phelps (Cambridge: Polity, 1994).

Cranfield, G. A., *The Development of the Provincial Newspaper, 1700–1760* (Westport, CT: Greenwood Press, 1962).

Crang, M., *Cultural Geography* (London: Routledge, 1998).

Cressy, D., *Bonfires and Bells: National Memory and the Protestant Calendar in Elizabethan and Stuart England* (Stroud: Sutton, 2004).

Critcher, C., Bramham, P., and Tomlinson, A. (eds), *Sociology of Leisure: A Reader* (London: E & FN Spon, 1999).

Croll, A., *Civilizing the Urban: Popular Culture and Public Space in Merthyr, c.1870–1914* (Cardiff: University of Wales Press, 2000).

Cronin, M., *Sport and Nationalism in Ireland: Gaelic Games, Soccer and Irish Identity since 1884* (Dublin: Four Courts Press, 1999).

Cross, G., *A Social History of Leisure since 1600* (State College, PA: Venture Publishing, 1990).

Cunningham, H., *Leisure in the Industrial Revolution, c. 1780–c.1880* (London: Croom Helm, 1980).

Cunningham, H., 'Leisure and Culture', in F. M. L. Thompson (ed.), *The Cambridge Social History of Britain*, vol. 2: *The People and Their Environment* (Cambridge: Cambridge University Press, 1990) pp. 279–339.

Dain, A., 'Assemblies and Politeness, 1660–1840' (unpub. PhD thesis, University of East Anglia, 2001).

Daunton, M. (ed.), *The Cambridge Urban History of Britain*, vol. 3: *1840–1950* (Cambridge: Cambridge University Press, 2000).

Davidoff, L., *The Best Circles: Society, Etiquette and the Season* (London: Hutchinson, 1986).

Davies, A., *Leisure, Gender and Poverty: Working Class Culture in Salford and Manchester, 1900–1939* (Buckingham: Open University Press, 1992).

Davies, A., 'Cinema and Broadcasting', in P. Johnson (ed.), *Twentieth-century Britain: Economic, Social and Cultural Change* (Harlow: Longman, 1994) pp. 263–80.

Defoe, D., *A Tour Through the Whole Island of Great Britain*, 1st pub. 1724–6, ed. G. D. H. Cole and D. C. Browning, 2 vols (London: Everyman, 1962).

Dolan, B., *Ladies of the Grand Tour* (London: HarperCollins, 2001).

Donaldson, W., *Popular Literature in Victorian Scotland: Language, Fiction and the Press* (Aberdeen: Aberdeen University Press, 1986).

Donnelly, J. S. and Miller, K. A. (eds), *Irish Popular Culture, 1660–1850* (Dublin: Irish Academic Press, 1999).

DeNora, T., *Music in Everyday Life* (Cambridge: Cambridge University Press, 2000).

Dumazedier, J., *Sociology of Leisure* (Amsterdam: Elsevier, 1974).

Durie, A. J., *Scotland for the Holidays: Tourism in Scotland, c.1780–1939* (East Linton: Tuckwell Press, 2003).

Durston, C. 'Puritan Rule and the Failure of Cultural Revolution, 1645–1660', in C. Durston and J. Eales (eds), *The Culture of English Puritanism, 1560–1700* (Basingstoke: Macmillan, 1996) pp. 210–33.

Durston, C. and Eales, J. (eds), *The Culture of English Puritanism, 1560–1700* (Basingstoke: Macmillan, 1996).

Ehrlich, C., *The Music Profession in Britain since the Eighteenth Century: A Social History* (Oxford: Clarendon Press, 1985).

Evans, N. and O'Leary, P., 'Playing the Game: Sport and Ethnic Minorities in Modern Wales', in C. Williams, N. Evans, and P. O'Leary (eds), *A Tolerant Nation? Exploring Ethnic Diversity in Wales* (Cardiff: University of Wales Press, 2003) pp. 109–24.

Fiennes, C., *The Journeys of Celia Fiennes*, ed. C. Morris (London: Cresset Press, 1947).

Fisher, S. (ed.), *Recreation and the Sea* (Exeter: University of Exeter Press, 1997).

Fowler, P. J., *The Past in Contemporary Society: Then, Now* (London: Routledge, 1992).

Fox, A., *Oral and Literate Culture in England, 1500–1700* (Oxford: Clarendon Press, 2000).

Fox, L., *The Borough Town of Stratford-upon-Avon* (Stratford: Corporation of Stratford-upon-Avon, 1953).

Fraser, W. H., 'Developments in Leisure', in W. H. Fraser and R. J. Morris (eds), *People and Society in Scotland*, vol. 2: *1830–1914* (Edinburgh: John Donald, 1990).

Geddes, O. M., *A Swing Through Time: Golf in Scotland, 1457–1743* (Edinburgh: HMSO, 1992).

Geertz, C., *The Interpretation of Cultures* (London: Fontana, 1975).

Giulianotti, R., *Football: A Sociology of the Global Game* (Cambridge: Polity, 1999).

Golby, J. M. and Purdue, A. W., *The Civilisation of the Crowd: Popular Culture in England, 1750–1900* (London: Batsford, 1984).

Golby, J. M. and Purdue, A. W., *The Making of Modern Christmas* (London: Batsford, 1986).

Gold, J. R. and M. M., *Imagining Scotland: Tradition, Representation and Promotion in Scottish Tourism since 1750* (Aldershot: Scolar, 1995).

Grassby, R., 'The Decline of Falconry in Early Modern England', *Past and Present*, 157 (1997) pp. 37–62.

Green, J., *All Dressed Up: The Sixties and the Counterculture* (London: Pimlico, 1999).

Greenway, J., *Drink and British Politics since 1830: A Study in Policy Making* (Basingstoke: Palgrave Macmillan, 2003).

Griffin, E., 'Popular Culture in Industrializing England', *Historical Journal*, 45 (2002) pp. 619–35.

Gurr, A., *Playgoing in Shakespeare's London*, 3rd edn (Cambridge: Cambridge University Press, 2004).

Harris, T. (ed.), *Popular Culture in England, c.1500–1850* (Basingstoke: Macmillan, 1995).

Harrison, B., *Drink and the Victorians: The Temperance Question in England, 1815–1872*, 2nd edn (Keele: Keele University Press, 1994).

Harrison, T. and Madge, C., *Britain by Mass Observation* (1st pub. 1939; London: Century Hutchinson, 1986).

Harvey, A., *The Beginnings of a Commercial Sporting Culture in Britain, 1793–1850* (Aldershot: Ashgate, 2004).

Hassan, J., *The Seaside, Health and the Environment in England and Wales since 1800* (Aldershot: Ashgate, 2003).

Haywood, L. et al., *Understanding Leisure*, 2nd edn (Cheltenham: Stanley Thomas, 1995).

Hembry, P., *The English Spa, 1560–1815* (London: Athlone Press, 1990).

Henricks, T., *Disputed Pleasures: Sport and Society in Pre-industrial England* (New York: Greenwood Press, 1991).

Herbert, T., 'Nineteenth-century Brass Bands', in T. Herbert (ed.), *Bands: The Brass Band Movement in the 19th and 20th Centuries* (Buckingham: Open University Press, 1991) pp. 7–56.

Herbert, T. (ed.), *Bands: The Brass Bands Movement in the 19th and 20th Centuries* (Buckingham: Open University Press, 1991).

Hignell, A., *A 'Favourit' Game: Cricket in South Wales before 1914* (Cardiff: University of Wales Press, 1992).

Hill, J., *Sport, Leisure and Culture in Twentieth-Century Britain* (Basingstoke: Palgrave Macmillan, 2002).

Hobsbawm, E. and Ranger, T. (eds), *The Invention of Tradition* (Cambridge: Cambridge University Press, 1992).

Hoggart, R., *The Uses of Literacy* (1st pub. 1957; Harmondsworth: Penguin, 1966).

Hollett, D., *The Pioneer Ramblers, 1850–1914* (North Wales Area of the Ramblers' Association, 2002).

Holt, R., *Sport and the British: A Modern History* (Oxford: Clarendon Press, 1992).

Holt, R., 'Sport and History: the State of the Subject in Britain', *Twentieth Century British History*, 72 (1996) pp. 231–52.

Holt, R. and Mason, T., *Sport in Britain, 1945–2000* (Oxford: Blackwell, 2000).

Howkins, A., *The Death of Rural England: A Social History of the Countryside since 1900* (London: Routledge, 2003).

Huggins, M., *Flat Racing and British Society, 1760–1914: A Social and Economic History* (London: Frank Cass, 2000).

Huggins, M. and Mangan, J. A. (eds), *Disreputable Pleasures: Less Virtuous Victorians at Play* (London: Frank Cass, 2004).

Hughes, M. and Stradling, R., *The English Musical Renaissance, 1840–1940: Constructing a National Music*, 2nd edn (Manchester: Manchester University Press, 2001).

Hutton, R., *The Rise and Fall of Merry England: The Ritual Year, 1400–1700* (Oxford: Oxford University Press, 1996).

Hutton, R., *The Stations of the Sun: A History of the Ritual Year in Britain* (Oxford: Oxford University Press, 1997).

Itzkowitz, D. C., *Peculiar Privilege: A Social History of English Fox-Hunting, 1753–1885* (Hassocks: Harvester, 1977).

Jarvie, G., *Highland Games: The Making of a Myth* (Edinburgh: Edinburgh University Press, 1991).

Jarvie, G. (ed.), *Sport in the Making of Celtic Cultures* (Leicester: Leicester University Press, 1999).

Jarvie, G. and Walker, G. (eds), *Scottish Sport in the Making of the Nation: Ninety Minute Patriots?* (Leicester: Leicester University Press, 1994).

Johnes, M., *Soccer and Society: South Wales, 1900–1939* (Cardiff: University of Wales Press, 2002).

Johnson, D., *Music and Society in Lowland Scotland in the Eighteenth Century* (London: Oxford University Press, 1972).

Johnson, P. (ed.), *Twentieth-century Britain: Economic, Social and Cultural Change* (Harlow: Longman, 1994).

Jones, R. A. N., 'Popular Culture, Policing and the "Disappearance" of the *Ceffyl Pren* in Cardigan, *c*.1837–1850', *Ceredigion*, 11 (1998–9) pp. 19–40.

Jones, S. G., *Workers at Play: A Social and Economic History of Leisure, 1918–1939* (London: Routledge and Kegan Paul, 1986).

Kift, D., *The Victorian Music Hall: Culture, Class and Conflict*, trans. R. Kift (Cambridge: Cambridge University Press, 1996).

Kirk, N. (ed.), *Northern Identities: Historical Interpretation of the 'North' and 'Northerness'* (Aldershot: Ashgate, 2000).

Langhamer, C., *Women's Leisure in England, 1920–60* (Manchester: Manchester University Press, 2000).

Leppert, R., *Music and Image: Domesticity, Ideology and Socio-cultural Formation in Eighteenth-century England* (Cambridge: Cambridge University Press, 1988).

Levinson, D. and Christensen, K. (eds), *Encyclopedia of World Sport from Ancient Times to the Present* (Oxford: ABC-Clio, 1996).

Longrigg, R., *A History of Horse Racing* (Basingstoke: Macmillan, 1972).

Lowerson, J., *Sport and the English Middle Class, 1870–1914* (Manchester: Manchester University Press, 1993).

Lowerson, J., 'Golf and the Making of a Myth', in G. Jarvie and G. Walker (eds), *Scottish Sport and the Making of a Nation: Ninety Minute Patriots?* (Leicester: Leicester University Press, 1994) pp. 75–90.

Lynch, M. (ed.), *The Oxford Companion to Scottish History* (Oxford: Oxford University Press, 2001).

McAleer, J., *Popular Reading and Publishing in Britain, 1914–50* (Oxford: Oxford University Press, 1992).

MacCarthy, F., *William Morris: A Life for Our Time* (London: Faber & Faber, 1994).

McCrone, K., *Sport and the Physical Emancipation of English Women, 1870–1914* (London: Routledge, 1988).

McKendrick, N., Brewer, J., and Plumb, J. H., *The Birth of a Consumer Society: The Commercialization of Eighteenth-century England* (London: Hutchinson, 1983).

Mackerell, B., 'Account of the Company of St George in Norwich', *Norfolk Archaeology*, 3 (1852) pp. 315–74.

McKibbin, R., *Classes and Cultures: England, 1918–1951* (Oxford: Oxford University Press, 1998).

McLean, T., *The English at Play in the Middle Ages* (Windsor: Kensall Press, 1983).

Macleod, D. S., *Art and the Victorian Middle Class: Money and the Making of Cultural Identity* (Cambridge: Cambridge University Press, 1996).

McVeigh, S., *Concert Life in London from Mozart to Haydn* (Cambridge: Cambridge University Press, 1993).

Magoun, F. P., *History of Football: From the Beginnings to 1871* (Bochum-Langendreer: Verlag Heinrich Pöppinghas O. H. G., 1938).

Malbon, B., *Clubbing: Dancing, Ecstasy and Vitality* (London: Routledge, 1999).

Malcolm, E., 'The Rise of the Pub: a Study in the Disciplining of Popular Culture', in J. S. Donnelly and K. A. Miller (eds), *Irish Popular Culture, 1660–1850* (Dublin: Irish Academic Press, 1999) pp. 50–77.

Malcolmson, R. W., *Popular Recreations in English Society, 1700–1850* (Cambridge: Cambridge University Press, 1973).

Mandler, P., *The Fall and Rise of the Stately Home* (New Haven, CT: Yale University Press, 1997).

Mangan, J. A., *Athleticism in the Victorian and Edwardian Public School* (Cambridge: Cambridge University Press, 1981).

Manning, R. B., *Hunters and Poachers: A Cultural and Social History of Unlawful Hunting in England, 1485–1640* (Oxford: Clarendon Press, 1993).

Marfany, J.-L. and Burke, P., 'Debate: the Invention of Leisure in Early Modern Europe: Comment', *Past and Present*, 156 (1997) pp. 174–97.

Marwick, A., *The Sixties: Cultural Revolution in Britain, France, Italy and the United States, c. 1958–c.1974* (Oxford: Oxford University Press, 1999).

Mason, T., *Association Football and English Society, 1863–1915* (Brighton: Harvester, 1980).

Mason, T. (ed.), *Sport in Britain: A Social History* (Cambridge: Cambridge University Press, 1989).

Mason, T., 'Sport and Recreation', in P. Johnson (ed.), *Twentieth-century Britain: Economic, Social and Cultural Change* (Harlow: Longman, 1994) pp. 111–26.

Matless, D., *Landscape and Englishness* (London: Reaktion, 1998).

Meller, H., *Leisure and the Changing City, 1870–1914* (London: Routledge and Kegan Paul, 1976).

Moorhouse, G., *A People's Game: The Centenary History of Rugby League Football, 1895–1995* (London: Hodder & Stoughton, 1995).

Morgan, M., *National Identities and Travel in Victorian Britain* (Basingstoke: Palgrave Macmillan, 2001).

Morris, R., 'Voluntary Societies and British Urban Elites, 1780–1850: an Analysis', in P. Borsay (ed.), *The Eighteenth-century Town: A Reader in English Urban History, 1688–1820* (Harlow: Longman, 1990) pp. 338–66.

Munting, R., *An Economic and Social History of Gambling in Britain and the USA* (Manchester: Manchester University Press, 1996).

Murray, W., *The Old Firm: Sectarianism, Sport and Society in Scotland*, revised edn (Edinburgh: John Donald, 2000).

O'Connell, S., *The Car and British Society: Class, Gender and Motoring, 1896–1939* (Manchester: Manchester University Press, 1998).

Ó Crualaoich, G., 'The "Merry Wake" ', in J. S. Donnelly and K. A. Miller (eds), *Irish Popular Culture, 1660–1850* (Dublin: Irish Academic Press, 1999) pp. 173–200.

Owen, T. M., *Welsh Folk Customs* (Llandysul: Gomer Press, 1987).

Owen, T. M., *The Customs and Traditions of Wales* (Cardiff: University of Wales Press and Western Mail, 2000).

Palliser, D. (ed.), *Cambridge Urban History of Britain*, vol. 1: *600–1540* (Cambridge: Cambridge University Press, 2000).

Patmore, J. A., *Land and Leisure in England and Wales* (Newton Abbot: David and Charles, 1970).

Perkins, M., *The Reform of Time: Magic and Modernity* (London: Pluto, 2001).

Phythian-Adams, C., 'Ceremony and the Citizen: the Communal Year at Coventry, 1450–1550', in P. Clark and P. Slack (eds), *Crisis and Order in English Towns, 1500–1700: Essays in Urban History* (London: Routledge & Kegan Paul, 1972) pp. 57–85.

Phythian-Adams, C., *Local History and Folklore: A New Framework* (London: Bedford Square Press, 1975).

Pimlott, J. A. R., *The Englishman's Holiday: A Social History* (Hassocks: Harvester Press, 1976).

Pittock, M., *Celtic Identity and the British Image* (Manchester: Manchester University Press, 1999).

Plumb, J. H., *The Commercialization of Leisure in Eighteenth-century England* (Reading: University of Reading, 1973).

Polley, M., *Moving the Goalposts: A History of Sport and Society since 1945* (London: Routledge, 1998).

Poole, R., *Time's Alteration: Calendar Reform in Early Modern England* (London: UCL Press, 1998).

Rappaport, E. D., *Shopping for Pleasure: Women in the Making of London's West End* (Princeton, NJ: Princeton University Press, 2000).

Reay, B., *Popular Cultures in England, 1550–1750* (London: Longman, 1998).

Reay, B. (ed.), *Popular Culture in Seventeenth-century England* (London: Routledge, 1988).

Reeves, A. C., *Pleasures and Pastimes in Medieval England* (Stroud: Sutton, 1995).

Reid, D. A., 'Interpreting the Festive Calendar: Wakes and Fairs as Carnivals', in R. D. Storch (ed.), *Popular Culture and Custom in Nineteenth-century England* (London: Croom Helm, 1982) pp. 125–53.

Reid, D. A., 'Playing and Praying', in M. Daunton (ed.), *Cambridge Urban History of Britain*, vol. 3: *1840–1950* (Cambridge: Cambridge University Press, 2000) pp. 745–807.

Richard Creed's Journal of the Grand Tour, 1699–1700, transcribed by A. Thomas (Oundle: Oundle Museum, 2002).

Richards, J., *The Age of the Dream Palace: Cinema and Society in Britain, 1930–1939* (London: Routledge and Kegan Paul, 1989).

Roberts, R., *The Classic Slum: Salford Life in the First Quarter of the Century* (Harmondsworth: Penguin, 1974).

Rojek, C., *Ways of Escape: Modern Transformations in Leisure and Travel* (London: Macmillan, 1993).

Rojek, C., *Decentring Leisure: Rethinking Leisure Theory* (London: Sage, 1998).

Ross, A. (ed.), *A Selection from* The Tatler *and* The Spectator *of Steele and Addison* (Harmondsworth: Penguin, 1982).

Rosser, G. and Dennison, E. P., 'Urban Culture and the Church, 1300–1540', in D. Palliser (ed.), *Cambridge Urban History of Britain*, vol. 1: *600–1540* (Cambridge: Cambridge University Press, 2000) pp. 335–69.

Rowntree, B. S. and Lavers, G. R., *English Life and Leisure* (London: Longmans, Green, 1951).

Russell, D., *Popular Music in England, 1840–1914: A Social History* (Manchester: Manchester University Press, 1987).

Russell, D., *Football and the English: A Social History of Association Football in England, 1863–1995* (Preston: Carnegie, 1997).

Russell, D., 'Football and Society in the North West, 1919–1939', *Journal of the North West Labour History Group*, 24 (1999/2000) pp. 3–14.

Sandiford, K. A. P., *Cricket and the Victorians* (Aldershot: Scolar, 1994).

Scott, C., *Poppy-Land: Papers Descriptive of the Scenery on the East Coast* (London: Carson & Comerford, 1886).

Sharpe, J. A., *Early Modern England: A Social History, 1550–1760*, 2nd edn (London: Arnold, 1997).

Simpson, J. and Roud, S., *A Dictionary of English Folklore* (Oxford: Oxford University Press, 2001).

Smith, D. B., *Curling: An Illustrated History* (Edinburgh: John Donald, 1981).

Smith, D. and Williams, G., *Fields of Praise: The Official History of the Welsh Rugby Union, 1881–1981* (Cardiff: University of Wales Press, 1980).

Solkin, D., *Painting for Money: The Visual Arts and the Public Sphere in Eighteenth-century England* (New Haven, CT: Yale University Press, 1992).

Spufford, M., *Small Books and Pleasant Histories: Popular Fiction and Its Readership in Seventeenth-century England* (Cambridge: Cambridge University Press, 1981).

Storch, R. D. (ed.), *Popular Culture in Nineteenth-century England* (London: Croom Helm, 1982).

Story, M. and Childs, P. (eds), *British Cultural Identities* (London: Routledge, 2002).

Strutt, J., *Glig-Gamena Angel-Deod, or The Sports and Pastimes of the People of England* (1st pub. 1801; 2nd edn, London: White, 1810).

Sweet, R., *Antiquaries: The Discovery of the Past in Eighteenth-century England* (London: Hambledon and London, 2004).

Swinglehurst, E., *Cook's Tours: The Story of Popular Travel* (Poole: Blandford Press, 1980).

Tardiff, A.-E., 'A Cultural History of Social Dance among the Upper Ranks in Eighteenth-century England' (unpub. PhD thesis, University of Cambridge, 2002).

Taylor, J., *A Dream of England: Landscape, Photography and the Tourist's Imagination* (Manchester: Manchester University Press, 1994).

Thomas, K., 'Work and Leisure in Pre-industrial Society', *Past and Present*, 29 (1964) pp. 50–66.

Thomas, K., *Man and the Natural World: Changing Attitudes in England, 1500–1800* (Harmondsworth: Penguin, 1984).

Thompson, E. P., *The Making of the English Working Class* (1st pub. 1963; Harmondsworth: Penguin, 1968).

Thompson, E. P., *Customs in Common* (Harmondsworth: Penguin, 1993).

Thompson, F. M. L., *The Rise of Respectable Society: A Social History of Victorian Britain, 1830–1900* (London: Fontana, 1988).

Torkildsen, G., *Leisure and Recreation Management*, 4th edn (London: E & FN Spon, 1998).

Towner, J., *A Historical Geography of Recreation and Tourism in the Western World, 1540–1940* (Chichester: John Wiley, 1996).

Tranter, N., *Sport, Economy and Society in Britain, 1750–1914* (Cambridge: Cambridge University Press, 1997).

Turner, V., *The Ritual Process: Structure and Anti-structure* (Chicago: Aldine, 1969).

Underdown, D., *Start of Play: Cricket and Culture in Eighteenth-century England* (London: Allen Lane, 2000).

Urry, J., *The Tourist Gaze: Leisure and Travel in Contemporary Societies* (London: Sage, 1990).

Urry, J., *Consuming Places* (London: Routledge, 1995).

Vamplew, W., *The Turf: A Social and Economic History of Horse Racing* (London: Allen Lane, 1976).

Vamplew, W., *Pay Up and Play the Game: Professional Sport in Britain, 1875–1914* (Cambridge: Cambridge University Press, 2004).

Veblen, T., *The Theory of the Leisure Class* (1st pub. 1899; London: Unwin Books, 1970).

Vickery, A., *The Gentleman's Daughter: Women's Lives in Georgian England* (New Haven, CT: Yale University Press, 1998).

Vincent, D., *Literacy and Popular Culture: England, 1750–1914* (Cambridge: Cambridge University Press, 1989).

Walton, J. K., *The Blackpool Landlady: A Social History* (Manchester: Manchester University Press, 1978).

Walton, J. K., *The English Seaside Resort: A Social History, 1750–1914* (Leicester: Leicester University Press, 1983).

Walton, J. K., *Fish and Chips and the British Working Class, 1870–1940* (Leicester: Leicester University Press, 1992).

Walton, J. K., *Blackpool* (Edinburgh: Edinburgh University Press, 1998).

Walton, J. K., *The British Seaside: Holidays and Resorts in the Twentieth Century* (Manchester: Manchester University Press, 2000).

Walton, J. K., 'Towns and Consumerism', in M. Daunton (ed.), *Cambridge Urban History of Britain*, vol. 3: *1840–1950* (Cambridge: Cambridge University Press, 2000) pp. 715–44.

Walvin, J., *Leisure and Society, 1830–1950* (London: Longman, 1978).

Waterfield, G. (ed.), *Palaces of Art: Art Galleries in Britain, 1750–1990* (London: Dulwich Picture Art Galleries in association with Lund Humphries, 1991).

Weber, W., *The Rise of the Musical Classics in Eighteenth-century England: A Study in Canon, Ritual, and Ideology* (Oxford: Clarendon Press, 1996).

Weideger, P., *Gilding the Acorn: Behind the Façade of the National Trust* (London: Simon & Schuster, 1994).

White, P. W., *Theatre and Reformation: Puritanism, Patronage and Playing in Tudor England* (Cambridge: Cambridge University Press, 1992).

Whyman, S., *Sociability and Power in Late-Stuart England: The Cultural World of the Verneys, 1660–1720* (Oxford: Oxford University Press, 2002).

Wilde, W. R., *Irish Popular Superstitions* (1st pub. 1852; Shannon: Irish University Press, 1972).

Wiles, R. M., *Freshest Advices: Early Provincial Newspapers in England* (Columbus, OH: Ohio University Press, 1965).

Williams, G., *1905 and All That* (Llandysul: Gomer, 1991).

Williams, G., *Valleys of Song: Music and Society in Wales, 1840–1914* (Cardiff: University of Wales Press, 1998).

Williams, J., *Cricket and England: A Cultural and Social History of the Inter-War Years* (London: Frank Cass, 1999).

Williams, J., *A Game for Rough Girls? A History of Women's Football in Britain* (London: Routledge, 2003).

Williams, L., ' "Rus in Urbe": the Greening of English Towns, 1660–1760' (unpub. Ph.D. thesis, University of Wales, 1998).

Williams, R., *Culture and Society, 1780–1950* (1st pub. 1958; Harmondsworth: Penguin, 1968).

Williamson, T., *Polite Landscapes: Gardens and Society in Eighteenth-century England* (Stroud: Alan Sutton, 1995).

Wilson, R. and Mackley, A., *Creating Paradise: The Building of the English Country House, 1660–1800* (London: Hambledon and London, 2000).

Wilton, A. and Bignamini, I. (eds), *Grand Tour: The Lure of Italy in the Eighteenth Century* (London: Tate Gallery, 1996).

Yeo, E. and S. (eds), *Popular Culture and Class Conflict, 1590–1914: Explorations in the History of Labour and Leisure* (Brighton: Harvester Press, 1981).

Index